Locating Postcolonial Narrative Genres

ROUTLEDGE RESEARCH IN POSTCOLONIAL LITERATURES

Edited in collaboration with the Centre for Colonial and Postcolonial Studies, University of Kent at Canterbury, this series presents a wide range of research into postcolonial literatures by specialists in the field. Volumes will concentrate on writers and writing originating in previously (or presently) colonized areas, and will include material from non-anglophone as well as anglophone colonies and literatures. Series editors: Donna Landry and Caroline Rooney.

Related Titles:

Locating Postcolonial Narrative Genres

Edited by Walter Goebel and Saskia Schabio

Routledge
Taylor & Francis Group

NEW YORK AND LONDON

First published 2013
by Routledge
711 Third Avenue, New York, NY 10017

Simultaneously published in the UK
by Routledge
2 Park Square, Milton Park, Abingdon, Oxon OX14 4RN

Routledge is an imprint of the Taylor & Francis Group, an informa business

© 2013 Taylor & Francis

Library of Congress Cataloging-in-Publication Data

Locating postcolonial narrative genres / edited by Walter Goebel and Saskia Schabio.
    p. cm. — (Routledge research in postcolonial literatures ; 43)
Includes bibliographical references and index.
1. Postcolonialism in literature.   2. Narration (Rhetoric)   I. Goebel, Walter.   II. Schabio, Saskia.
PN56.P555L63 2012
809'.93358—dc23
2012011678

ISBN13: 978-0-415-53960-9 (hbk)
ISBN13: 978-0-203-09886-8 (ebk)

Typeset in Baskerville
by IBT Global.

Printed and bound in the United States of America on sustainably sourced paper by IBT Global.

Contents

PART III
Longue Durée Perspectives and Orature

PART IV
Emerging Narrative Genres

     Blessed House"   195
     RENATE BROSCH

14   Postcolonialism and Nostalgia in Michael Ondaatje's *Divisadero*   208
     GEORGIANA BANITA

     Contributors   223
     Index   227

Acknowledgments

Our thanks go first and foremost to our contributors, who have, over the years, engaged in the sustained exchange of ideas and critical debate from which this project emerged. We have been fortunate to receive generous support from the *Deutsche Forschungsgemeinschaft*, and the Centre for Cultural and Technological Studies (IZKT), in helping establish a series of postcolonial conferences at Stuttgart University, enabling stimulating collaboration and networking. Furthermore, we would like to thank Athina Ballasch for her excellent proofreading and help in preparing the manuscript for the press. We are grateful to Julius Haager for his invaluable assistance, as well as to Jessica Bundschuh for her careful readings and expert help at proof stage.

Furthermore, grateful acknowledgment is due to L. Fogarty for granting copyright approval to Bill Ashcroft to quote from his poem "Farewell Reverberated Vault of Detentions" in his contribution "Post-colonial Utopianism: The Utility of Hope." We are grateful to Amina Elbendary and *Al Ahram Weekly* for granting permission to use her translation of *State of Siege* by Mahmoud Darwish, *Al Ahram Weekly* (2002), 11–17 April in Patrick Williams's chapter. Thanks are also due to Syracuse University Press for permission to Patrick Williams to quote from *The Adam of Two Edens* by Mahmoud Darwish (Syracuse University Press, Syracuse, NY 2000) as well as to *MPT* for approval to quote from Mahmoud Darwish, *State of Siege*, trans. S. Maguire and S. Hafez, *Modern Poetry in Translation*, 3/1 (2004): 4–33. An extract from the poem can be found at www.mptmagazine.com.

Introduction
Towards a Postcolonial Narrative Aesthetics
Walter Goebel and Saskia Schabio

Genres classify and order the textual world and have allowed us to talk economically about it at least since Aristotle's *Poetics*. They do not exist *a priori*, but in the texts themselves and in the interpreters' heads. They are communicative constructs which depend upon family resemblances or structural homologies between a number of texts. What makes them so interesting as an object of analysis is that they have limited life-spans (Fowler 1987). These—while also following an internal logic of the evolution of literary forms and of the devolution from genre to mode—seem to often correspond to long-term dispositions in societies, reflecting on social structures, communal vs. individualized concepts of interaction, ontological beliefs, forms of self-fashioning, and—especially in satires, parodies and utopian forms of literature—on shortcomings and tensions within a given society. This volume aims to find out how postcolonial texts have determined the evolution or emergence of specific formal innovations in narrative genres.

In the field of postcolonial studies questions of subversion, parody, and mimesis have predominated over other aspects of aesthetic form. It is high time to attempt to explore wider dimensions of a postcolonial aesthetics, a main aspect of which being specificities of generic evolution or emergence. This collection of essays presents a first foray into this most complex field. Lukács and Bakhtin have frequently been quoted as avant-garde theoreticians who explored the links between aesthetic form and general cultural formation typologically. They provide inspiration for this collection, however Eurocentric and dated some of the questions they posed may appear today, and this volume obviously moves beyond their main concern with epic and novel. Some of the findings open up and also subvert Western narratives about the development of genres, narratives which in our postmodern days generally stress a liberal fluidity or even lead to the postulation of the death of genre as such, in the wake of Derrida's sceptical comments on the prescriptive dimension of the laws of genre (Derrida 1981). Notwithstanding postmodern and poststructuralist visions of a transgeneric free for all, however, the evolution of new narrative forms continues even in the West with e.g., fantasy, neo-gothic, magic realism, neo-realism, metafictional novels, along with many hybrids like the epic novel, a form most popular today, or varieties of the fictionalized autobiography. Deconstruction and construction appear to be—and always have been—parallel and interlaced movements. Even in the Renaissance, when hierarchies of genres were supposedly more stable, forms like the utopia and the autobiography evolved along with hybrids like the tragicomedy—and the pastoral has been the most hybrid of forms since antiquity.

The vision of a totally hybridized and transgeneric literature in a transnational and globalized world appears to some extent to be germane to the satiated and in some respect parasitical culture of the Western metropolis. Its very freedom of aesthetic play and experiment depends on the existence of the genres it deconstructs, inverts or fuses while ignoring the continual articulation of new generic forms. This vision also neatly dovetails with a world of rootless, transnationally available labour forces and ubiquitously marketable commodities. On the so-called margins, however, it is to be expected that questions of self-definition and of the provincializing of the dominant discourses of Others will trigger off more clearly articulated aesthetic trajectories. Some of these return to early, often precolonial, non-Western narrative forms, to Sheherazade's legacy or to early Indian narratives—and thus direct our attention towards the Oriental roots of Western narrative self-fashionings and of Western histories of the novel as the ultimate form of modernity. To de-centre Western aesthetics means to develop a susceptibility for earlier forms of orature, myth, tale, and forms of communal storytelling (Wiemann, Trivedi, Ghazoul, Msiska below) which were at a later stage individualized. Here Bakhtin's observations on the evolutions of new genres from popular—often oral and communally shared—forms are inspiring (Bakhtin 1986). The socio-historical long-term opposition between forms of *Gemeinschaft* and of *Gesellschaft* (Tönnies 1963) often dovetails with the *longue durée* of narrative forms, for example the autobiography and the autobiographic novel, as both were and are intimately linked to articulations of Western individualism and as both form the nucleus of Ian Watt's grand narrative about the rise of the novel.

Another focus of the collection concerns the re-articulation of the amazingly fecund epic form as a mould for the creation of traditional or emerging national, communal, and also individualized voices. Here it is fascinating to follow Patrick Williams's argument concerning the birth of a new kind of lyrical epic which is to some extent also an anti-epic: an epic of Palestine suffering and defeat which questions the very foundations of imperialist modernization and its ramifications in the ideology of heroism, dovetailing neatly with Paul Gilroy's concept of the Black Atlantic and the concomitant traumatic experiences of Western modernization. Williams speaks of the 'resistant epic.'

A central concern and perhaps even conundrum of this collection is the predominance of Western aesthetics and its terminology. The evolution of the new appears to be only describable and even discernible through the lenses of established generic concepts and their transcendence. It is difficult to introduce a new terminology after so many centuries of Eurocentric aesthetic and narratological reflection. Only by forming new and often paradoxical compounds can the limitations of narratology itself and the necessity of its very provincialization be hinted at between the lines. We hope that this effort at aesthetic decolonization is felt here and there in peculiar terms like "non-teleological autobiography," "heterobiography," or "anti-heroic epic." As long as an awareness of the dialectics of blinding terminology and partial insight is maintained and of the linguistic and conceptual limitations of a hermeneutics of cultural alterity (see Trivedi), it seems, we may blunder on with limited access and often somewhat parochial analytic tools. The assimilable artifacts of the more or less alienated and Western-educated elites will, because of such aesthetic and epistemological distortions, always be acknowledged first: Achebe, for example, is the acclaimed father of the Nigerian novel, and not Tutuola.

Generally speaking, we know two main patterns for generic evolution/ devolution: the earlier formalist one and Bakhtin's, that is, a more elitist devolutionary one and an evolutionary popular one. According to the first, new genres are born more or less spontaneously by the craft of the gifted author/ artist who can assemble intertexts and remould them effectively, which then in the course of productive reception become automatized and popularized, ending up as mass-produced formulaic literature, e.g., from Ben Franklin's autobiography to *Ragged Dick*. Bakhtin, on the other hand, highlights the formation process and emphasizes the influence of popular and communal forms, e.g., of speech genres and orality in general, on the evolution of the new. Bakhtin's approach is essential for aesthetic decolonization and for a new respect for the precolonial too, but is hampered by some difficulties. In order to discover the power of popular forms, for example in Amos Tutuola's or in Ben Okri's novels, we need a quasi-anthropological familiarity with the cultures and languages concerned (e.g., for Tutuola with Yoruba mythology). Unfamiliarity with the specific culture will lead to the imperialist projection of assimilative comparative literature agendas and possibly allow "that generic definitions are simply drawn from Western theory and then applied in a suspiciously general fashion all over the globe" (Hitchcock 2003: 317). The other, more decolonizing and Bakhtinian model of aesthetic emergence would allow postcolonial genres to "denature repressive modes of classification, such that its task as genre is to reconfigure genre, as speech genres perhaps" (Hitchcock 2003: 320). It goes without saying that there are many modes of the productive reception of forms between these two prototypical models of generic evolution and devolution.

We know that this collection offers only a few inroads into a complex topic, but we have—after this volume was completed—been confirmed in our endeavours to link the aesthetic and the socio-historical once more by discovering a cognate publication by Eli Park Sorensen, who also turns to

Lukács—if not to Bakhtin—to analyse the emergence of aspects of a postcolonial narrative aesthetics. Sorensen specifically questions the streamlining of interpretive techniques in the postcolonial field, what he calls the predominance of the "modernist ethos," which correlates (post)modernist aesthetic features, such as formal disruptions, meta-fiction, or language games with political subversion. He demands a more differentiated approach to postcolonial literary form beyond the "modernist ethos" which, he believes, has come to act as a prescriptive formula. One of the strands of his investigation takes him to the defence of a version of Lukácsian utopian realism which is not at all compatible with modernist aesthetics as the only expression of resistant form. In spite of a marked defence of utopian gestures in our volume (Ashcroft, Schabio), Sorensen's support of utopian realism seems, as it were, somewhat limited to us, as it does not consider the lack of teleology in many postcolonial (utopian) texts. Sorensen does, however, add a formal paradigm to our investigations, while fighting the same battle against a lack of aesthetic latitude and susceptibility in postcolonial studies.

A main difference is to be observed between Sorenson's and our approaches to aesthetic form, however, a basically temporal one. Sorensen opposes what he calls the modernist ethos, which supposedly streamlines interpretations of postcolonial literature, by concentrating on features such as formal disruptions, meta-fictional strategies, or language games and which, while turning away from supposedly 'naïve' realism, are, as it were, apparently unable to decode the formal complexity and the hidden utopian agendas in realist texts. Thus, according to Sorensen, postcolonial literature has been divided into two parts: the neglected realist texts, often in languages other than English, and the texts which are accessible to modernist interpretive strategies. He quotes Neil Lazarus, whom he follows in his argument, claiming that basically all postcolonial literature was by Western critics reduced to the modes of reading usually applied to *Midnight's Children* (Lazarus 2002), a prototypical novel for the postcolonial canon. To escape the 'modernist ethos' Sorensen offers his approach to apparently silenced realist voices.

We observe a somewhat bizarre quality in this debate between two groups of Western interpreters who hold the keys to postcolonial literature and who project Western dilemmas which we have been familiar with at least since the so-called expressionism debate in the Germany of the 1930s, if not before (e.g., in the classical opposition of *mimesis* and *poiesis*), onto the postcolonial field—without taking into account the possibility of entirely new approaches which may have originated in non-Western societies with their unfamiliar formal traditions. Western aesthetic debates seem to offer the formal boundaries for all world literatures. But more important and to the point concerning our volume: Lukács in his *Theory of the Novel* encompasses a *longue durée* timespan from the heroic epics to the modern novel and correlates ontological changes with aesthetic forms, while Sorensen and others reduce the postcolonial perspective to approaches to literature and modes of presentation prevalent in the twentieth century. By this they cut off the precolonial history of narratology and narrative, from the vantage point of which postcolonial narrative, let alone what Lazarus calls pomo-postcolonial readings and narratives, are little more than an episode (cf. Trivedi). If we want to investigate the evolution/emergence of literary forms in socio-historical perspective, we must take into account Lukács' (and Bakhtin's) *longue durée* approach, e.g., include Sheherazade or the history of the autobiography since and predating Montaigne, for example in China and Arabia. Only then are comparative formal studies of a 'planetary' dimension, as they have been demanded by Gayatri Spivak in *Death of a Discipline*, truly rewarding. We do not want to deny that the differences between formal templates can be analysed in a synchronic comparative view—as some of the essays in this volume also do, but such a view must be informed by a sensitive *thick description* of long-term cultural differences, rather than by the short-lived theoretical debates of Western scholars (e.g., about modernism and utopian realism). Otherwise we will only be able to discover grades of assimilation to varieties of Western aesthetics—and here Lazarus' attack upon pomo-postcolonial readings (Lazarus 2002: 774) indeed has a valid point—instead of at least attempting to provincialize Western aesthetics itself.

The discussion Sorensen highlights is also bizarre because he implicitly assumes that modernist aesthetics are predominantly a Western form of discourse, while many investigations have shown that its central categories were products of an intercultural African-European exchange. *Heart of Darkness*, the locus classicus of a modernist aesthetics of alienation, dissociation, bricolage, and the transcendence of the verbal by the visual was a (post)colonial novel. Modernism is definitely not a European product, in spite of prolonged attempts to present it as inspired mainly by European demi-gods like Marx, Nietzsche, Bergson, etc. Such intertextual, but not intercultural, yarns mask the breakdown of European logocentric dominance in the baffling postcolonial encounter and the African roots of European modernism—which were never denied for the visual arts and music (cf. Göbel 2006). That Eliot's original epigraph for *The Waste Land*, which was taken from *Heart of Darkness*, was rejected in favour of a canonized European classic, symbolically unveils a much longer battle to Europeanize modernism and to deny its intercultural origins. The effective refunctioning of modernist tropes and strategies in African literature equally prove the intercultural nature of the movement (Brown 2005). Eliot's version of modernism was later creolized by Walcott, Brathwaite, and others, emphasizing the cosmopolitan quality of modernist artefacts (cf. Pollard 2004).

In fact, the official version of the literary history of modernism and its Eurocentric intertextualities are little more than examples of epistemological imperialism. This imperialism is partly based on the privileging of the written text over both the situatedness of experience and over orality and visual culture—the latter to be counterbalanced by a return to Bakhtin's investigations into the genre-forming potential of popular (and oral) cultural forms. As Adriana Cavarero has maintained: "The whole affair about the centrality of the text [. . .] depends on the well-known tendency of intellectuals to represent the world in their own likeness and image" (Cavarero 2000: 76). Our agenda in this volume, however, is rather to trace "the reinvention of the novel [and other narrative forms] in postcolonial writing," a "vast and extremely difficult topic" (Hitchcock 2003: 324), which will along the way allow us to redefine our concept of a critical comparative literature, inspired by anthropological knowledge and modes of thick description, in a search for "alternative canons," "indigenous theory," and local experiences (Budholia 2008: 17).

In our collection, debates about more mimetic/realistic versus more explorative concepts of literature are reflected, between socio-historical correspondences and the emergence of new generic forms. Our first section reaches out beyond narratology towards the general positioning of a postcolonial aesthetics, which considers precolonial and utopian trajectories. The opening essay by Harish Trivedi voices a general critique of Western histories of the novel, whose non-Western roots—e.g., in Bangladesh or in Palestine—have been generally neglected, partly because of the lack of linguistic and cultural competence on the part of postcolonial scholars. Trivedi insists on the importance of precolonial narrative forms for the development of the novel, and especially of short fiction in the Indian context, challenging the term 'postcolonial' as referring to a rather short-lived phase within the rich literary traditions of India. In this respect Trivedi seconds Wiemann's and Ghazoul's contributions, which also evoke the importance of shorter forms of narrative for generic evolution.

Bill Ashcroft emphasizes the importance of 'anticipatory consciousness' for narrative evocations of the utopian—with special reference to Ernst Bloch, thus salvaging clear aesthetic trajectories from the metropolitan, postmodern spirit of 'anything goes.' What may sound like a traditional Marxist aesthetics, gains postcolonial validity by relating the utopian to the supranational, rather than the international. According to Ashcroft, this means reaching out beyond the national towards forms of cultural community, racial identity etc., which are not easily reduced to geo-political formations. As examples the concept of Aztlán in Chicano culture, Gandhi's *Hind Swaray* and the myth of 'Mother India,' which link India with peasant traditions, are analysed. It is upon the tendency to transcend the practical and the political that Ashcroft bases the postcolonial utopian mode, a position at odds with traditional Marxist ideas and also at odds with Trivedi's more localized view of cultural identity.

Finally, Saskia Schabio explores the utopian dimensions of Glissant's poetics of creolization. If for him the 'Novel of the Americas' prefigures the appearance of the 'New Man,' whose lineaments, however, are already realized in literature, a radical questioning of the Western division of genre is crucial to his enterprise. While pointing out the dangers of folkloristic deformation, Glissant strategically introduces the "poetics of the oral African text" and ponders notions of 'oraliture,' unsettling received concepts of both epic and novel (Glissant 1989: 137; 245). The "irruption into modernity" that has shaped Caribbean experience has engendered particular inflections of the novel genre and informs Edouard Glissant's attempt to delineate the specificity of the 'novel of the Americas' (Glissant 1989: 146).

The second part is mainly concerned with narrative genres responding to or in dialogue with Western forms, subverting, parodying, or transcending them. Patrick Williams reads Darwish's lyrical epic as postcolonial resistance genre. The recoding of the epic formula leads to a non-heroic, non-national, fragmentary, but polyphonic form, which Darwish calls his 'epic of Troy,' that is, an epic told from the perspective of the losers or the besieged, and which in some respect appears to be closer to the novel than the epic. In Darwish, the epic, much as in Glissant (cf. Schabio) is not a clearly defin-able, idealized, or dated genre (Lukács, Bakhtin), but quite alive again and expressive of the hybrid, the transitory, and cross-breeding.

Like Harish Trivedi, Mpalive Msiska challenges the postcolonial from the vantage-point of precolonial literacy and orature, which he engages in a dialogue with marginalized Western literatures. His topic is no more and no less than a re-interpretation of the history of the African novel, which he positions in opposition to what he calls the 'racial romances' of Conrad and Cary. The postcolonial African novel is, according to Msiska, inspired by British literature from the Scottish and Irish margins and by aspects of avant-garde modernism, on the one hand, on the other by Ngugi's concept of orature, leading to a radical transformation of modernist-realist traditions. As an example Msiska mentions Ngugi's *Matigari* (1987), a kind of textual-ized oral performance which is conversant with Bakhtin's concept of the multigenre novel.

Sharae Deckard demands a form of comparative literature for the "capi-talist peripheries," a chapter of which Msiska can be said to have offered. She seeks structural homologies in postcolonial African crime fiction and focuses on the failed narrator/investigator and on grotesque elements in novels by Mabanckou and Pepetela, which register social deformations and uneven developments in Angola and the Congo respectively. Deckard links this aes-thetic template to the function of some of Dostoevski's deformed figures and to Bakhtin's theory of the grotesque as well as to his concept of carnivaliza-tion. The perspective becomes even more planetary by comparative glances at similar aesthetic strategies used in Machado de Assis's *Brás Cubas*.

Walter Goebel finally focuses on V.S. Naipaul's truncated autobiog-raphies and what he calls heterobiographical narratives, which on the one hand seem to parody Western models of Cartesian individualism, as well as the official history of the individualist novel, as presented e.g. by Ian Watt, while on the other exploring the existential dimensions of a pervasive postcolonial melancholia, grounded in experiences of alienation and discrimination. It is this existential dimension which distinguishes Naipaul's mosaic fictionalized autobiographical texts from the epistemological and semiotic decentring prevalent in postmodern metropolitan autobiographies. Melancholia for a lost communitarian ideal and traumatic experiences of alienation prevail over any form of postmodern playfulness in what can be called his fractured and mosaic heterobiographical texts.

In our third section the evolution of oral forms into literature (Bakhtin) is the uniting theme, which was also focussed on by Trivedi. Ferial Ghazoul opposes a more spatial-horizontal approach to literature, in the terms of Self and Other, to a vertical one, which delves into the oral past and local memories. She explores the powerful influence of folktales, proverbs, and myths in Achebe's *Things Fall Apart* and in Rushdie's *Haroun or the Sea of Stories*, and emphasizes their kinship to the *Arabian Nights* and the *Panchatantra*. Ghazoul's third example of orature is Radna Ashour's novella *Siraaj*, which wavers between the genre of political allegory and the folktale, while combining African and Asian intertexts. All three examples, however different, deconstruct the opposition between native or nativist and modernist aesthetics.

Nadia El Kholy's contribution on the Gayer-Anderson-Museum in Cairo offers a markedly contrastive view of orality. While for Ghazoul orature transforms the modernist novel from within, especially with embedded forms, her argument basically following a Bakhtinian trajectory, El Kholy's essay questions the very basis of orature. Gayer-Anderson bought an old Mamluk house which had belonged to a family from Crete, and turned it into a museum for Arab monuments, paintings, and furniture. He then interlaced these objects with legends collected from the head of the Kretan family, a holy old man. Recording, cutting, editing, and annotating the stories he deemed noteworthy, finally even commissioning an artist to produce 14 copper plates corresponding to the legends collected, Gayer-Anderson produced and lived in his own self-contained version of the Orient. El Kholy thus calls into question the idea that oral culture can generally offer access to an unadulterated version of a communal past, questioning the, as it were, largely unmediated reception of orature in Trivedi's, Ghazoul's, and Msiska's contributions.

Dirk Wiemann emphasizes the socio-historical and communal dimensions of genres, much like Msiska, and at the same time aims at a transmodern re-writing of the centre. He focuses on Indian short story cycles as updated forms of the village sketch which traditionally, e.g., in the *Canterbury Tales*, in Mitford's *Our Village* or in the caravanserai of *Arabian Nights*, projected idealized communitarian chronotopes—though often under siege. These kinds of chronotopes implicitly oppose Eurocentric theories of the novel as the form of enlightened individualism by presenting what Wiemann calls fictions of localization.

The fourth section targets 'emerging' genres. Sue Kossew introduces Australian 'Sorry Novels,' which apologize for colonial injustice against the indigenous population. She emphasizes the ambivalent quality of such literature, which can lead, on the one hand, to white self-righteousness, but on the other can open up shared spaces for ethical understanding. Noha Hamdy interprets Soueif's *A Map of Love* as a 'translational' novel with double cultural encodings. She speaks of a code-switching aesthetics, which generally vacillates between Oriental tale and travelogue. Renate Brosch focuses on the postcolonial as a "mode of reading" for which the aesthetics of the short story, which privileges opacity, density, and complex imagery, proves especially suggestive, as well as being conducive to the social functionalization of literature and the formation of a communal cultural imaginary. In particular, the visual semiotic qualities of the short story form allow for active reader immersion and for the formation of communal audience responses, thus being especially open to postcolonial readings. For Georgiana Banita a growing heterogeneous transnational readership implicated in the process of writing gives rise to a larger strategy to dialogize narrative culture. Her examples are Ondaatje's *Divisadero* and *Anil's Ghost*, novels not usually categorized as postcolonial. All the more her contribution elucidates the danger of fuzziness in the concept of a postcolonial aesthetics, as it comes to include aspects of postmodernism and the world novel. Banita can also show that postcolonial nostalgia still influences the transnational paradigm of the emergent genre of the world novel. Read in this light, her contribution is a counterpoint to our initial emphasis on the utopian dimensions of a postcolonial aesthetics. At the same time, the tension between a postcolonial and a transnational and in this case also postmodern perspective on genre prompts us to critically review current debates on the scope of the novel (e.g., Wai Chee Dimock and Franco Moretti) as a planetary form, and the implications for a world literature perspective—the globalizing tendencies of which our project implicitly calls in question.

Besides a marked emphasis on oral literature and its problems of transmittance (El Kholy) and on orature, our collection attempts to cautiously approach some emerging genres, however difficult to define, and even to name, these may be. With such tentative and sometimes overlapping terms as lyrical epic, resistance epic (Williams), postcolonial utopia (Ashcroft), transgressive novel (Msiska), heterobiography (Goebel), sorry novel (Kossew), fiction of localization (Wiemann), translational novel (Hamdy), 'Novel of the Other America,' or creolized novel (Glissant/Schabio), we hope to have, however dimly, lit up a few paths towards a postcolonial narrative aesthetics.

Works Cited

Bakhtin, M.M. (1986) *Speech Genres and Other Essays*, trans. V.W. McGee, ed. C. Emerson and M. Holquist, Austin, TX: University of Texas Press.

Brown, N. (2005) *Utopian Generations: The Political Horizon of Twentieth Century Literature*, Princeton: Princeton University Press.

Budholia, O.P. (2008) *Generic Manifolds: Indian Literature Since 1950*, New Delhi: Adhyayan Publishers.

Cavarero, A. (2000) *Relating Narratives: Storytelling and Selfhood*, trans. P.A. Kottmann, London and New York: Routledge.

Derrida, J. (1981) 'The Law of Genre', trans. A. Ronell, in W.J.T. Mitchell (ed.) *On Narrative*, Chicago: University of Chicago Press, 51–77.

Fowler, A. (1987) *Kinds of Literature: An Introduction to the Theory of Genres and Modes*, 3rd edn, Oxford: Oxford University Press.

Glissant, É. (1989) *Caribbean Discourse: Selected Essays*, trans. J.M. Dash, Charlottesville: University Press of Virginia.

Göbel, W. (2006) 'The Birth of Modernism in the Heart of Darkness' in J. Mildorf, H.U. Seeber and M. Windisch (eds) *Magic, Science, Technology and Literature*, Münster: LIT Verlag, 153–63.

Hitchcock, P. (2003) 'The Genre of Postcoloniality', *New Literary History*, 34/2: 299–330.

Lazarus, N. (2002) 'The Politics of Political Modernism', *The European Legacy*, 7/6, 771–82.

Lukács, G. (1971 [1920]) *Die Theorie des Romans: Ein geschichtsphilosophischer Versuch über die Formen der großen Epik*, Berlin: Luchterhand.

Pollard, C.W. (2004) *New World Modernisms: T.S. Eliot, Derek Walcott, and Kamau Brathwaite*, Charlottesville and London: University of Virginia Press.

Sorensen, E.P. (2010) *Postcolonial Studies and the Literary: Theory, Interpretation and the Novel*, London: Palgrave Macmillan.

Spivak, G.C. (2003) *Death of a Discipline: The Wellek Library Lectures in Critical Theory*, New York: Columbia University Press.

Tönnies, F. (1963) *Gemeinschaft und Gesellschaft: Grundbegriffe der Reinen Soziologie*, Darmstadt: Wissenschaftliche Buchgesellschaft.

Part I

Pre- and Post-colonial Aesthetic Templates

1 Love, Marriage, and Realism

The Novel in Pre- and Post-colonial India

Harish Trivedi

The novel is of the West [...]. [In India] it is part of the mimicry of
the West, the Indian self-violation. (Naipaul 1964: 214)

Beginning effectively in the eighteenth century, the genre of the novel arose
in the West and quickly established a still unchallenged supremacy over all
the other literary genres. Beginning at about the same time, the military
power of the West won for it political and economic supremacy over large
territories in other parts of the world which continued until the middle of the
twentieth century. It has been argued from widely different points of view
that these synchronic developments were not entirely coincidental. To cite
just two examples, the Bangladeshi critic Firdous Azim, in her ambitiously
titled book *The Colonial Rise of the Novel* (1993), discussed works by Aphra
Behn, Defoe, but mainly Charlotte Brontë to highlight the issues not only
of colonialism but equally of race, gender, and the spread of the English
language. While speaking of a 'colonial encounter,' she nevertheless scrupu-
lously specified that her study "does *not* position itself along with the rhetoric
of a 'decolonizing' mission, which dismisses the English text as that of the
colonial master" (Azim 1993: 6; my emphasis). On the other hand, Edward
Said in his *Culture and Imperialism* (1993) put forward the argument that Western novelists right from Jane Austen to Salman Rushdie needed to be read
'contrapuntally' to bring out the almost symbiotic connection between the
Western novel and Western Empires, in particular the British. He proceeded
to deliver magisterially an inadequately instantiated but characteristically
sweeping assertion: "Without Empire, I would go so far as saying, there is no
European novel as we know it" (Said 1993: 69).

Said is as forthrightly 'postcolonial' as a critic of the novel as Azim is
tentative, but an academic proclivity they share is that despite their common
colonial provenance, they both discuss only the Western novel and work
exclusively out of the Western archives. If the novel also arose as a popular literary form in Bangladesh (formerly a part of India) or the Palestine,
arguably under colonial influence, they show no awareness of it. In numerous other works of literary criticism as well, postcolonial discourse remains
similarly situated in the colonizing metropolis rather than in a postcolony, a
circumstance that seriously circumscribes the radical potential of postcolonial discourse.

The purported complicity of the Western novel in the imperialist enterprise is a subject that may be well worth exploring, though Said's discussion of Jane Austen on the basis of extremely limited textual evidence in just one novel, *Mansfield Park*, amounts to scraping the bottom of his ideological barrel. Rather more productive may be an exploration of the coercive literary example that the Western novel set for the literatures of the colonies. With the spread of English education and the induction of colonial modernity in cultural and literary matters, a colony that did not seek to produce novels of its own on the model of the Western novel was seen to be even more backward and retarded than otherwise. The rise of the novel in the colonies constitutes a postcolonial narrative of its own, with its own examples of resistance to the tyranny or at least oppressive hegemony of this alien form that paralleled the resistance generally to colonial rule.

The traditional understanding of the matter has been that the colonies and indeed the rest of the world lacked the literary genre of the novel, and when these non-European expanses of the world became aware of this Western invention, they promptly attempted to imitate it and thus to supply the lack. In this version of literary history, numerous early attempts in the colonies to imitate this literary form fell well short of the model and were to be accounted as failures. It was only gradually, with growing experience, that the colonial subjects learnt to write the novel and to draw abreast of the West, as indeed in numerous other cultural and political matters. In this view, the novel thus proved to be a measure of the potential capability of the colonies to learn from and successfully follow the example of the West.

But in a recent counter-narrative, the Western novel did not come as such a great novelty to the colonies, for the good reason that they already had their own indigenous narrative forms, many of which could be traced back to a period long before the rise of the novel in the West. And if the early colonial attempts to write a novel did not come close to the Western model, it was not because of a failure to imitate assiduously enough, but rather because of a conscious or unconscious wish to combine this imported Western form with the older local forms of narration, to accommodate and appropriate it according to the local traditions rather than slavishly to imitate it. If the novel was a 'gift' of the West, the receiving subjects often looked it full in the mouth before accepting it.

Western Realism, Indian Reality

In the particular case of India, which of all the British colonies had probably the oldest and richest tradition of a literature of its own, existing in a large variety of classical and modern languages and dating back to 1500 BC, the local reception and appropriation of the Western genre of the novel provides a complex case of literary interaction. What is of utmost interest here is not whether the novel in India arose in imitation of the Western model, but how, right since its beginnings under colonial auspices in the latter half of the nineteenth century up to the present postcolonial times, the Indian novel has remained distinct from the Western novel in significant ways.

A profound distinction between the novel in the West and in India was articulated by V.S. Naipaul in his account of a personal voyage of exploration to India, *An Area of Darkness* (1964). In it, Naipaul discussed in detail the fiction of R.K. Narayan (1906–2001), a highly regarded and widely popular Indian novelist writing in English, and proceeded to make several generalizations about both the novel and India:

> The novel is of the West. It is part of [the] Western concern with the condition of men, a response to the here and now. In India thoughtful men have preferred to turn their backs on the here and now and to satisfy [. . .] 'the basic human hunger for the unseen.' It is not a good qualification for the writing or reading of novels. (Naipaul 1964: 214)

This is probably as categorical an assertion of a basic contradiction between being an Indian and being able to produce or even consume novels as ever enunciated. It was rendered even more remarkable for the fact, firstly, that Naipaul was no mere critic but himself established as a major novelist (having already published in 1961 *A House for Mr Biswas*, which now ranks as one of the greatest postcolonial novels in English) and secondly, that he was, though born in Trinidad, a high-caste Hindu by lineage, a Brahmin, just as R.K. Narayan was, and genetically programmed, presumably, to turn his back too on the real world and to attend instead to a hunger for the unseen. Nevertheless, he went on here to speak of the "*aimlessness* of Indian fiction— which comes from a profound doubt about the purpose and value of fiction," and added that younger Indian novelists too were only producing novels that were "documents of the Indian confusion" regarding fiction (Naipaul 1964: 216; original emphasis).

A dozen years later, on a subsequent sojourn in India, Naipaul remained convinced that Indians could not write novels because they entertained a view of the world that prevented them from realistically engaging with it. Almost obsessively, he returned to the singular example of R.K. Narayan to re-read slowly a major novel by Narayan, *Mr Sampath* (1949), and now complained that the life he depicted was on such a small and inconsequential scale that it seemed bracketed off from reality: "The writer [Narayan] contemplates the lesser life that goes on below: small men, small schemes, big talk, limited means: a life so circumscribed that it appears whole and unviolated . . . " (Naipaul 1977: 19). The small town where most of his fiction was located was for Naipaul "to some extent artificial, a simplification of reality," and even the realistic weapons of comedy and irony with which Narayan treated his material were "part of a Hindu response to the world" (Naipaul 1977: 21). Narayan's novels were not like proper Western novels, which they outwardly resembled, for the reason that they were not "social comedies" but rather, "religious books, at times religious fables, and intensely Hindu" (Naipaul 1977: 22).

One may smell in these remarks more than a whiff of the all too familiar odour of essentialist Orientalizing, according to which the East is more spiritual than the West and not concerned with mere material reality. Naipaul seemed to be unaware of the possibility that in terms of human existence, a hunger for the unseen must necessarily coexist with other hungers, a hunger for food and sustenance, for example. A high-minded philosophical view of the world according to Hinduism may lay down that the world is 'unreal'—as contrasted with the eternal Supreme Spirit which alone in this view is 'real.' But it also prescribes, as famously in the scriptural teachings contained in the *Bhagavad-Gita*, that while one lives on this earth, one has a duty to act in the right cause according to one's *dharma* (inherent duty) and that such action may involve killing one's enemies, even if they happen to include one's own kin. The classic statement of this understanding of the world is to be found in the *Bhagavad-Gita*, especially in Chapter 2, verses 19 to 38, where Lord Krishna exhorts the reluctant warrior Arjuna to stand up and fight in accordance with his ordained duty, explaining that though those he is about to kill are unreal and therefore dead already, he yet must kill them in order to fulfil his duty as a warrior (*Bhagavad-Gita* 1986: 99–122).

Anyhow, at a more mundane level, Naipaul himself as he travelled around India registered instance after instance of all kinds of Indians thinking and acting as materialistically as anyone in the West or indeed as he himself did. For example, he recorded that the staff of a hotel in Kashmir where he was a long-term resident, and for whom he claimed he had even declared 'my affection,' seemed to blatantly overcharge him nevertheless, whereupon, even though he was ill and lying in bed, he flew (physically) into a rage and threw a mighty tantrum. Naipaul's account of this episode is as novelistically realistic as could be wished for; he quoted in full, complete with misspellings, an elaborate nine-item estimate of expenditure that he was handed by the hotel staff, and derived considerable satisfaction from the fact that he was able to beat it down (Naipaul 1964: 156–157).

In both philosophical and pragmatic terms, Naipaul's view that Indians, or at least Hindus (for numerous Indian novelists are Muslims, including Salman Rushdie), were congenitally incapable of writing novels, perhaps betrayed to some extent his own anxiety and apprehensions about the capability of the novel, a form that he has repeatedly declared to be dead. The main issue he raised, that Indians are incapable of engaging with reality, must be interpreted, if it is to make any sense, to mean that some Indian writers tend to represent the reality around them in a manner that is at variance with the mode of realism largely practiced by novelists in the West.

According to Edward Said, the realism of the Western novel has served as a tool to expose the unreality of the bourgeois aspiration of its protagonists:

Almost without exception the protagonist of the late nineteenth-century [European] novel is someone who realizes that his or her life's project—the wish to be great, rich, or distinguished—is mere fancy, illusion, dream. (Said 2011: 323)

In this respect, Said argues, these protagonists "are like the archetypal hero of the novel form itself, Don Quixote," whose birth "marks off the world of the novel in its fallen, unhappy state, its 'lost transcendence' [in Georg Lukács's phrase] from the world of the epic, which is happy, satisfied, full" (Said 2011: 324). This seems not too far a cry from Narayan's novels with their 'small men, small schemes, big talk, limited means,' in Naipaul's own characterization. The novel is neither the epic nor the romance; its greater realism means that it is unlikely that many dreams and fancies will be fulfilled and realized in it, whether they have arisen out of the Hindu view of the world or out of the Protestant work ethic.

It may then appear that a rather more plausible formulation in this regard would be not that the Indian reality is essentially different from Western reality, but that it is represented in fiction through a different mode of realism. This is basically the position Meenakshi Mukherjee argued from in her book *Realism and Reality*:

the conventions of [Western] realism [. . .] could not be transferred to the Indian situation, where the nature of social reality was substantially different, without causing certain inadvertent mutations in the mode itself. (Mukherjee 1985: vii)

The 'mutations' introduced in the form of the Western novel in India may not always have been 'inadvertent,' but Mukherjee was right to focus on 'the nature of social reality' in India, unlike Naipaul who saw the Indian reality as philosophically transcendent and beyond the grasp of literary realism. Mukherjee discussed in particular what she called "the Novel of Purpose," also called by others "the Christian novel" (Mukherjee 1985: 27), a category which included fictional works by foreign missionaries and Indian converts to Christianity, in which the authors excoriated the 'evils' of Hindu society and motivated their readers to convert as well. Such novels were among the first to be written in several Indian languages and showed how the new literary form came as part of a package with Christianity and with colonialism (which facilitated such proselytization in India); such novels also exemplified a close adherence to the form of the Western novel.

Love and Marriage

On the other hand, there is perhaps a need equally to highlight the fact that what may be called more indigenous novels, written by unconverted authors on 'traditional' themes, were rather more numerous in all the Indian languages, and it is such works that embodied a basic modification in both the themes and the form of the Western novel. For example, few of these novels ended with the hero and the heroine getting married to each other at the end of the novel, an event that forms the culmination of a vast proportion of Western novels. Indeed, one of the most popular plot-lines of the Western novel throughout the hey-day of realism in the eighteenth and the nineteenth centuries was how boy meets girl, how the girl sets her cap on the boy who is usually wealthier and in the beginning rather less attracted to her than she is to him, and how after realizing the true nature of their feelings for each other and overcoming certain material obstructions, they achieve the fulfilment of their most ardent wish and desire and indeed of their individual selves by getting married in the last chapter, with the confident narratorial projection that they will live happily ever after. This was the template of human conduct that somehow proved most amenable to novelistic treatment in the West, and it became enshrined in the English novel in particular after the supreme example of Jane Austen, who has been seen by numerous common readers (mistakenly, as it happens) to endorse this pattern of human growth and development.

But if this tale of love and marriage is realism, what would be fantasy? The assumption that 'falling' in love (as if one were not looking where one is going) was a kind of epiphany, that marrying the person one had fallen in love with was an obligation that must overrule all others, and that such a marriage was a culmination of a young life and would by itself ensure that one would live happily ever after, were all a make-believe, an unexamined romantic convention, in every sense of the word 'romantic,' which showed that the so-called 'realistic' novel of the West was still half-embedded in older non-realistic traditions of the distinctly romantic genre of the 'romance.' A basic assumption here was that prenuptial love does not alter when it alteration finds in the mundane nitty-gritty of marriage, and another that the act and bond of marriage concerned only the two individuals who were getting married and hardly at all the extended family.

In India in the latter half of the nineteenth century, when the form of the novel arose and gained popular circulation, and by and large even now for a vast proportion of the population at large, the social reality has been radically different. To start with, child marriages were common in the nineteenth century with many boys and nearly all girls getting married in their teens; in fact, in one of the earliest Hindi novels, an enlightened father announces his radical intention that he will marry his son off not until he has reached the mature age of eighteen and his daughter (who grows up to be the heroine of the novel and an exemplary new woman) not at the age of nine but at eleven (Phullauri 1877: 8–9)! Such marriages were 'arranged' by parents and other relatives or even professional go-betweens, with the boy and the girl not even getting to meet before they were married off, restrictions of caste were observed in the selection of the bride and the groom, and astrological charts were consulted to predict not only the compatibility of the couple, but also to fix an auspicious date for the wedding, to the hour if not the minute. Following marriage, the young bride and groom lived (happily) ever after under the same roof as the parents of the groom and numerous other relatives as well. If conjugal 'love' came into it, and it perhaps inevitably did through long years of close intimacy and procreation, it succeeded, and did not precede, marriage. Divorce was not an option, nor remarriage, even when either spouse was widowed; the rate of divorce even now amongst even the highly educated, affluent, and Westernized class of Indians is so low as to be nearly invisible. "India still has one of the lowest divorce rates in the world, with about one in 1,000 marriages collapsing, according to recent studies" (Dummet 2011: npn).

Much of this may sound shockingly backward and uncivilized to a Western reader—but then Western mores in this regard, such as courtship, dancing especially with persons other than one's spouse, kissing in public, or disobeying one's parents in the crucial business of marriage, seemed horribly shameless, morally corrupt, and even sinful to Indians; the compliment was returned with interest (See Trivedi 2005). In the early decades of the arrival and adaptation of the form of the novel, a public controversy arose in the Hindi journals centred round some Hindi novels which were thought, under the influence of the Western model, to be excessively concerned with romantic love or *shringara* and even the champions of the novel in this debate admitted that novels with a love-interest were indeed deleterious from a moral point of view, while pleading in extenuation that not all novels had a love-interest (Chaturvedi 1986: 162–163). Anyhow, whether for ill or good, such was, and still substantially remains, the Indian social reality, which the novel in India, as imported from or via Britain, was now called upon to represent.[1]

A major consequence of such *mésalliance* or even miscegenation between Western form and Indian reality was that one of the most prominent and attractive themes of Western fiction, romantic love leading eventually to marriage, had to be thrown out of the window. What replaced the novel of love-and-marriage in India was what has been called 'the domestic novel,' i.e., the novel of life after marriage, or more accurately, the *'garhasthya upanyas'* (Shukla 1929: 595), i.e., the novel concerned with depicting the discharging of one's duties as a householder, in the second of the four prescribed phases of a man's life according to the traditional Hindu pattern. (Ruth Prawer Jhabvala attempted to catch some of these cultural connotations in the title of one of her early Indian novels, *The Householder* (1960), which was turned into one of the first literary films made by the team of James Ivory and Ismail Merchant under the same title in 1963).

A work of fiction with an arguable claim to be the first novel to be published in Hindi was *Devrani Jethani ki Kahani* (1870), which translates as 'The Story of the Younger Sister-in-law and the Elder Sister-in-law' except that for each of these specific kinships, indicating the wives of two brothers, Hindi has a single word, *devrani* and *jethani* respectively. How real and intimate these kinships are is indicated by the fact that Hindi has similarly short, simple, and clearly disambiguated terms for what in English would in awkward circumlocution be called the maternal grand-father and grandmother (*nana* and *nani*) and paternal grand-father and grand-mother (*dada* and *dadi*), maternal uncle (*mama*) and paternal uncle (*chacha*), a paternal uncle elder to one's father (*tau*), mother-in-law and father-in-law (*saas* and *sasur*—and no deployment of the curiously impersonal and officious qualifier 'in-law' just because they are not blood relations), parents of the bride and the groom as addressed by each other (*samadhi* and *samadhin*), a brother-in-law who is one's wife's brother (*sala*) and a brother-in-law who is one's sister's husband (*jija*), a sister of one's husband (*nand*), the husband of an elder sister as addressed by the husband of a younger sister (*sarhu*), and a set of especially connotative terms for what one's younger brother (or sister) would call one's wife and she him (*bhabhi* and *devar*)—and this is only a select list. Such close kinships and the distinct and specific terms for each of them were a source of fascination for many British observers of India; Rudyard Kipling in *Kim* attempted to imitate this native linguistic-cultural feature but ended up immediately tying himself in a knot when he referred to "My sister's brother's son," who would, of course, be simply "my brother's son" (Kipling 2011: 31 and 341)—and would in Hindi be *bhatija*, as distinct from a sister's son, *bhanja*, though in English both would be just 'nephew.'

A highly popular Hindi novelist of the same generation as Kipling, Gopalram Gahamari (1866–1946), produced a series of novels whose titles indicate a focus on precisely such relationships: *Saas-Patohu* (1899; 'Mother-in-law and Daughter-in-law'), *Bada Bhai* (1900; 'Elder Brother'), *Devarani-Jethani* (1901; 'The Younger Daughter-in-law and the Elder Daughter-in-law,' the same as in the novel published in 1870 cited above), *Do Bahin* (1902; 'Two Sisters'); and *Tin Patohu* (1904; 'Three Daughters-in-law'). Even more remarkable perhaps is an early novel in a neighbouring language, Gujarati, *Sasu Bahuni Ladai* (1866; 'The Quarrel between Mother-in-law and Daughter-in-law') by Mahipatram Nilkantha (1866), who apparently sought to demonstrate that a harmonious relationship at home between these two members of the household would then lead to greater welfare of the family, community, and society. Incidentally, Nilkanth was apparently the first Gujarati to be sent to England to be educated ('D.B.M.' 1991: 2949).

In the twentieth century too, some of the best known short stories by the greatest writer of fiction in both Urdu and Hindi, Premchand (1880–1936), focus on such familial relationships, such as 'Bade Bhai Sahab' (Respected Elder Brother), and 'Bade Ghar ki Beti' (A High-Born Daughter) who through her noble conduct mediates between mutually discontented brothers and reconciles them to each other in the household of her in-laws (for which again Hindi has a single word, *sasural*). Similarly, it is brothers and sisters or sons and father who constitute the fabric of some of the best short stories by Nirmal Verma (1929–2005), a high modernist Hindi writer who spent nine years in (the erstwhile) Czechoslovakia, set his first novel entirely in Prague, and also wrote some especially evocative short stories set in London and Venice.

Such family relations are so intimate and intricately interwoven that the conjugal relationship always exists in their wider context. Further, all these relationships, including the conjugal, are often played out within the shared space of a populous extended family under the same roof. Privacy as a value is seen to be a peculiar Western oddity in such a setting, like individuality. The large extended family has not only constituted a staple of Hindi fiction; it now dominates television too, with shows such as the phenomenally popular 'Kyunki Sas Bhi Kabhi Bahu Thi' ('For the Mother-in-Law too was once a Daughter-in-Law'), which was the longest running soap on Indian TV, earned the highest viewership ratings in that category for eight years, and was "Asia's most watched and awarded [TV] show" ('Kyunki': Wikipedia).

Even beyond the sphere of Hindi literature and Indian TV, one of the best known English-language novels of the twentieth century, not Indian in provenance, offers a particularly detailed and complex depiction of the Hindu extended family. This is Naipaul's masterpiece *A House for Mr Biswas* (1961), which is set in the 'East Indian' migrant community in Trinidad, which remains typically Hindu and Indian in many ways. The 'Hanuman House,' in which a substantial part of the novel is set, is populated by the grand matriarch Mrs Tulsi, her nine daughters, and their respective husbands, living under the same roof in the one room allotted to each nuclear unit of the family while cooking and eating together the same food and sharing other common spaces, in a cheek-by-jowl coexistence and sometimes in a state of unspoken tension and little jealousies. Mr Biswas is the only one of Mrs Tulsi's sons-in-law who proves rebellious and challenges her time and again, often in the privacy of his own mind or room but sometimes in the open, with comically ineffectual and even humiliating consequences. At the end of the novel, however, he is able to break away and buy the eponymous house where he is at last rid of his hated mother-in-law:

> He thought of the house as his own, though for years it had been irretrievably mortgaged. [. . .] he was struck again and again by the wonder of being in his own house, the audacity of it [. . .] since his marriage he felt he had lived nowhere but in the houses of the Tulsis, at Hanuman House [. . .], at Shorthills, [. . .] in Port of Spain. And now at the end he found himself in his own house, on his own half-lot of land, his own portion of the earth. (Naipaul 1961: 2)

Thematically, Naipaul fully endorses the long trajectory through which Mr Biswas is able to fight free of the large family household and to set up his own home, and the transition from a traditional Indian way of living to a modern, Westernized life-style. But it is the bustling and often bristling life in the crowded Hanuman House (which Naipaul had himself experienced as a child in the 'Lion House' of his 'Nanie'/Nani or maternal grand-mother) that comes alive with particular vividness in the novel and forms its imaginative and emotional core. Naipaul's biographer tells us that Mrs Capildeo, on whom Mrs Tulsi is modelled, had over forty grand-children and all of them and their parents lived their lives together and slept under her family roof (French 2008: 23–25). Naipaul's marvellous fictional evocation of the communal life of this extended Indian family is in my bilingual view probably unmatched by anything even in Hindi literature (Trivedi, qtd. in French 2008: 199), though Naipaul himself may be intrigued to know that, without realizing it, he had in this regard written one of the great Hindu/Indian novels of all time, a genre whose very possibility he later called into question.

In *A House for Mr Biswas*, the hero realizes, as soon as he has got married, that by marrying one member of it he has been drafted into the whole Tulsi clan: "He was expected to become a Tulsi" (Naipaul 1961: 99). This aspect of marriage in the context of an Indian extended family has been comically exaggerated in a recent novel, *2 States: The Story of My Marriage* by Chetan Bhagat, in which, though the girl whom the hero wants to marry has already accepted him, the hero realizes that he must get her parents and her younger brother to consent to the idea as well, and therefore invites all of them to dinner, pulls out four rings and goes down on his knee to say: "I, Krish Malhotra, would like to propose to all of you. Will all of you marry me?" (Bhagat 2009: 183). Though largely unheard of in the West, Bhagat is, as attested by some extracts from reviews of his earlier works quoted at the beginning of this book, "the biggest-selling English-language novelist in India's history" according to the *New York Times*, and "a rockstar of Indian publishing" according to the *Times of India*. His dedication of this novel reads: "This may be the first time in the history of books, but here goes: Dedicated to my in-laws" (Bhagat 2009: ii, v).

A House for Mr Biswas also conforms to another important aspect of the Indian novel as it evolved in the nineteenth century: The hero gets married early on in the narrative, on page 99 in an edition that runs to 623 pages. This is, of course, radically unlike numerous Western novels in which the author saves up this connubial event or eventuality for the last chapter if not the last page—apparently oblivious of the reality-check that as a rule, it is only after one has got married that the fun (or the real mature business of living) begins. Such premature conventional closure of numerous Western novels may be regarded as a literary device so artificial as to serve to undermine retrospectively much of the realism that may have preceded it. It was mocked two hundred years ago by Jane Austen in her very first novel *Northanger Abbey* (written 1798–1799; published 1817), in which she wrote with a meta-fictional flourish in the last chapter that though the hero and the heroine were still anxiously in suspense as to whether they will be able to marry each other and when, such anxiety could not possibly infect "the bosom of my readers, who will see in the tell–tale compression of the pages before them, that we are all hastening together to perfect felicity" (Austen 1817: ch. 31, par. 4).

Of the major English novels of the nineteenth century written in the high realist mode, George Eliot's *Middlemarch* is an exception in this regard, for it depicts its main characters as marrying early to repent at leisure in the rest of the long novel. Virginia Woolf, in a highly appreciative assessment of George Eliot on the occasion of her birth-centenary in 1919, acclaimed as her masterpiece "the mature *Middlemarch*, the magnificent book which, with all its imperfections, is one of the few English novels written for grown up people" (Woolf 1966: 201). This remark occurs somewhat as a *non sequitur* and has puzzled many readers. But, arguably, Woolf was here drawing attention precisely to the fact that this 'mature' novel does not conform to the romantic convention that just getting married is the be-all and the end-all of life. Incidentally, though Virginia Woolf herself followed the nineteenth-century convention in this regard in her two earliest novels, *The Voyage Out* (1915) and *Night and Day* (1919), she never went back to the old template in any of her seven subsequent novels, and the greatest among them, such as *Mrs Dalloway* (1925), *To the Lighthouse* (1927) and *Between the Acts* (1941), in fact begin with the central characters already long married and clearly not living very happily ever after.

Conclusion

"The novel arrived in India much as Athena did in Greek mythology, fully formed from the heads, and hands, of a paternalistic ruling power," says Priya Joshi whose own pioneering work in book history focuses on the import and circulation of British novels in India in the latter half of the nineteenth century (Joshi 2006: 495). The British novel may have arrived in India in an already fully developed state in terms of its own tradition, but it clearly did not carry any divine authority or sanction in India and was soon re-moulded into something of local relevance and meaning. Whether Western or Black in origin (as argued by Martin Bernal), this Athena was seen by Indian writers to be a false goddess and soon transformed into a Brown Athena, in a thoroughly refashioned avatar. The novel in India successfully resisted the tyranny of this Western form and adapted and domesticated it radically to the local cultural scene.

In this chapter, an attempt has been made to explore and assess the claims and counter-claims of Western and Indian reality and realism as they relate to the writing of novels, and to view in a comparative light a major theme and staple of the Western novel, love and marriage, and its radically different treatment in the Indian novel. In an earlier discussion elsewhere, I had examined the varied nomenclatures by which the novel came to be known in the different Indian languages; the continuing presence in some early examples of the Indian novel of the supernatural and of passages in verse; the incursion in early Hindi novels of some White characters and Western objects and of other manifestations of colonial modernity; the remote physical spaces in the hinterland of India nearly exempt from colonial authority that some early Hindi novelists identified as their preferred fictional locales and exploited with spectacular success; and the continuing debate in India on the issue whether we have been able truly to 'master' the genre of the Western novel (cf. Trivedi 2003: 999–1007). There remain, of course, numerous other aspects of this complex literary and cultural interaction to be studied and analyzed, of which just one may be briefly noted here by way of an inconclusive conclusion.

This concerns the apparently mechanical and mundane matter of the norms regarding the length of a novel. The Western novel has traditionally been required to be 'of a certain length' and if it falls short of that, it is regarded as a novella or a long short story. This is presumably because novels are seen as modern prose equivalents of the classic epics in verse and thus expected to possess a similar fullness of scope and treatment. But this Western norm is again not necessarily universal. No categorical difference is made in several literary cultures between a novel and a novella,[2] and the lack of logic in the term 'short story' in English is exposed as soon as we look at its equivalents in other languages. To start with, why should the 'short story' be called short when if it were long it would not be called a 'long story' but rather a novella or a novel? Is the mere length of a fictional work the major criterion behind this distinction, or is it possible to take into account other intrinsic factors? And what happens to this mechanically metric distinction when we find that, unlike in English, it is not the novel but the (short) story which is the major fictional form in many other literary cultures in which most important novelists have been equally important short story writers. In the case of Hindi, both the twentieth-century writers of fiction named above, Premchand and Nirmal Verma, are in common critical regard quite as significant as short story writers as they are as novelists.

The persistent Indian predilection for the short story and the high critical regard accorded to it may arguably derive from some phenomenally successful collections of loosely linked stories produced in India right at the beginning of the narrative tradition in Sanskrit and Pali. The most famous of these, the *Panchatantra*, comprises fables with animals as well as stories with human characters which relate to a wide variety of situations and psychological motivations, are wittily told with a comic enjoyment of life, and contain a brief moral expressed in an aphoristic *shloka* or verse couplet appended at the end.

No less remarkable than this work, composed probably in the 3rd century B.C., is its transmission all over the world, from China and Japan in the East to Persia, Arabia, and Europe in the West. It was translated into Persian in the sixth century, into Arabic in the eighth, into Greek in the eleventh, into Spanish in the thirteenth, into Latin and German in the fifteenth, into Czech in 1528, and eventually into English (from the Italian) under the title *The Moral Philosophie of Doni* by Sir Thomas North in 1570 ('R.T.' 1991: 3064–3066). This was two decades before Shakespeare began to write, three decades before the East India Company was set up, and one and a half centuries before the novel arose in English or the British Empire in India. According to the Russian Indologist S.F. Oldenburg, it "became one of the most widely circulated books in the world after the Bible" (Oldenburg qtd. in Galik 1989: 120). In the present context, to think of the *Panchatantra* and its lively 'short' stories and of their global spread and influence as a foundational text of storytelling is a salutary reminder of genres of fictional narration other than the novel and of the long pre-colonial period in the literatures of the world before the advent of the postcolonial.

Notes

1. For a rare instance in Hindi fiction of caste-defying love, see *Shyamasvapna* by Jagmohan Singh, 1885.
2. See for example the discussion of the traditional pre-novelistic Arabic narrative form, the *qissa*, by Abdelfattah Kilitto 2006: 262–268.

Works Cited

Austen, J. (1817) *Northanger Abbey*, http://www.pemberley.com/etext/NA/chapter31.htm. Accessed: Nov. 12, 2011.

Azim, F. (1993) *The Colonial Rise of the Novel*, London: Routledge.

Bhagavad-Gita, The (1986) Ed. and trans. Bhaktivedanta Swami Prabhupada, A.C. Mumbai: The Bhaktivedanta Book Trust.

Bhagat, C. (2009) *2 States: The Story of My Marriage*, New Delhi: Rupa & Co.

Chaturvedi, R. (1986; reprinted 1994) *Hindi Sahitya aur Samvedana ka Vikas* [The Development of Hindi Literature and Sensibility], Allahabad: Lok Bharati.

'D.B.M.' [Deepak B. Mehta] (1991; reprinted 1999) 'Nilkanth, Mahipatram Rupram', in M. Lal (ed.) *Encyclopedia of Indian Literature*, vol. IV, New Delhi: Sahitya Akademi, 2950.

Dummett, M. (2011) 'Not so happily ever after as Indian divorce rate doubles', *BBC News*, 1 January 2011. http://www.bbc.co.uk/news/world-south-asia-12094360. Accessed: Nov. 12, 2011.

Dutt, P.G. (1870; reprinted 1986) *Devrani Jethani ki Kahani*, New Delhi: Rishabh Charan Jain evam Santati.

French, P. (2008) *The World is What It Is: The Authorized Biography of V.S. Naipaul*, London: Picador.

Galik, M. (1989) 'East-West Interliterariness: A Theoretical Sketch and a Historical Overview', in A. Dev and S.K. Das (eds) *Comparative Literature: Theory and Practice*, New Delhi: Indian Institute of Advanced Study/Allied Publishers, 116–128.

Joshi, P. (2006) 'India, 1850–1900', in F. Moretti (ed.) *The Novel: Vol. I: History, Geography and Culture*, Princeton: Princeton University Press, 495–508.

Kilito, A. (2006) 'Qissa', in F. Moretti (ed.) *The Novel: Vol. I: History, Geography and Culture*, Princeton: Princeton University Press, 262–268.

Kipling, R. (2011) *Kim*, H. Trivedi (ed.), London: Penguin Classics.

'Kyunki Saas Bhi Kabhi Bahu Thi' [TV programme] (2011) http://en.wikipedia.org/wiki/Kyunki_Saas_Bhi_Kabhi_Bahu_Thi. Accessed: Nov. 10, 2011.

Mukherjee, M. (1985) *Realism and Reality: The Novel and Society in India*, Oxford: Oxford University Press.

Naipaul, V.S. (1961; reprinted 2002) *A House for Mr Biswas*, London: Picador.

———. (1964; reprinted 1975) *An Area of Darkness*, Harmondsworth: Penguin Books.

———. (1977; reprinted 1979) *India: A Wounded Civilization*, New Delhi: Penguin Books India.

Narayan, R.K. (1949) *Mr. Sampath–The Printer of Malgudi*, London: Eyre & Spottiswoode.

Phullauri, S. (1877; reprinted 1973) *Bhagyavati*, New Delhi: Sharada Prakashan.

Prawer Jhabvala, R. (1960) *The Housholder*, New York: W.W. Norton.

Said, E. (1993) *Culture and Imperialism*, New York: Knopf.

———. (2011) 'Appendix: Introduction to *Kim* by Edward W. Said [Penguin Classics 1987]', in H. Trivedi (ed.) *Kim*, London: Penguin Books.

Shukla, R. (1929; reprinted 1940) *Hindi Sahitya ka Itihas* [A History of Hindi Literature], Allahabad: Indian Press.

Singh, T.J. (1885; reprinted 1954) *Shyamasvapna* [Dreaming of Shyama], Kashi [Banaras/Varanasi]: Nagaripracharini Sabha.

'R.T.' [Radhavallabh Tripathi] (1991; reprinted 1999) 'Pachatantra', in M. Lal (ed.) *Encyclopedia of Indian Literature*, vol. IV, New Delhi: Sahitya Akademi, 3064–3066.

Trivedi, H. (2003) 'The Progress of Hindi Part 2: Hindi and the Nation', in S. Pollock (ed.) *Literary Cultures in History: Reconstructions from South Asia*, Berkeley: University of California Press, 958–1022.

———. (2005) 'Colonizing Love: *Romeo and Juliet* in Modern Indian Disseminations', in P. Trivedi and D. Bartholomeusz (eds) *India's Shakespeare: Translation, Interpretation and Performance*, Newark: University of Delaware Press, 74–91.

Woolf, V. (1966) 'George Eliot', in *Collected Essays*, vol. I, London: Hogarth Press.

2 Post-colonial Utopianism

The Utility of Hope

Bill Ashcroft

"Farewell Reverberated Vault of Detentions"
Lionel Fogarty

Today up home my people are
indeedly beautifully smiling
for the devil's sweeten words are
gone.
Today my people are quenching
the waters of rivers without grog
Today my people are eating delicious
rare food of long ago.
Tonight a fire is made round
for a dance of leisuring enjoyment
where no violence fights stirs.
Certainly my people are god given
A birthright of wise men and women
Our country is still our Motherland
Our desires ain't dying in pitifully
lusting over contempt and condition
Tonight my peoples sleep
Without a tang of fear
No paralysed minds
No numbed bodies
No pierced hearts hurt
The screams of madness ends.
[. . .]
Today my people feel precious as
human beings burials and birth
Mankind demands imperative love
for all, And my people never
wants to escalating barbarous century.
For now Today up home they free,
Tonight they learn to fight consciences. (Fogarty 1996: 266)[1]

Locating a Genre

I begin with this poem to suggest a movement that has developed almost unnoticed in post-colonial writing, a persistent hope for the future that refuses to be snuffed out however much it is couched in irony, however impossible it seems. Fogarty's hope, expressed as much in terms of recovery and critique of the present as in terms of possibility, concerns his people conceived as a group connected to the earth, survivors of devastation, a people in country, a people at home. But what is the manner of its dwelling in the *nation*? It is that last word round which the ambivalence, complexity, and contradiction of post-colonial utopianism revolves. For in whatever way we frame it, this genre takes a form that ignores, or repudiates, the concept of nation inherited from the colonial state. The word 'nation' itself is absent as post-colonial writers conceive a hope that takes various shapes: geographical, historical, cultural, racial—shapes that may constitute an emerging genre of post-colonial utopianism.

The suggestion that such a genre may exist is made possible by the disruption of the idea of genre itself, a disruption suggested by Adena Rosmarin when she asks:

> Does genre constitute the particular or do particulars constitute the genre? Are genres found in texts, in the reader's mind, in the author's, or in some combination thereof? Or are they not "found" at all but, rather, devised and used? Are they "theoretical" or "historical"? Are they "prescriptive" or "descriptive"? Are they used deductively or inductively? Can we "see" them or do they hover on the hermeneutic "horizon," always potentially but never actually in view? Is their use in literary explanation inevitable? If so, should it be foregrounded? Can genres be used to explain "literariness"? Or are they the enemy of all that makes literature seem "literary"? Might they be the enemy of the reader as well, a too rigorous constraint on the interpretive act? How many genres are there? Where do they come from? How, exactly, do they work? And change? (Rosmarin 1986: 7)

These questions, and, we might say, the proliferation of *doubt* with which they surround the concept of genre, open a space for the emerging genre of post-colonial utopianism. While genre seems wedded, traditionally, to the concept of form, the excessive horizonality of form, its recalcitrant resistance to definition, is itself conducive to the identification of new post-colonial genres revolving around conceptual rather than formalistic criteria.

The different manifestations of this genre are nearly always at least an implicit critique of state oppression of one kind or another. If such a genre can be identified, it does so by means of a set of relations: the relation between liberation, nationalism, and the nation-state; between the sacred and the secular; between memory and the future; and between the material conditions of post-colonial societies and the particular nature of their imagined possibilities. I am particularly concerned with the ways in which they are conceived in literary narrative, but I want to consider their relation to the concept of nation in general to assess the utility of hope. In literature, the utility of utopia lies in the generation of hope itself. But is there any political instrumentality in utopian thinking?

Why utopia? Utopia is by definition impossible, an unachievable ideal, a fanciful dream, unrealistic, and naive. Yet utopian theory has undergone a vigorous renaissance during the post-Cold War period of global empire. A curious combination of Marxist theory and science fiction has led the way in utopian thought in the latter part of the twentieth century. Indeed, between Ernst Bloch in the 1930s and Fredric Jameson in the 1990s Marxist thinkers have taken most of the theoretical initiative. But utopianism has also been flourishing unobserved in post-colonial literatures during that same period. The concept of the utopian remains an anchor to any theory of a better world, any hope for social change and amenity. In using the word *utopianism* we already make a distinction between the fantasy, the 'placeless place,' of Thomas More's imagined island, and the irrepressible belief in a liberated future. The issue is not what is imagined, the *product* of utopia so to speak, but the *process* of imagining itself.

Indeed, for most contemporary utopian theory Utopia is no longer a place but the spirit of hope itself. For Fredric Jameson, 'practical thinking' everywhere represents a capitulation to the system. "The Utopian idea, on the contrary, keeps alive the possibility of a world qualitatively distinct from this one and takes the form of a stubborn negation of all that is" (Jameson 1971: 110–111). This linking of utopia and hope begins with Bloch who sees what he calls 'the anticipatory consciousness' as the fundamental internalization of the utopian in human experience. It is through the *novum*–the idea of the new–that we orient ourselves and reshape questions about the nature of human existence in concrete ways so that we can see more clearly the direction of utopia. It is this spirit that lies at the heart of post-colonial liberation. But this, in turn, is built upon a profound paradox, which underlies all our encounters with the genre: All achieved utopias are degenerate, yet without *utopianism*, without the spirit of hope, liberation is not possible.

We might also ask 'Why literature?' Literature, according to Ernst Bloch, is inherently utopian because its *raison d'être* is the imaging of a different world–what he calls its "anticipatory illumination." The anticipatory illumination is the revelation of the "possibilities for rearranging social and political relations to produce *Heimat*, Bloch's word for the home that we have all sensed but have never experienced or known. It is *Heimat* as utopia [. . .] that determines the truth-content of a work of art" (Zipes 1989: xxxiii). This is the home of Lionel Fogarty's poem, and *Heimat* becomes the promise in post-colonial writing that replaces the promise of nation. It may lie in the *future* but the promise of *Heimat* transforms the present.

Imagination forms the basis of the utopian in literature, and it is the process of imagining that forms the basis of the utopian in post-colonial transformation. The idea that literature has a utopian function is nevertheless apt to confuse people: It does not mean that literary works themselves are always utopian, nor even necessarily hopeful, but rather that the imaging of a different world in literature is the most consistent expression of the anticipatory consciousness that characterizes human thinking. It is the function of imagining that forms the basis of the utopian in literature and the basis of the utopian in post-colonial resistance. Utopia is a vision of possibility that effects the transformation of social life. It is desire in the act of imagining, and imagination that can be at once oppositional and visionary, a state of affairs that explains the importance of the literary and other creative arts in post-colonial representation.

Post-colonial Utopia and the Nation

There is a certain irony in the existence of post-colonial utopianism since the colonialist ethic present in Thomas More's *Utopia*—which was founded by King Utopus subduing the indigenous inhabitants of Abraxa—was extended in the eighteenth century by the literary imagination of various kinds of colonial utopias. James Burgh's *Cessares* (1764), Thomas Spence's *Crusonia* (1782), Carl Wadstrom's *Sierra Leone* (1787), Wolfe Tone's *Hawaii* (1790), Thomas Northmore's *Makar* (1795), and Robert Southey's *Caermadoc* (1799) were all utopias established in isolated regions of Africa, the Caribbean, South America, or the Pacific, with a blithe absence of moral qualms about setting up a colonial utopia on someone else's land. These were necessarily distant utopias of defined and bounded geographical space, an ambiguous precursor of the *national* utopias that were to give a vision of a post-colonial liberation.

This is not an idle paradox. The pre-independence utopia of a liberated post-colonial nation provided a very clear focus for anti-colonial activism in British and other colonies, but this appeared to come to an abrupt halt once the goal of that activism was reached and the sombre realities of post-independence political life began to be felt. The post-colonial nation, a once glorious utopian idea, was now replaced in the literature, particularly in Africa, by a critical rhetoric that often landed authors in gaol. But gradually, in writers such as Ayi Kwei Armah, Ngugi wa Thiong'o, or Ben Okri, and latterly women writers such as Chimamanda Adichie, Sade Adeniran, and Unomah Azuah, post-independence despair gave way to a broader sense of future hope. Post-colonial utopian thought now gains its particular character from its *problematic* relationship with the concept of the nation. The utopian vision takes various forms, but it is always a form of hope that transcends the boundaries of the nation-state, because that concept represents disappointment and entrapment rather than liberation.

This suggests a considerable revision of the now somewhat notorious idea of Frederic Jameson's that all Third World texts are national allegories (Jameson 1986: 69). Aijaz Ahmad's equally notorious response was to accuse Jameson of turning all Asian and African critics and writers into mystified 'civilizational others' by reducing all the issues they dealt with to the problem of a nationalist struggle against colonial oppressors and their post-colonial successors (Ahmad 1987). Ahmad underestimated the importance of the word 'allegory' and the undoubted prominence of national concerns. But by the same token, 'national allegory' fails to embrace the complexity of the relationship between literature and the idea of nation. In particular, it "fails to adequately describe the dissolution of the idea of nation and the continuous persistence of national concerns" (Franco 1989: 211). Indeed, we could also say that the term 'nationalism' itself fails to grasp the complexity of writing that expresses a future hope that in some respects might fall into the category of 'national concerns,' and yet appears to completely supersede the idea of nation as a failed, or at least contested, category. But whether expressing 'national concerns' or not, contemporary utopian thought works beneath, above or outside the concept of the nation-state.

The core of the problem of the post-colonial nation was the inheritance of colonial boundaries. As Wole Soyinka put it, the Berlin Conference in 1884 carved up Africa "like some demented tailor who paid no attention to the fabric, colour or pattern of the quilt he was patching together" (Soyinka 1994: 31). The problem was that individual nations and the OAU itself, which might have done something about it, kept the colonial boundaries sacrosanct. Likewise, the catastrophic partitioning of India not only institutionalized ethnic hatred as a strategic enmity that still dominates South Asian politics, but exposed the real absurdity of boundaries, as Amitav Ghosh reveals in *The Shadow Lines*. In the case of Africa, anti-colonial nationalism was always going to be undermined by the fracturing reality of colonial boundaries.

Post-independence nations have almost inevitably taken over the role of the colonial state and maintained its administrative and class structure. As Fanon says:

> National consciousness, instead of being the all-embracing crystallization of the innermost hopes of the whole people, instead of being the immediate and most obvious result of the mobilization of the people, will be in any case only an empty shell, a crude and fragile travesty of what it might have been. (Fanon 1963: 148)

I will return to Fanon's phrase "the innermost hopes of the whole people" in a moment, but he goes on to describe the way the newly created middle class will "look toward the former mother country and the foreign capitalists who count on its obliging compliance" (Fanon 1963: 149). This merely confirms the structural reality which colonialism installs and which the nation cannot escape. Just as boundaries and colonialism went hand in hand, so they locked incipient nationalisms into a discourse that in most cases amounted to a political prison.

This prison wasn't entirely inherited in Africa. Ali Mazrui made the point nearly three decades ago that "while the greatest friend of African nationalism is race consciousness, the greatest enemy of African nationhood is ethnic-consciousness" (Mazrui 1982: 23–24).

> Modern African nationalism was born and prospered under the stimulation of racial solidarity and shared blackness. On the other hand, the struggle for viable modern nations within Africa is considerably hampered by ethnic cleavages. (Mazrui 1982: 24)

An early vision of escape from this prison came with the idea of a post-colonial transnationalism. The symbolic moment of anti-colonial solidarity came in 1955 with the Asian-African conference in Bandung, Indonesia, in which twenty-nine formerly colonized nations met in a groundbreaking conference that was meant to establish what today might be called a 'new world order.' The African contingent was, in reality, quite small—only Egypt, Libya, Ethiopia, and Liberia were independent, and if we look at a map of African independence we see why. Most African colonies didn't receive independence until the 1960s. But Richard Wright's 1956 travelogue *The Color Curtain*, written after he attended the conference, "depicts the moment of transition from anti-colonial dream to postcolonial reality as one already rife with failure" (Ahmad 2009: 179).

The moment that might have been the realization of W.E.B. Du Bois' "world of colored folk" is depicted as "a world of irrationality, mysticism, lack of specificity and internal incoherence" (Ahmad 2009: 179). But even more problematic than the conditions eliciting this rebuke from black American modernity, a problem very soon to be elaborated in African literature, was the political betrayal of colonial nationalist hopes. Wright may have urged newly independent nations to foreswear mysticism and become "secular and practical" (Wright 1994 [1956]: 218), but these nations proved themselves more than capable of learning the lessons of their former masters, including the pull of Cold War polarities. In his words, all the men at the Bandung conference "represented governments that had already seized power and they did not know what to do with it" (Wright 1994 [1956]: 207). Despite its symbolic importance, the conference showed "how the newly independent nations have lost the energy of resistance and gained an unwelcome accountability without achieving anything resembling the motivating utopia" (Ahmad 2009: 180). This betrayal of nationalist hope provided the themes for much post-colonial writing in the years to come.

But the utopianism of post-colonial writing began to overcome the trauma of independence, and the spirit of hope replaced the vision of particular national utopias. At the same time, it took a different direction from the hopeful spirit of transnational unity that dominated the Bandung conference. Post-colonial utopianism after independence went beyond national boundaries and also beyond transnationalism. Although it might still be based in the concept of a people, it embraced a fluidity, mobility, and multiplicity, that while still recognizable as 'African,' 'Indian,' 'Chicano/a,' or 'Oceanic' conceived of freedom, identification or self-representation in a space beyond the nation-state. This is true, paradoxically, even when writers used the concept of 'nation' to identify a people with a cultural or ethnic unity. The distinction between a nation, which represented a people, and the nation state, which represented the political and administrative structures providing identifiable boundaries to that people, became a marked feature of the new utopianism.

Varieties of Utopian Heimat

When we look closely at the genre of utopian writing after independence, we see immediately its expansive supra-national character. Indeed it seems that the vision of a future beyond the nation is the one shared characteristic of post-colonial literary utopianism. African utopianism, for instance, reverts either to a historic sense of pharaonic identity or embeds a sense of cultural 'Africanness' in a mythic consciousness that extends beyond any particular nation. Caribbean utopianism is most familiarly situated in Rastafarianism with a vision of return to Ethiopia, and the nation features hardly at all in discussions of Caribbean arts or sport. Neither does the African past represent utopia, rather the memory of Africa in Caribbean writing is seen as something that can transform the present with a vision of the future. The Indian literary transnation is perhaps most identifiable in its 'transnational' character, while still retaining a sense of 'India.' Indeed the exuberant vibrancy and hybridity of South Asian writing in writers such as Rushdie, Mistry, Tharoor, and Ghosh has had an extensive global impact. At the other end of the scale, the utopianism of the tiny island nations of the Pacific rests in the vision of a region called Oceania. By encompassing a *Heimat* based on traditional patterns of migration and trade, Oceania is markedly distinct from, and markedly more impressive than a collection of island nations.

The utopianism of indigenous people is one that exists categorically within yet beyond the nation and is also deeply invested in cultural memory. A beautiful description of this occurs in Alex Miller's *Landscape of Farewell* when the narrator goes with an Aboriginal man to visit his ancestral country:

> It was still the country of his Old People, as he called his ancestors, the term familiar and intimate, as if they were not remote beings whose individual features had been forgotten long ago, but were known to him and were a people still in occupation of their lands. It was a term that seemed to suggest that the entire colonial enterprise had never taken

place, and that the old reality, like the Old People themselves, had not become extinct but had defied our belief in history and had survived. The Old People, indeed, suggested to me another way altogether of look ing at reality and the passage of time than my own familiar historical sense of things, in which change and the fragmentation of epochs and experience is the only certainty. (Miller 2007: 233–234)

The journey is later described as one made by Dougald to the spiritual centre of his life, a centre that exists in a place that is somehow outside of geography as it is outside time.[2]

The implication of this of course is that nationalism, or more specifically, the post-colonial nation-state, may well be incommensurable with the cultural realities of colonial peoples, a fact that becomes obvious in post-independence states from Africa to the Caribbean to Asia. It is this incommensurability that provides some of the energy and most of the direction of post-colonial utopian literature after the disillusion with the post-colonial nation state. If there is one thing post-colonial writers share in their very different material and cultural circumstances, it is that *Heimat* is not the nation.

In all these literary versions of post-colonial hope there is a vision of *Heimat* in either a geographical region, a culture, a local community, a racial identity, in a disruption of conventional boundaries, a dynamic operation of memory, and most often a sense of the sacred. This *Heimat* indeed, is where we can say this genre of post-colonial utopianism is 'located.' One of the most striking examples of the political utility of utopia can be seen in the Chicano myth of Aztlán. Rudolfo Anaya's novel *Heart of Aztlan* captured the spirit of this myth which was politically embedded in the pronouncement of *El Plan Espiritual de Aztlán* at the First Chicano National Conference in Denver in 1969, which confirmed three important things: a Chicano ethnicity, a homeland, and a nation. The Chicano version of utopian thinking, the Aztlán myth, proved to be a surprisingly resilient weapon in the Chicano political arsenal because it so comprehensively united ethnicity, place, and nation. It differs from other post-colonial utopias because it combined the mythic and the political so directly: on one hand it was a spiritual homeland, a sacred place of origin; on the other it generated a practical (if impossible) goal of re-conquering the territories taken from Mexico. But this union of sacred and political proved to be its secret power. Aztlán, the Chicano utopia, became a focus for Chicano cultural and political identity and a permanent confirmation of the possibility of cultural regeneration. For a people dwelling in the cultural, racial, and geographical borderlands, Aztlán represented its national hope.

Gandhi and Hind Swaraj

These different regions and literatures indicate the variety of the utopian impulse, and the various visions of home. But a question that must be put to all forms of literary resistance is: 'How is the literary vision implicated in political life?' I want to focus on a specific non-literary utopian vision to engage this difficult question of its *utility*, and in particular to trace the utility of one form of post-colonial utopianism in its very ambivalent orientation to the nation. This is Gandhi's vision of *Hind Swaraj* or Indian Home Rule—one of the most potent forms of utopianism in modern times, and one with a deep sense of sacred vision. How did this locate itself in the nationalist drive to independence? Utopianism and politics are not necessarily identical, nor always compatible. Jameson sees Utopianism "not as some unlocking of the political [. . .] but rather a whole distinct process in its own right" (Jameson 2005: 10), and this is a useful caution, particularly where literary utopianism is concerned. But what does *Hind Swaraj* tell us about the relation of the utopian to the political? The reason for turning to this radical social movement is that it demonstrates, more directly than literary visions of possibility, the point at which utopian thinking leads to social change, and thus helps us assess the political utility of utopian thinking.

The reason *Hind Swaraj* is so interesting is that it was able to achieve what Fanon thought nationalism could not do: mobilize the "innermost hopes of the whole people." It is arguable that Nehru's modern industrial socialist nation could not have been established without the utopia of *Hind Swaraj*. But paradoxically this vision, so critical in the birth of Indian nationalism, was anti-nationalist, anti-Enlightenment and anti-modern. 'Home rule' imagined an India outside any conception of the modern nation state—an India much closer to Bloch's conception of *Heimat* than to the modern idea of nation. This paradox emerges in Partha Chatterjee's foundational *Nationalist Thought and the Colonial World* (1986), which, while it doesn't mention utopia, exposes the ambivalent relationship between utopian thinking and nation building and the actual process by which utopian thinking may evolve, or 'degenerate,' into an organized nation-state machine.

Chatterjee offers the thesis that post-colonial nationalism emerges in three stages: the moment of departure, the moment of manoeuvre, and the moment of arrival. He identifies these stages in the three Indian thinkers Bankimchandra Chattopadhyay, Mohandas Ghandi, and Jawaharlal Nehru, all of whose philosophies exhibit a particular relation to the problematic and thematic of Orientalism, which underlies the nationalist discourse it inherits from Enlightenment thinking. Nationalist thinking might reverse the *problematic* of Orientalist thought which sees the 'Oriental' as a passive and essentialized subject, but still operates within the Orientalist *thematic*—the post-Enlightenment framework of Knowledge, Science, and Reason within which it re-defines that subject.

> There is, consequently, an inherent contradictoriness in nationalist thinking because it reasons within a framework of knowledge whose representational structure corresponds to the very structure of power nationalist thought seeks to repudiate. (Chatterjee 1986: 38)

For Chatterjee, this contradictoriness signifies both the theoretical insolubility of the national question in a colonial country and the extended problem of social transformation in a post-colonial country, within a strictly nationalist framework (Chatterjee 1986: 39).[3] But one solution to this problem was a utopianism that was able to step outside *both* the problematic and thematic of Enlightenment thinking. Gandhi's *Hind Swaraj* was able to transcend the imperatives of modernity and of global capitalism and repudiate the nation-state as a symptom of the problem. Ironically, this came to be seen as a foundation on which an alternative Indian modernity could emerge.

Gandhi's conception of *Swaraj* is an almost perfect utopianism, a classic utopia that existed by repudiating post-Enlightenment thought itself. Gandhi is, in fact, the firmest believer in a classical utopian system that we can find in anti-colonial thought. *Swaraj* is so important because there are very few classic utopias of the kind found in the history of utopian literature—ideal societies located either in the future or in a distant land, characterized principally by absence of private property. The paradox of Gandhi's *Swaraj* is that a utopian moment so critical in the development of Indian nationalist thinking was fundamentally opposed to that modernity on which the nation was founded. For him:

> It is not the backwardness or lack of modernity of India's culture that keeps it in continued subjection [. . .] it is precisely because Indians were seduced by the glitter of modern civilization that they became a subject people. And what keeps them in subjection is the acceptance by leading sections of Indians of the supposed benefits of civilization. (Chatterjee 1986: 86)

Swaraj is not just an attack on capitalism, but an attack on civil society itself. Industrialization would lead to the exploitation of villages and socialism would not change this (Chatterjee 1986: 88). The pamphlet *Hind Swaraj or Indian Home Rule*, first published in the columns of *Indian Opinion* and written in 1908 on a voyage home from London, stylistically avoids the doctrinaire by setting up a dialogue between Reader and Editor. In this way utopia emerges as a conversation rather than a program, which tends to domesticate its radical utopian vision but also reinforces the fact that the utopian agenda is an ethical rather than economic imperative.

Gandhi's critique of 'modern civilization' is a condemnation of the

> entire edifice of bourgeois society: its continually expanding and prosperous economic life, based on individual property, the social division of labour, and the impersonal laws of the market. (Chatterjee 1986: 90)

In his essay "Enlightened Anarchy: A Political Ideal," Gandhi's rejection of modern civilization includes its system of democratic government, which will become unnecessary if the national life becomes so perfect as to be self-controlled. It will then be a state of enlightened anarchy in which each person will be his own ruler. He will conduct himself in such a way that his behaviour will not hamper the well-being of his neighbours. In an ideal State there will be no political institution and therefore no political power. (Gandhi 1958, vol. 68: 256)

The sheer breadth of Gandhi's moral expectation brings him to the critical point at which utopias inevitably dissolve into dystopias—the need for some kind of controlling force or structure to guarantee this moral imperative. But the formalization of *Swaraj* into a political program is something Gandhi refused to envisage no matter how often he was asked to provide a practical structure of *Swaraj*. While Marxist critics condemn Gandhi for failing to endorse the kind of structural program that might have institutionalized a mass grassroots textile industry, Gandhi remains the most radical utopian for this very refusal. Indeed he remains the most radical anarchist in history because he constantly refused to systematize the processes of worker control. Whatever the merits or possibilities of Gandhi's belief in human behaviour, his position transcends both the problematic and the thematic of colonial nationalism. Marxist critique of Gandhi, by contrast, operates firmly within the Enlightenment thematic of such nationalism.

Gandhi's was not a literary utopianism but a social movement, and it provides a fascinating test case for the political utility of utopian thinking. In its essence it shows very clearly the distinction between nation and state, because the colonial state was opposed by a concept of the nation as a whole. The 'science' of non-violence, *satyagraha*, "provided for the first time in Indian politics," says Chatterjee, "an ideological basis for including the *whole people* within the political nation" (Chatterjee 1986: 110). This whole people, in its multiplicity, its mobility, and annoying capacity to render the boundaries of the state porous, may also be referred to as a 'transnation.' The nation had its own boundaries and divisions, most notably the caste system which Gandhism worked strenuously to overturn. But the utopian vision of the whole people could be kept quarantined from the business of state politics and the business of Congress. "Swaraj can only come through an all-round consciousness of the masses" (Gandhi 1958a: 9–10).

The interesting feature of Gandhism is the ease with which it maintained a vision of the apparently unobtainable, such as the ideal of property in trust. This, like all other ideals, would "remain an unattainable ideal, so long as we are alive, but towards which we must ceaselessly strive" (Gandhi 1958b:318). This may go some of the way to explaining one of the greatest changes of direction in Gandhi's program—the change to the principle of Khadi or village based weaving. In 1944, Gandhi proposed a 'New Khadi Philosophy.' Whereas khadi workers had sold their cloth to small khadi shops in the city, now Gandhi demanded that khadi stop being sold but that each village (and ideally each peasant) should become self-sufficient in cloth. Again Gandhi was interested in the moral significance but it had a potentially huge impact on the khadi industry already developed. Although it represented a major change in direction, it was consistent with Gandhi's vision of a system lying quite outside the system of industrial capitalism that the emerging nation-state could not avoid.

Here lies the profound and defining paradox in utopian thinking as radical as Gandhi's: In order to remain true to its ideals it must divorce itself from the possibility of even a partial success, which is precisely what 'national development' now represented. *Swaraj* could only maintain its character as a social possibility if it separated itself from the emerging machinery of the post-colonial nation state. This is because Ghandi's, like all utopias, is a critical utopia, and utopian interventions "like those of the great revolutionaries, always aim at the alleviation and elimination of sources of exploitation and suffering" (Jameson 2005: 12), rather than at blueprints for a perfect world.

Gandhi and Nehru's Statism

How then did Gandhi's *Hind Swaraj* pave the way for Nehru's statism? First, it showed that an organized support could be built on the 'whole' of the peasantry. But second, it did so because the politics of non-violence could not achieve what Gandhi intended, that is, "to train the masses in self-consciousness and attainment of power" (Jameson 2005: 124). The political mobilization of the peasantry not only took a different form than Gandhi had envisaged, but took a form that could be said to have contradicted his vision. This is because, according to Chatterjee, the next stage of the nationalist project, its moment of arrival, was to "situate nationalism within the domain of a *state ideology*" (Chatterjee 1986: 132). This was the position of Nehru who believed that a strong nation-state structure was essential to the provision of social justice, which was impossible under the decadent colonial state. A new set of modern institutions must be established so that the economic structures of society could be reorganized and enough wealth created to ensure social justice for all. This, unlike Gandhi's, must be an achievable utopia, in which the state has a central coordinating and directing role. In Nehru's mind, only a modern socialist state could provide for all.

Mother India

Here then, is the paradox: Gandhi's radical utopia—which transcended not only capitalism but also civil society itself and the very concept of the modern nation—became the vision on which the Indian nation was built. The process by which national modernity appropriated Gandhi's utopian vision can be seen to be uncannily replicated in the iconic *ur-text* of the Indian film industry: *Mother India* (also known as *Bharat Mata*, directed by Mehboob

Khan in 1957). This is a film that not only embodies India's development of its own modernity, but metonymically reproduces the contradictions of that development. It re-invents the foundational myth of Nehruvian socialism—the nation-state will provide for the marginalized and needy—by appropriating the maternal embodiment of land and community. Just as Nehru founded the nation-state on the back of Gandhi's ability to mobilize the whole cross-section of the Indian people with *Hind Swaraj*, so the film shows the modern state built on the foundation of a communal peasant tradition. Crucially, and not surprisingly, the mother myth of India, of *Bharat Mata*, persists despite the plight of actual women, whose back-breaking life is enacted by the heroine in a hymn of sacrifice and suffering.

In 1949, the Film Enquiry Committee commissioned by the Ministry of Information and Broadcasting appealed to Indian producers and directors to co-operate with the government, and share the responsibility of nation-building. Indian cinema should serve as an "effective instrument" for "national culture, education and healthy entertainment" to promote and further induce "a national character with its multifaceted aspects" (Government of India 1951: 46). Mehboob Khan, under his studio's banner of hammer and sickle, completed this monumental saga eight years later. Indian cinema became a protector of the official culture and the history of the nation, and gained the status of the generally accepted social and ethical consciousness of India.

Mehboob reproduced "the Indian woman" as an icon of national martyrdom and submission to the nation-state, although for one critic "[it] is neither in touch with the reality of the largely economic, social and political exploitation of Indian women, nor does it sympathise in any way with the real plights of peasants" (Schulze 2002: 75). Ever since *Mother India*, filmmakers have been adapting and reproducing its national iconic imagery and emotional set-up, albeit as the same scenario of the individual sacrificing for the collective.

The effect is to make this vision of India appear a discovery rather than an invention, just as Nehru's *The Discovery of India* was the invention of an India that could lead into the new utopia of Indian nationhood. The core of this invention was of course 'Indian Civilization,' which had never existed as a homogeneous entity and was as removed from daily reality as *Mother India* from peasant women. Nehru's invention of Indian national culture lay well within the thematic of Orientalism which traditionally constructed India under the rubric of an unchangeable 'Hinduism,' based on the Sanskrit epics and the "golden Aryan past" which very few upper castes ever inhabited.

In the opening credits of *Mother India* we see the deeply wrinkled face of a woman, Radha, "Mother India" lifting a lump of earth close to her face and then letting the earth slowly crumble in her work-worn hands. The camera draws back a little, to take in her surroundings. The old woman is squatting in the furrow ploughed by a tractor driving behind her. We see the technological progress taking place in rural India: high-tension wires, a tarred road, cars, construction vehicles and tractors, a bridge construction, and a dam site in the making, with cranes moving busily. We follow a jeep to the village. A group of men, their Gandhi caps indicative of official status and their INC links, are respectfully positioning themselves in front of the old woman: "Mother, your village is now provided with water and electricity." Held in high esteem by all, the mother is being requested to inaugurate the new dam. She refuses in humble timidity, though her son convinces her to go along. At the dam site, our eyes glide over the vast water surface. The mother is to be adorned by flower garlands. Here, too, she modestly declines. She does not approve of such honour bestowed upon her. She bows her head, and again her son convinces her. Ultimately, she is decorated with flowers, their fragrance evoking memories in the old woman.

In the following two and half-hours, we see how Radha is transformed into "Mother India." It begins with the memory of her wedding day and her virtuously downcast countenance. But in time her husband who loses his arms in an agricultural accident is too ashamed to be a burden and so leaves. She resists the sexual advances of the local moneylender and she remains poor, virtuous, and highly respected by all in the village. Her youngest son Birgu tries many times to retrieve the bangles that she wore at her wedding and which are now with the moneylender. Eventually joining a dacoit gang, he returns one day to humiliate the moneylender and retrieve the bangles.

His childhood love is going to be married off. He rides wildly through the apparently idyllic village and aims straight for the moneylender. He takes his mother's bangles from the moneylender and without any hesitation sets fire to all the debt records and account books that bonded the village people to him. But when riding away from an angry village with his childhood sweetheart, his mother runs after him, calls his name, and then shoots him with a gun from behind. She rushes to the dying son and holds him. He hands over, with his last strength, the bangles to her. His blood runs over his mother's hand and in a superimposition of images, in mother's memory, the blood mixes with the water flowing from the dam sluice into the canals. However, as it does so the red becomes clear—she has sacrificed her son that the nation may be purified.

The symbolism is disturbing: Honour is to be preserved above justice; tradition to be maintained against disruption at all costs; strangest of all, the traditional structure of village life must be preserved to avoid hindering the process of modernization. The mother—India herself—must ensure this. The shooting of the son is the sign of the violent cessation of a certain kind of order in which resistance is still possible. The nation has no room for lawlessness. Its utopia, like all achieved utopias, is one in which the regulation of the individual is necessary for the good of the collective. The collective of the modern nation-state rests on the solid foundation of Indian civilization— *Bharat Mata*.

The Utility of Utopia

I do not equate Gandhi's vision of *Hind Swaraj* in any simple way with that romantic vision of a Mother India produced by Mehboob's film. Gandhi's vision was neither an economic nor a cultural romanticism because he lay completely outside the problematic and thematic of Enlightenment thought—the very thematic that mobilizes the Mother India image. Neither can we see in Birgu an example of Gandhi's enlightened anarchy in which each man ruled, because that form of anarchy assumed the leadership of the wise and moral *satyagrahi*—the local leader of the non-violence movement. But I make the comparison to show the process by which Nehru's modern Indian nation-state was able to build on the idea of *Swaraj*, just as it built on the myth of Indian civilization that he claimed to have 'discovered.' Both of these encompassed Fanon's phrase "the innermost hopes of the whole people." In the film that 'whole' is a mythic fantasy, whereas in reality Indian independence was successful because Gandhi had paved the way for a belief that the Indian people, regardless of caste division, and in particular including the peasantry, could be instrumental in the project of national self-determination. Paradoxically this occurred, not through a concept of the nation, but a vision of *Heimat* on which all that hope for liberation was projected.

What then of the utility of utopia? And what is Gandhi's relation to literary utopianism? If we examine *Hind Swaraj* in order to address the question of the political utility of literary utopianism, we see that the literary vision and the social movement have something in common. Their value lies not in their capacity for producing social change directly, but for encapsulating that intensity of desire for *Heimat* without which change cannot take place. That desire is founded on a thorough critique of the conditions of exploitation and oppression. The fact that political change in India meant Nehru adopting the statism Gandhi's *Swaraj* explicitly rejects, does not alter the fact that it was the vision of *Swaraj* which mobilized the Indian peasantry into a sense of being a whole people, despite the disruptions and divisiveness of caste. To put it another way, it may have been Gandhi's vision that enabled Indians to imagine a national community, the very imagined community on which Nehru built the post-colonial nation.

> Paradoxical as it is, the fact still remains that Gandhism, originally the product of an anarchist philosophy of resistance to state oppression, itself becomes a participant in its imbrication with a nationalist state ideology. (Chatterjee 1986: 155)

This is not the only contradiction in the trajectory of utopian thought, nor does it need to stand as an argument for or against political utility, but in the Indian case, it is one of the most fascinating. Did Nehru hijack the utopian vision of Gandhi's *Swaraj*, or did *Swaraj* infuse Indian modernity with its particular character? Did Gandhi's radical vision fail because it stood so far outside the problematic and thematic of modernity? Or did it succeed because it mobilized the "innermost hopes of the whole people," providing the vision and the energy for the Nehruvian nation-state? This conundrum lies embedded deep in the very concept of utopia because it reveals the complex and ambivalent relationship between utopian vision and politics. What emerged was a new utopia, modern, scientific, industrial—a state that existed to provide identifiable political, economic boundaries within which the Indian transnation could embrace modernity. What is undeniable is that Gandhi's vision and the virtually beatified memory of the man himself remain deeply imprinted on the Indian cultural psyche.

The conclusion we reach is that the power of utopian thought may well lie in its transcendence of the practical. The power and hence, we may say, the utility of Gandhi's vision was maintained by his adamant, impractical refusal to reduce his vision of *Swaraj* to a structured political program. Ironically, it was this refusal that gave his vision its attraction, mobilized a whole people, and ultimately conceived the Indian nation. This, I believe, is why utopianism manifests itself so widely and so powerfully in post-colonial literatures, and why literature is such an important vehicle of the utopian. Literature is not called upon, in fact importuned, to produce a practical program in the way Gandhi was. But literature is important because what can be imagined always exceeds that which can be achieved. The energy and utility of this genre of post-colonial utopianism might lie in its similar refusal to be reduced to a practical program, because what literature anticipates, what it illuminates, is the power of desire itself.

Notes

1.   Thanks are due to L. Fogarty for granting copyright approval to Bill Ashcroft to quote from his poem.
2.   There are many examples I could take from contemporary Aboriginal writers to describe the indigenous feeling for country, but I use this quote from a white writer to indicate the degree to which the Aboriginal sense of *Heimat* in the Dreaming is becoming understood in Australia.
3.   We should note in passing that where Chatterjee talks about nationalism and the nation-state he is talking about India where nationalist discourse is both historically long-lived and well developed. Although many inferences can be made to post-colonial nationalism around the world, the case he discusses is not identical with them all.

Works Cited

Ahmad, A. (1987) 'Jameson's Rhetoric of Otherness and the "National Allegory"', *Social Text*, 17: 3–25.

Ahmad, D. (2009) *Landscapes of Hope: Anti-Colonial Utopianism in America*, Oxford, New York: Oxford University Press.

Chatterjee, P. (1986) *Nationalist Thought and the Colonial World: A Derivative Discourse*, Minneapolis: University of Minnesota Press.

Fanon, F. (1963) *The Wretched of the Earth*, trans. C. Farrington, New York: Grove Press.

Fogarty, L. (1996) 'Farewell Reverberated Vault of Detentions', in P. Porter (ed.) *The Oxford Book of Modern Australian Verse*, Melbourne: Oxford University Press, 266.

Franco, J. (1989) 'The Nation as Imagined Community', in H.A. Veeser (ed.) *The New Historicism*, London: Routledge, 204–212.

Gandhi, M.K. (1958a) Speech at AICC Meeting, Patna, 19 May 1934; in *The Collected Works of Mahatma Gandhi*, New Delhi: Publications Division, vol. 58: 9–10.

———. (1958b) Interview 9 Nov 1934; in *The Collected Works of Mahatma Gandhi*, New Delhi: Publications Division, vol. 59: 318.

Government of India (1951) Ministry of Information and Broadcasting: Report of the Film Enquiry Committee, New Delhi: Government of India Press, 46.

Jameson, F. (1971) *Marxism and Form: Twentieth Century Dialectical Theories of Literature*, Princeton: Princeton University Press.

———. (1986) 'Third World Literature in the Era of Multinational Capitalism', *Social Text*, 15: 65–88.

———. (2005) *Archaeologies of the Future: The Desire called Utopia and Other Science Fictions*, London, New York: Verso.

Mazrui, A. (1982) 'Africa Between Nationalism and Nationhood', *Journal of Black Studies*, 13/1: 23–44.

Miller, A. (2007) *Landscape of Farewell*, Sydney: Allen & Unwin.

Rosmarin, A. (1986) *The Power of Genre*, Minneapolis: University of Minnesota Press.

Schulze, B. (2002) 'The Cinematic "Discovery of India": Mehboob's Re-Invention of the Nation in Mother India', *Social Scientist*, 30/9–10: 72–87.

Soyinka, W. (1994) Interview with Nathan Gardels, 'Bloodsoaked Quilt of Africa', *Weekly Mail and Guardian* (South African), 20–26 May 1994: 31.

Wright, R. (1994 [1956]) *The Color Curtain*, Jackson, MS: University of Mississippi Press.

Zipes, J. (1989) 'Introduction: Toward a Realization of Anticipatory Illumination', in E. Bloch, *The Utopian Function of Art and Literature: Selected Essays*, trans. J. Zipes and F. Mecklenburg, Minneapolis: University of Minnesota Press, xi–xliii.

3 " . . . At the Edge of Writing and Speech"

Shifting Genre, Relocating the Aesthetic

Saskia Schabio

Shifting Genre—Relocating the Aesthetic

In her discussion of postcolonial aesthetics, Deepika Bahri observed a "remarkable lack of a sufficiently developed critical framework for addressing 'the aesthetic dimension' (in Herbert Marcuse's words) of post-colonial literature" (Bahri 2003: 1). Invoking the aesthetic in postcolonial literature is an enterprise with an inherent predicament. Arguably, "aesthetics" as a discipline was founded on orientalism and the dialectics of East and West.[1] And yet, postcolonial studies seems currently to be preoccupied with a recalibration of the 'aesthetic,' in which a sustained interest in 'genre' is observable. With some scepticism, invocations of the aesthetic may be traceable to disciplinary concerns —as if raising postcolonial studies to the ranks of the philosophy of art.

With less scepticism, what seems at stake is a preoccupation which would pose a challenge to the aesthetic as a "First world discipline" (Bahri 2003: 104).[2] Just how to pose that challenge is the issue. The problem is, partly, one of choosing between the alternatives of understanding postcolonial aesthetics as a descriptive enterprise—even in the absence of neutral standards of comparison—or consciously acknowledging the 'generic' nature of postcolonial agendas, with a recognizable normative orientation—as Bahri does when, *pace* Marcuse, positing an ineliminable utopian and liberatory dimension of the aesthetic.

I take an interest in 'genre' itself as a particularly viable tool in this discussion, offering a way of enhancing reflection on the often unexamined evaluative standards and contexts that tend to shape the reception of postcolonial literature.[3] How does genre help us to understand, in Brennan's words, "why third-world art is so neglected, condescended to, or homogenized before it appears in cosmopolitan packaging . . . ?" (Brennan 1997: 315). Such a line of inquiry would also include models of generic evolution themselves, that is, generic histories and the particular locales of their emergence (Cf. Hitchcock 2003). A pertinent example is the ascription of value to oral forms in accounts of generic evolution and poetic invention—which is often invoked in approaches that would not pander to metropolitan audiences.

The Vernacular and the New

Such a view on generic innovation invites comparison with Dante's *De vulgari eloquentia* (ca. 1305), and the fashioning of the vernacular self in the deviation from classical models, as in Montaigne's invention of the autobiographic mode in his *Essais:*

> OTHERS fashion man, I repeat him; and represent a particular one, but ill made; and whom were I to forme a new, he should be far other than he is; but he is now made. And though the lines of my picture change and vary, yet loose they not themselves. The world runnes all on wheeles. All things therein move without intermission [. . .] I cannot settle my object; it goeth so unquietly and staggering, with a naturall drunkennesse. [. . .] I describe not the essence, but the passage; not a passage from age to age, or as the people reckon, from seaven yeares to seaven, but from day to day, from minute to minute. I may soone change, not onely fortune, but intention. (Montaigne 1946: vol. 2, 392)

As this excursion to incipient European modernity and its exemplary conjunction of inventiveness and self-invention reminds us, the 'irruption' of speech into the supposedly stable nature of the written word and decorum of self-representation is foundational for the emergent genre of the *Essais.* Even so, the example reveals the extent to which the staggering, transitional subject, 'in passage,' is at the core of liberal humanism. (Montaigne's own unstable positioning as a member of the lower ranks of the aristocracy, and located at the periphery, is pertinent.) Such a view on genre serves to put into perspective claims of the autonomy of the Western self, and dependency models along with claims of originality. In the following, I propose to discuss Édouard Glissant's notion of the 'Novel of the Americas' and approach to orality in *Caribbean Discourse* as a viable intervention into this discussion.

We see him ostentatiously place the work of decolonization, with which *Caribbean Discourse*, first published in French in 1981, is so intensely concerned, within the context of genre, and, in particular, the novel genre. Writing at about the same time, Glissant arrives at a conclusion as radical as Derrida's contemporary call to make "light of all the tranquil categories of genre-theory and history in order to upset their taxonomic certainties, the distribution of their classes, and the presumed stability of their classical nomenclatures" (Derrida 1980: 63). For him, however, such questioning is existential in eliminating the basis of any 'dependency complex'[4] (Glissant 1989: 136) and prerogative of a 'First world aesthetics,' a prerequisite to his thinking on cultural renewal *tout court*; this is seen through the angle of a particular Caribbean experience of modernity, and with clear political and material implications. At the same time, *Caribbean Discourse* offers a sustained critique of the evolution of the Western novel as an evaluative standard in discussions of postcolonial literature (cf. also Brennan 1990; Edwards 2004).

Orature and Utopia

Arguably, Che Guevara's "el hombre nuevo" had inspired Édouard Glissant's vision of the "New Man" in *Caribbean Discourse*.[5] One may deem this excessively airy, yet to achieve such 'newness,' Glissant set great stakes by what he named the "Novel of the Americas." In this context, he stated:

> The issue (experienced in the specific struggles that take place more or less everywhere along the chain of the Americas) is the appearance of a new man, whom I would define, with reference to his "realization" in literature, as a man who is able to live the relative after having suffered the absolute. (Glissant 1989: 147)

By "relative" he refers to "the obscure need to accept the Other's difference," by absolute the "dramatic endeavor to impose a truth on the Other." He feels, that "the man from the Other America 'merges' with this new man, who lives the relative;" and he sees this "new creation" "witness[ed]" in the people's fight for survival across the American continent (Glissant 1989: 147–148).

Of the Americas, often figuring in the European utopian imagination either as the "Paradise islands," or a "non-place" to be conquered, Glissant cannot speak in a language of origins and pure beginnings. Instead, his work may be taken as a pivotal example of "the critical inflection" the European utopian tradition "has received in Caribbean writing" (cf. Schabio 2009: 315, 322). While "occidental utopia," as he states in a later piece, designs "a perfect shape," and is driven by 'normative' intent (Glissant 2005: 141), the utopianism he has in mind emerges from 'living the relative,' an ontological "need to accept the Other's difference" (Glissant 1989: 147–148) yet most pertinent in the Caribbean in the political struggle of peoples for survival across the Americas. The term "utopia" gains currency in later writing, such as *La Cohée du Lamentin* (2005). Even so, Glissant does not detail the utopian dimensions of such writing in his chapter on what he deems, in *Caribbean Discourse*, the "Novel of the Americas" (Glissant 1989: 144). But his remarks on the "cross-cultural poetics," or "poetics of creolization" (Glissant 1989: 142) strongly intimate a utopian intent, inspiring the people's "self-renewal," which he develops in later work alongside his poetological considerations and expanding vision of creolization (Glissant 1989: 223–224). This, originating in the Caribbean, but applicable across the world, past and future. If creolization is observable across the world, in the current accelerated "entanglements of world-wide relation" (Glissant 1997: 31), this is a tendency always present in literature. In an interview on his *La Terre, le Feu, l'Eau et les Vents: Une Anthologie de la Poésie du Tout-monde* (2010), he pronounced that

"Tout-Monde" forms the new condition of all literatures and contemporary authors to have severed all regional or national ties in search of the Other across time ["quêtes de l'Autre à travers les âges," Glissant 2011: npn]. The lineaments of such thinking are also perceivable in his *Poetics of Relation* (1997), where he urges to "renew the visions and aesthetics of relating to the earth" (Glissant 1997: 148). Here, it becomes clear that this potential is deeply connected with his expanding vision of creolization. As in *Caribbean Discourse*, Glissant establishes a close relation between the utopian and the particular "insular" or "archipelagic" nature, of which Caribbean experience of creolization seems to present an exemplary case. In *La Cohée du Lamentin*, once again, the "Archipels" emerge as utopian 'mode'—abstaining from violence and embarking on the mission to inspire, sharing and participating in the languages of the world (my paraphrase):

Jeudi 1er mai. Archipels

Qui ne participent pas de la force et se donnent mission d'inspirer. Qui partagent la parole entre toutes les langues du monde. (Glissant 2005: 27)

This is taken from the chapter titled "Au jour le jour, en un recoin de l'année 2002" (Glissant 2005: 21). It brings together, in a style reminiscent of both diary and aphorism, a particular day, often referring to world political events in the news, and one of Glissant's key terms such as *mondialité, identité, la relation*, as if to point out the contrapuntal nature of "Art" (Glissant 2005: 27).

To whom this persona is speaking in such a manner, at once impressionistic and magisterially apodictic, and which community this speech of utopia is heard and read by, is open to debate and an issue in itself: Is it Martinique, where his bearings lie—the title *La Cohée du Lamentin* will remain opaque to those unfamiliar with the particulars of this place—in the Caribbean archipelago, is it the Americas, or, is the addressee indeed a world (literary) community? Or even "un peuple qui manque," 'a people that is missing' (Glissant 2005: 16), which Glissant invokes in a previous chapter boastingly entitled "Incipit absolu" (Glissant 2005: 15)?[6] This title, at once, indicates simply the "opening line," marking off the incomplete nature of what is said, as well as a practice predating the advent of the printed word and ascription of titles to texts (a 'non-title title').

I take this to be programmatic: While, as he stated in *Caribbean Discourse*, Glissant doubted whether Creole would offer a way of reconciling "the rules of writing and the teeming, irrepressible element in 'oralture'" (Glissant 1989: 245), the relation between speech and writing seems crucial, both in his poetological and in his literary work. Furthermore, if Glissant's poetics bears a close relation to the utopian, a radical questioning of the Western division of genre, I will argue in the following, is vital to this enterprise. If genres are always emergent, but the novel is taken to be particularly so, precisely for its close contact with the vernacular, Glissant offers an alternative to an evolutionary model based on 'novelization.' With his acknowledgment of popular and communal forms, of speech genres, and orality, his notion of creolization seems deceptively close to Bakhtin's evolutionary model. However, Glissant's concept differs from Bakhtin's in important ways, not least for its challenge of the Western novel. Giving its famed "cannibalistic" nature a negative turn, the novel, according to him, was monoglot, rather than polyglot, a genre which "increasingly caused all exploration of time and all related techniques to be restricted to this genre" (Glissant 1989: 136). These considerations are perhaps most fully fleshed out in *Caribbean Discourse*, departing from what he deems the "poetics of the oral African text" (Glissant 1989: 137). Preceding the lines cited at the outset, which so boldly parallel the aesthetic, the birth of this "new man," and the liberation struggles across the Americas, Glissant had specified his image of the "Novel of the Americas" in terms "of a tortured relationship between writing and orality" (Glissant 1989: 144, 147).

Observing a transition from oral to written forms in Martinique, what he gleans from his experience as a writer, is a keen sense of a literature "under constraint," true for both "traditional oral literature" and "a written nontraditional literature" (Glissant 1989: 147). As he footnotes, these considerations refer to the novel of the "Other America," that is "the Caribbean and South America," and not part of the northern "urban, industrial world" of the U.S. (Glissant 1989: 147). Such a broad vision allows him to align Faulkner with the "Other America" for a common experience of diaspora and the plantation system. Extrapolating from Faulkner, the novel of this Other America is for Glissant the marked expression of a shared history, experienced as "exploded, suffered time," as "nonhistory" (Glissant 1989: 144, 223).

Such regional alignment and new geopolitical formation seemed politically desirable at the time Glissant was writing. He references, for example, the second Latin American Congress of Negro-African cultures held in 1980 in Panama and the responsibilities he sees for the intellectual in bringing about an alternative future (Glissant 1989: 225). Obviously, he was contributing to the project of economic, political, and cultural self-empowerment behind the formation of the Caribbean federation (cf. also Niblett and Oloff 2009: 13). In this context, the fact of creolization as an experience shared across the Caribbean, and including the French, Spanish, and Anglophone territories, provided a major argument within that cause, as did his notion of a "cross-cultural poetics." Clearly, this was a concrete strategic and political project—even if maintained against all odds, as Glissant concedes with an eye on the failure of a Caribbean federation in the Anglophone Caribbean (Glissant 1989: 222). Yet it meant devising a whole new basis for the aesthetic, one that would neither be strangled by notions of belated imitation, nor submit to nativism: Describing his quest, Glissant claims: "My language attempts to take shape at the edge of writing and speech." Here, he refers to moving beyond the novelist's use of "every-day speech" as he is striving for a "synthesis of written syntax and spoken rhythms, of 'acquired' writing and oral 'reflex,' of the solitude of writing and the solidarity of the collective voice" (Glissant 1989: 147).

Glissant is making space for a revaluation of the oral that is not folklore. Neither is this the naturalist's positivist and documentary way of recording pieces of real-life conversations and the mundane. He rather presents the (utopian) idea of a fusion, or creation of a spatial and temporal continuum, between the written records of history and lived experience, the individual and the communal. At the same time, we are given a version of relating anew the people and the poet, "a new man," "in touch with a new audience of the spoken word" (Glissant 1989: 108). In other words, Glissant takes us beyond the opposition between nativist and modernist aesthetics—here I see him as conversant with the examples given by Ferial Ghazoul in her contribution in this volume, as much as with Pio Zirimu's endeavours of emphasizing both the richness of oral traditions and their pertinence in literate societies (*orature*).[7] Instead, the "synthesis" he mentions emerges as the effect of a shared, if specific and local, experience of modernity in the Americas: As he states, the "landscape has its language," positing a deep structural relation, in what he deems "our world," between the wording of the 'American Novel' and the surrounding landscape, which he perceives as ever-changing and mobile. He values the particulars of each landscape, as for example when turning to the particulars of his own, that of Martinique, that of the forest, so unlike that of the "meadow" or the "serenity of the spring." Yet while acknowledging the entanglement of man and the specific locale, he asserts the shared experience in the "*irruption into modernity*" across the Americas (Glissant 1989: 146).

One may, in search of an equally powerful enterprise, think of Kamau Brathwaite's *History of the Voice* (1979) and his reminder that the "hurricane does not roar in pentameter," noting the inappropriateness of Western forms to Caribbean self-expression (Brathwaite 1993: 265). "Nation language," Brathwaite memorably stated, "largely ignores the pentameter" (Brathwaite 1993: 265). This is certainly not an exact analogy. But, like Brathwaite, Glissant also recognizes the book as "the tool of forced poetics" (Glissant 1989: 244–245), while he deems "orality" "the instrument of natural poetics" (Glissant 1989: 245). Yet he remains aware of the "trap of the 'official' strategy of promoting folklore" (Glissant 1989: 218), and uncertain whether Creole would offer a way of mediating "the rules of writing and the teeming, irrepressible speech in 'oraliture'" (Glissant 1989: 245). Instead he suggests a critical analysis of forms such as the folktale, in which he sees "[n]ational consciousness" take hold, even though not fully developed and, potentially stifling any truly liberatory impulse; an instance of this being, as he observes in folktales, the absence of "daily techniques of work or creation"—the means of production are always the colonizer's possession—and the inability to "undertake the transformation of his [Man's] landscape" (Glissant 1989: 131, 132).

With their emphasis on the "language of landscape" (Glissant 1989: 145), these considerations are reminiscent of Glissant's first novel, *The Ripening*

(1958), in which his characters seek "full knowledge of this land, the full taste of each hidden corner" (Glissant 1985: 90). "This is the place," said Thaël. "And we discovered it. We can say we have made it ours. Yesterday, it had the blood of our forefathers, today it has our voice" (Glissant 1985: 185). In *Caribbean Discourse*, Glissant seems to be extending the concern of *The Ripening* with nation building, and expanding it, to the strategic image of an enlarged Caribbean, as he is concerned with the American writer in "search for temporal duration" (Glissant 1989: 144).

First and foremost then, his considerations of genre thrive on the insight, pointed out in Wiemann's essay, that genres, "in structuring the sphere of reading practices, serve also to condition writing practices" for very prag-matic reasons (Bennett 1990: 103–104; qtd. Wiemann in this volume, p. 155).

At the same time, Glissant's project is of a more categorical nature, as he strikes at the heart of the Western division of genres, and the foundations, indeed, of a first world aesthetics. Conspicuously, his point of entry is a cri-tique of the opposition between epic and novel, an opposition which, for all their difference of approach, has proven so formative to both Lukács's, as well as Bakhtin's writing on genre, and has been endowed with their particu-lar correlations of modernity and the rise of the novel. Glissant strategically introduces the "poetics of the oral African text" (Glissant 1989: 137)—his wording expressly casts the oral in terms of the structuralist terminology of text and, hence, unhinges any simple nativist projection. In fact, to be raising the issue of a deep relation between the oral and the written appears to be the main issue: In other words, that "synthesis of written syntax and spoken rhythms" (Glissant 1989: 147). Such writing would be particularly relevant to the Caribbean and thrive on the "ruptures in Caribbean culture," in which the African element and the "dignity of the group" was faced with the impossibility of "the collective non-possession of the land" and "in which the explicitness of the song (the traditional oral culture)" was disrupted by Western forms (Glissant 1989: 137).

Even so, he cautions against a polarized perception of genres and their ascription to a "poetics so diametrically opposed," so as to "neutralize these poetics in relation to each other" as well as confining them to "their conven-tions instead of allowing the latter to be challenged" (Glissant 1989: 136–137). In other words, this is Glissant's way of saying that 'genres are always emergent.' Still, when he interprets "relation" as an evolutionary principle in an on-going process of generic transformation, this also connects with the transformation 'at large,' which he envisages in the "appearance of the New Man"—"able to live the relative after having suffered the absolute" (Glissant 1989: 147).

Longue Durée Perspectives—Novel or Epic?[8]

In the course of *Caribbean Discourse*, Glissant discusses a number of forms such as folktale, epic and tragedy. The audacity with which he correlates the question of genre and the work of decolonization is breathtaking. An important part of these efforts revolves around definitions of 'epic' and 'novel.' His point of departure is the African epic of the Zulu Emperor Chaka (Mofolo 1981), which he takes as an exemplary case for the African epic. Yet his first move is to note similarities with Western epic forms, such as tyranny and communal participation in the hero's dramatic downfall as well as the magical moment which cannot be claimed as specific to the African epic. Neither does this apply to the oral form of its presentation, as he states with an eye on Homer's poems. However, the African epic deviates from Western examples in that it "is not concerned with the *origin* of a people or its early history." It also does not recount a "creation myth" (Glissant 1989: 134). But, instead, in a way reminiscent of Darwish's 'poetry of Troy' (cf. Williams in this volume, p. 68), it is an epic of "conquered heroes," which was also that of their communities—but not asserting, neither legitimizing these (Glissant 1989: 135). At this point Glissant marks its difference from the *Illiad*, the *Odyssey*, and the *Old Testament*. He ends these considerations with a reference to Hegel's notion of the epic (Glissant 1989: 135), and reaches the conclusion that "the epic is disruptive. History comes to an abrupt end," anticipating the violent arrival of the white man—"that this contact with another culture *would come*" (Glissant 1989: 135–136).

By this, Glissant expressly refutes Hegel's explanation of the epic as "'naive consciousness'," and by implication also refutes Lukács who follows Hegel's interpretation.[9] The African epic as a precolonial form is marked by a "strangled awareness" that will be felt and experienced throughout colonization "in the life of African peoples" (Glissant 1989: 135).

In other words, Glissant establishes a *long durée* perspective (as outlined in the introduction) by anchoring an experience of modernity in the African epic, and effectively cancelling established postcolonial perspectives on narratology. As Harish Trivedi demonstrates, Edward Said still adheres to Lukács's view, when referring to the "world of the novel in its fallen, unhappy state," as marked off "from the world of the epic, which is happy, satisfied, full" (Said 2011 [1987]: 324; qtd. Trivedi in this volume, p. 17). Glissant's move is precisely to question the concept of the epic as chanting of a world that is "happy, satisfied, full," dynamizing both Edenic projections of the African past and a generic nomenclature clustered around the Western novel. Even more pertinent than Lukács, whom Glissant might be referencing *pace* Hegel, are potential cross-references to Bakhtin's notion that the epic "has been from the beginning a poem about the past" (Bakhtin 1981: 13)—a past, that is "absolute and complete," ignorant of "openendedness, indecision, indeterminacy" (Bakhtin 1981: 16). This allows him to cast the novel as "the only genre born of this new world and in total affinity with" it and novelization as a principle of change (Bakhtin 1981: 7). The 'new world' Bakhtin refers to is a "world become[s] polyglot, once and for all and irreversibly," with the "period of national languages, coexisting but closed and deaf to each other," having "come[s] to an end" (Bakhtin 1981: 12).

Glissant challenges ossifying perspectives on epic and novel, Bakhtinian or Lukácsian. Their approaches to generic evolution were related to a particular trajectory of modernity and a specific interpretation of changes in society. If Bakhtin traces the emergence of the novel to a "very specific rupture in the history of European civilization," namely its "entrance into international and interlingual contacts and relationships" (Bakhtin 1981: 11), the "Novel of the Americas" (Glissant 1989: 144) emerges from the "ruptures in Caribbean culture" Glissant evokes (Glissant 1989: 137).

Where does this leave us? The "mere invocation of the novel as a sign of modernity," Peter Hitchcock states, "is also a sign that alternative local modernities may be sacrificed for Western prerogatives" (2003: 324–325). Expanding on Bakhtin's "The Problem of Speech Genres," he proposes to specify the "process of novelization in relation to the primary speech genres of a particular location" (Hitchcock 2003: 319).

Glissant may provide the point of departure for such a reconsideration, taking his project of recalibrating writing and speech as a starting point— born from his particular notion of modernity and poetic investment in political and economic decolonization.[10]

Such a transformed approach to genre is to be traced from *Caribbean Discourse*, and the 'Novel of the Americas,' through his *La Cohée du Lamentin*, to his notion of *la poésie du Tout-Monde* in *La Terre, Le Feu, L'Eau et les Vents* (2010). Here, he explicitly shuns traditional generic distinctions and advances "la poésie" in terms of a "mélange" or "mixture" of genres, beyond purely formal concerns, and as if indeed advancing an alternative to the 'novel,' and the evolution of poetic newness from this genre. His strategic refutation of the "dependency complex" in *Caribbean Discourse* is restated in the preface to his anthology and in his refutation of the opposition between "anthropological literature," on the one hand, and literature *tout court*, on the other. What the texts assembled in his anthology solicit, he claims, is a shared "intelligence" and "opening of the spirit" (Glissant 2011: npn).

Conclusion

We have observed Glissant interpret creolization as an evolutionary principle in an ongoing process of generic transformation. He boldly equates this with both a utopian and a political process, first in the struggles across the Americas, "carrying forward our people to self-renewal" (Glissant 1989: 223) and, then, with reference to what he deems *Tout-Monde*, or *mondialité*, a "prodigious reality" ["realité prodigieuse"], to which "our utopias belong," and which is contrarian to globalization ["le revers négatif"] (Glissant 2005: 15).

Whatever objections there may be to the dangers of such culturalism,[11] and to such a correlation of genre and socio-political reality, a radical questioning of traditional Western concepts of novel and epic, I have been arguing, is crucial to this project. We see him thus weave an inevitable connection between genre and utopian thinking, as if also underwriting the close link between the disruption of genre and an emergent genre of postcolonial utopianism that Bill Ashcroft has traced: "The issue is not what is imagined, the *product* of utopia so to speak, but the *process* of imagining itself" (cf. Ashcroft in this volume, pp. 28-29). Furthermore, if Ashcroft aligns that emergent genre in particular with Bloch's notion of the *novum*, Glissant's statement in *La Cohée du Lamentin*, that occidental utopia, above all, designs 'the perfect shape' (Glissant 2005: 141), is normative, parallels a Blochian approach. As a "place," "utopia" is a good place, only in as much as it is the "proper place" of the "missing people" ["le lieu même de ce peuple", "un peuple qui manque"]. Glissant then plays on the difference between, as Ashcroft has it, "the 'placeless place,' of Thomas More's imagined island," and "the irrepressible belief in a liberated future" (cf. Ashcroft in this volume, p. 29), a future, of which Glissant can only speak in terms of repetition and *correctio*, ostentatiously figuring "it" forth and negating "it." "It" is "not a dream," "it is what is missing in the world," "this is what it is; that which we are missing in the world" (my translation).

> L'Utopie n'est pas le rêve. Elle est ce qui nous manque dans le monde. Voici ce qu'elle est: cela, qui nous manque dans le monde. (Glissant 2005: 16)

Glissant hence also refers to the interrelation between utopia and space, striking at the very foundations of the genre of narrative utopia, a genre which, Wegner explains, is predicated on the birth of the "singularly modern construct of the nation-state" as an "original spatial, social, and cultural form" (Wegner 2002: 15, xvi). However, as much as Glissant critiques deformations of nationalism in the postcolonial state throughout his work, his notion of an ongoing process of generic transformation also allows for reflecting, in essentially generic terms, on the persistence of an "Orwellian nemesis" (Harris 1983: xv), and on the confinement within the narrative of a "largely" Western "dystopian" "modernity," of utopian as well as dystopian perspectives on the nation state.[12] This, for Glissant, may have been a way of wrenching the postcolonial and utopianism from inscription within the confines of these "tranquil categories" of genre as well (Derrida 1980: 59), while, at the same time, making space for enlarged thinking on the 'crosscultural' in *Caribbean Discourse*.[13] These are large claims, I realize, requiring further analysis, and I have been unable to give more than a glimpse of the ground Glissant is shifting, or to contextualize his approach to genre and to orality. Yet, for one who memorably wrote, "We do not fear utopia, it is our sole Act : our sole form of Art" ["Nous ne craignons pas l'Utopie, elle est notre seul Acte : notre seul Art"] (Glissant 2005: 27; my translation), such questioning is existential *and* a way of wrenching the aesthetic from the premises of orientalism. Glissant's audacity in coupling the aesthetic and the political in his understanding of genre may appear extremely culturalist, and, for that matter, evasive. Nonetheless, it is also a way of recalibrating the notion that to "look at literature through genres is to grasp the former historically," and, thereby, reconsider the way literature engages the historical and the political (Heath 2004: 168; qtd. Wiemann in this volume, p. 155).

Notes

1. While heeding the dangers of a false universalism in discussions of non-Western art, anthropologist and cognitivist studies at the same time posit a new universalism. Hogan hopes that in expanding on the possibilities of comparative literature, one may arrive, finally, at the "isolation of universal principles of literary composition, structure, reception, etc.," challenging this dialectics (Hogan 1995: 3). Cf. his later *The Mind and Its Stories* for a continuation of this discussion and Chari 1995. On "universal aesthetic value" versus "relativism" see Dutton 2001: 289. For a sustained analysis of Hegel's position, see P.G. Stillman 2005.
2. Cf. Spivak: "It would work to make the traditional linguistic sophistication of Comparative Literature supplement Area Studies (and history, anthropology, political theory, and sociology) by approaching the language of the other not only as a 'field' language . . . " (Spivak 2003: 9).
3. Examples are the relative transparency of the novel versus poetry, the novel as a popular form, or as an allegory of the postcolonial nation, nativism versus modernism, and in particular, the written versus the oral. However, as Brennan observed, " . . . under conditions of illiteracy and shortages, and given simply the leisure-time necessary for reading one, the novel has been an elitist and minority form in developing countries when compared to poem, song, television and film. [. . .] It has been, in short a naturally cosmopolitan form that empire has allowed to play a national role, as it were, only in an international arena" (Brennan 1990: 18).
4. Glissant explicitly takes sides with Fanon's refutation of Mannoni's notion of a "dependency complex" (Glissant 1989: 136).
5. See Niblett and Oloff 2009: 15 for this connection. For a discussion of Glissant's notion of the 'Other America,' see also Dash 1998. The following discussion draws on Glissant's notion of "cultural newness" (Schabio 2009: 317ff.), with respect to a common Caribbean identity and federation (cf. Schabio 2009: 316ff.), his approach to the nation, and emphasis on relating to the particulars of landscape, evolving from *The Ripening* to *Poetics of Relation* (cf. Schabio 2009: 314, 317–321).
6. This requires further exploration of Glissant's Deleuzean references (Glissant 2005: 16) and their relation to the Blochian overtones of his thinking—in particular in light of his engagement in the "Utopia Station" project (2003) which had referenced Bloch's phrase "something's missing" (cf. Nesbit et al. 2003 npn; Schabio 2009: 310). I have first discussed tensions with a Deleuzean approach in Schabio 2009: 311, 319, 321.
7. I am aware that this is to grossly simplify Glissant's complex discussion of modernity in *Caribbean Discourse*.
8. My approach to Glissant is indebted to Williams's reading of Darwish in this volume. I explore Glissant's notion of epic and novel in greater detail in a forthcoming paper, in particular his distinction between a "poetics of duration" and a Western "poetics of the moment" (Glissant 1989: 136 ff.).

9. Later, in *Intention Poétique* (1995) he again references Hegel, when he deems the epic the "poetic cry of the arising consciousness," which as the cry of a community "uncertain of itself," is the cry of an "excluding consciousness," and therefore markedly not naive (Siemerling 2005: 19; Siemerling's translation).

10. It is perhaps helpful to contextualize Glissant's profound engagement with the literary to better gauge what he is attempting to achieve. Glissant is writing at a time when Walter Ong's thoughts on orality and literacy gained currency. If compared, Ong's notion of the evolution of "interiorized states of consciousness" and "communal structures" (Ong 2002: 175), finds significant modification from the particular angle from which Glissant is looking at modernity. This is performed at about a time, when Frederick Jameson deemed the poor reception of "a popular or realistically social third-world-novel" as shaped by "our own modernisms," reminding us of "outmoded stages of our own first-world cultural development" (Jameson 1986: 66). On the other hand, Jameson's own view of 'Third World' literature might be more indebted to an account of the evolution of the novel, clustered around a nostalgic (Lukácsian) opposition between the epic and the novel (cf. George 1999: 114).

11. See Chris Bongie in *Friends and Enemies* for an analysis of late Glissant's "excessive culturalism" (Bongie 2008: 362) and Schabio 2009: 320–321.

12. Cf. Schabio 2009: 305f., 313f., 322; on Wegner's approach see Schabio 2009: 302. Ashcroft, in his work on future thinking and postcolonial utopianism (e.g. Ashcroft 2007), explores the import of Bloch's concept of utopia as a "strategic place to begin thinking about the concept and its post-colonial textual constructions" (Ashcroft 2007: 411). On Caribbean utopia and Glissant see Ashcroft 2007: 423, 427–429.

13. For Glissant and recalibration of "dystopian visions of the nation" see Schabio 2009: 306; on Glissant's Blochian affinities, the utopian dimension of the aesthetic, and response to globalization cf. Schabio 2009: 310ff. Here, I wish to stress the 'generic' aspect of Glissant's approach which seems conversant with Wilson Harris's strategic invocation of "cross-cultural imaginations" as a challenge to "claustrophobic ritual," "bear[ing] upon the future through mutations of the monolithic character of conquistadorial legacies of civilization . . . " beyond "Orwellian nemesis" (Harris 1983: xv). On Orwell and Harris see Pordzik 2001: 7–8; Schabio 2009: 305, 315.

Works Cited

Ashcroft, Bill (2007) 'Critical Utopias', *Textual Practice*, 21 (3): 411–431.
Bahri, D. (2003) *Native Intelligence: Aesthetics, Politics, and Postcolonial Literature*, Minneapolis and London: University of Minnesota Press.
Bakhtin, M. (1981) 'Epic and Novel', in M. Holquist (ed.) *The Dialogic Imagination: Four Essays*, trans. C. Emerson and M. Holquist, Austin, TX: University of Texas Press, 3–40.
———. (1986) 'The Problem of Speech Genres', in C. Emerson and M. Holquist (eds) *Speech Genres and Other Late Essays*, trans. Vern W. McGee, Austin, TX: University of Texas Press, 60–102.
Bennett T. (1990) *Outside Literature*, London and New York: Routledge.
Bongie, C. (2008) *Friends and Enemies: The Scribal Politics of Post/Colonial Literature*, Liverpool: Liverpool University Press.

Brathwaite, E.K. (1993 [1979]) 'History of the Voice', *Roots: Essays in Caribbean Literature*, Ann Arbor: University of Michigan Press, 259–304.

Brennan, T. (1990) 'The National Longing for Form', in H.K. Bhabha (ed.) *Nation and Narration*, London and New York: Routledge, 44–70.

———. (1997) *At Home in the World: Cosmopolitanism Now*, Cambridge, MA: Harvard University Press.

Chari, V.K. (1995) 'The Genre Theory in Sanskrit Poetics', in P.C. Hogan and L. Pandit (eds) *Literary India: Comparative Studies in Aesthetics, Colonialism, and Culture*, Albany: State University of New York Press, 63–79.

Dash, M. (1998) *The Other America: Caribbean Literature in a New World Context*, Charlottesville and London: University Press of Virginia.

Derrida, J. (1980) 'The Law of Genre', *Critical Inquiry*, 7/1: 55–81.

Dimock, Wai. C. (2007) "Introduction: Genres as Fields of Knowledge", *Special Topic: Remapping* Genre, PMLA, 122/5: 1377–1388.

Dutton, D. (2001) 'Aesthetic Universals', in B. Gaut and D. McIver Lopes (eds) *The Routledge Companion to Aesthetics*, London: Routledge, 279–291.

Edwards, B. Hayes (2004) 'The Genres of Postcolonialism', *Social Text*, 78, 22/1: 1–15.

George, R.M. (1999) *The Politics of Home: Postcolonial Relocations and Twentieth-Century Fiction*, Berkeley and London: University of California Press.

Glissant, É. (1985 [1958]) *The Ripening*, trans. and introd. J.M. Dash, London and Kingston: Heinemann.

———. (1989) *Caribbean Discourse: Selected Essays*, trans. J.M. Dash, Charlottesville: University Press of Virginia. [*Le Discours Antillais*. Paris: Les Éditions du Seuil, 1981].

———. (1995) *Introduction à une Poétique du Divers*, Montreal: Presses de l'Université de Montreal.

———. (1997) *Poetics of Relation*, trans. B. Wing, Ann Arbor: The University of Michigan Press.

———. (2005) *La Cohée du Lamentin: Poétique V*, Paris: Éditions Gallimard.

———. (2010) *La Terre, le Feu, l'Eau et les Vents: Une Anthologie de la Poésie du Tout-monde*, Paris: Galaade.

———. (2011) 'Le Tout-Monde est la nouvelle condition des littératures,' interview with T. Chanda, RFI. par MFI le 3 mars 2010. http://www.rfi.fr/culture/20110203-edouard-glissant-le-tout-monde-est-nouvelle-condition-litteratures. Accessed: Aug. 20, 2011.

Harris, W. (1983) *The Womb of Space: The Cross-Cultural Imagination*, Westport, CT, and London: Greenwood.

Heath, S. (2004) 'The Politics of Genre', in C. Prendergast (ed.) *Debating World Literature*, London and New York: Verso, 163–174.

Hitchcock, P. (2003) 'The Genre of Postcoloniality', *New Literary History*, 34/2: 299–330.

Hogan, P.C. (2003) *The Mind and Its Stories: Narrative Universals and Human Emotion*, Cambridge: Cambridge University Press.

———. (1995) 'Beauty, Politics, and Cultural Otherness: The Bias of Literary Difference', in P.C. Hogan and L. Pandit (eds) *Literary India: Comparative Studies in Aesthetics, Colonialism, and Culture*, Albany: State University of New York, 3–43.

Jameson, F. (1986) 'Third World Literature in the Era of Multinational Capitalism', *Social Text*, 15: 65–88.

Lukács, G. (1971 [1920]) *Die Theorie des Romans: Ein geschichtsphilosophischer Versuch über die Formen der großen Epik*, Berlin: Luchterhand.

Marcuse, H. (1978) *The Aesthetic Dimension: Toward a Critique of Marxist Aesthetics*, Boston: Beacon.

Mofolo, T. (1981) *Chaka*, London and Nairobi: Heinemann.

Montaigne, M. de (1910; 1946) *Essays by Michel Lord of Montaigne*, trans. J. Florio [1603], ed. E. Rhys, 3 vols, Everyman's Library, London: J.M. Dent.

Niblett, M. and Oloff, K. (2009) 'Introduction,' in M. Niblett and K. Oloff (eds) *Perspectives on the 'Other America': Comparative Approaches to Caribbean and Latin American Culture*, Amsterdam and New York: Rodopi.

Nesbit, M. et. al. (2003) 'What is a Station', <www.e-flux.com/projects/utopia/about.html>. Accessed: 20 Feb. 2005.

Ong, W. (2002 [1982]) *Orality and Literacy*, London: Routledge.

Pordzik, R. (2001) *The Quest for Postcolonial Utopia: A Comparative Introduction to the Utopian Novel in the New English Literatures*, New York: Peter Lang.

Ramazani, J. (2001) *The Hybrid Muse: Postcolonial Poetry in English*, Chicago: Chicago University Press.

Said, E. (2011) 'Appendix: Introduction to *Kim* by Edward W. Said [Penguin Classics 1987]', in H. Trivedi (ed.) *Kim*, London: Penguin Books.

Schabio, S. (2009) 'Peripheral Cosmopolitans: Caribbeanness as Transnational Utopia?' in R. Pordzik (ed.) *Futurescapes: Space in Utopian and Science Fiction Discourses*, Amsterdam: Rodopi, 301–322.

Siemerling, W. (2005) *The New North-American Studies: Culture, Writing, and the Politics of Re/Cognition*, London and New York: Routledge.

Spivak, G. (2003) *Death of a Discipline*, New York: Columbia University Press.

Stillman, P. (2009) 'Hegel as a Colonial, Anti-Colonial, and Postcolonial Thinker', in A. Davison and H. Muppidi (eds) *Europe and Its Boundaries: Words and Worlds, Within and Beyond*, Lanham and New York: Lexington Books, 25–47.

Wegner, P.E. (2002) *Imaginary Communities: Utopia, the Nation, and the Spatial Histories of Modernity*, Berkeley and Los Angeles: University of California Press.

Part II

Resistant and Subversive Genres

4 "Writing the Poetry of Troy"

Mahmoud Darwish and the Lyrical Epic as Postcolonial Resistance Genre

Patrick Williams

"All beautiful poetry is an act of resistance"

(Darwish, 'The essence of the poem,' 2009)

This is principally an essay about a genre-shift in poetry and why that matters. It is also about the difficult relation of aesthetics and politics as lived by one poet. It will get around to questions of the postcolonial eventually; the postponement being partly based on the assumption that the colonized nature of Palestine does not need to be urgently argued for. First of all, however, it is necessary to offer a brief introduction on the context of Darwish's intervention, and why it has particular significance within Arabic culture, in a way in which it would not in European or Western culture, not least because of the widely reiterated belief that, as Darwish puts it, "Poetry is the Arabic art *par excellence*" (Darwish 1999: 10). That introduction, combined with the necessary discussion of the epic context, means that a more detailed examination of Darwish's poetry will be slightly delayed.

The politics of 'modernizing': The concept of the 'modern' in Arabic literature is very old indeed, and the battle of the traditionalists and the modernizers has a long history. The original modernizing of poetic form and content carried out by the eighth and ninth century writers Abu Nuwas (757–814) and Abu Tammam (788–845) was seen as politically subversive and theologically heretical, with an impact far beyond the realm of the poetic. It was regarded as challenging the idea that truth and knowledge are given—from positions of authority, whether political, theological, or textual—and not the product of individual thought or research. Although, as Adonis points out, the battle between traditionalists and modernizers has not been a constant factor in Arab poetry, at those times when it has come to the fore, such as over the last century and a half, it remains a powerful one (Adonis 1990). Darwish's development of the lyrical epic therefore automatically places him in the ranks of the problem-causing modernizers, but embracing the modern clearly does not frighten him: "The most significant leap Arabic poetry has made has been the acceptance by the Arab reader of a poetry no longer bound by the rigid rules of the past" (Darwish 1999: 10).

The politics of modernity: A related issue for Arab poets concerns the extent to which it is acceptable, useful or profitable to be influenced or inspired by Western poets, Western poetic developments or Western cultural politics, especially as encapsulated in modernity. Modernity itself constitutes a particularly thorny issue, routinely regarded as a Western import or imposition—a process which is inherently problematic—and one which supposedly stands in opposition to the perceived authenticity of Arab culture. (So far, however, the import or imposition does not appear to be having a great deal of success: Darwish says that in Arab society, only poetry and the security services have achieved modernity!) Beyond this, the engagement of Palestinian cultural production with modernity is not straightforward: at best, perhaps, it might figure as one of the peripheral modernities analyzed by the Warwick Centre's current project. At the same time as modernity is appearing a less than desirable attainment for Palestinian culture, there is the view from the opposite side, where Palestinian access to modernity is to be resisted at all costs: Derek Gregory, for instance, in *The Colonial Present* (2004) talks about Ariel Sharon's determination to remove Palestinians from modernity altogether. The Israeli approach encapsulates the fact that modernity in Palestine/Israel is very much a case of what Trotsky termed "combined and uneven development," both in the unequal level of development in the two component parts, and in the deliberately engineered, in Andre Gunder Frank's phrase, "development of underdevelopment" in the dominated area (Trotsky 1967: 21–33).

Another way in which Darwish's genre shift matters is because of the importance of poetry as *diwan* in Arabic culture, an intellectual or cultural reservoir and archive, which is referred to and drawn on in a manner which has no obvious correlate in Western culture. Its status as *diwan* is also connected to the function of poetry as a public form able to attract large audiences—especially in the case of Darwish, who can fill football stadia for his performances. The question of the relation of the writer to his (very large) audience, and one with definite expectations, is especially relevant to Darwish. In poetry recitals, Darwish's audiences routinely want him to perform his early, famous, and most unambiguously political, works; when it is time for a new collection of poems, overt political commitment is taken for granted (and its perceived absence can be the occasion for bitter criticism). For his part, Darwish repeatedly disorients and potentially disappoints his audience by offering them something different in poetic form or content, or both. He refuses to be dictated to, and insists on the necessary development of his poetry as poetry, and not, as he terms it, sloganeering. That remains the case even when the poetry in question is politically engaged: "I think poetry must protest while affirming its status as poetry, and not in offering direct commentary or taking up positions" (Darwish 2006: 16). This approach can result in collections such as *A Bed for the Stranger* (1999), where overt politics scarcely appears, or *Mural* (2000), where the political risks being eclipsed by the metaphysical. In the context of his culture, this constant challenge to audience expectations is seen as a particularly high-risk strategy, but as Darwish comments, "Taking risks is the primary condition of poetry" (Darwish 2006: 25).[1]

Finally, Darwish's poetic intervention, however small-scale it might seem from the vantage point of Western literature, matters because of the broad context of cultural production by and for Palestinians, inside or outside of Palestine. The vulnerable, frequently struggling, nature of Palestinian culture makes the presence of someone of the stature of Darwish all the more important, while everything he does and says takes on a greater than usual significance.

* * * * *

What, then, does Darwish's genre shift consist of? From the 1980s onwards, he was working on a hybrid or compound form, more extensive than he had hitherto tackled, which his friend the Greek poet Yiannis Ritsos named the "lyrical epic" (Darwish 1997: 86). This in itself might seem quite a bold move, given that the epic has for a considerable amount of time, and especially in the West, been a contested genre: among early dismissals one might mention John Stuart Mill: "an epic poem, though in so far as it is epic (i.e., narrative) it is not poetry at all, is yet esteemed the greatest effort of poetic genius" (Mill 1833: 352). A century later, for Mikhail Bakhtin, in what has become the *locus classicus* of denunciations of the genre, the epic encapsulates all of the negative qualities which the novel is deemed to overcome: "We speak of the epic as a genre that has come down to us already well-defined and real. We come upon it when it is already completely finished, a congealed and half-moribund genre" (Bakhtin 1983: 14).

Even a critic like Walter Benjamin, sympathetic to the epic form, and with none of the sort of agenda which motivates Bakhtin's comments in terms of polemically valorizing one genre over another, felt that the epic was not appropriate to, or even possible within, modernity. In "The Storyteller," Benjamin elegiacally comments:

> The art of storytelling is reaching its end because the epic side of truth, wisdom, is dying out. This, however, is a process that has been going on for a long time. And nothing would be more fatuous than to want to see in it merely a 'symptom of decay', let alone a 'modern' symptom. It is, rather, only a concomitant symptom of the secular productive forces of history, a concomitant that has quite gradually removed narrative from the realm of living speech and at the same time is making it possible to see a new beauty in what is vanishing. (Benjamin 1982: 87)

Though he would reject Benjamin's elegiac pessimism, Darwish was well aware that reworking the epic in and for the contemporary world is neither easy nor straightforward: "I believe the space for epics in our national life is shrinking: our sentiments thirst for what is normal, the achievements of normal life. Perhaps we are bored of heroism . . . " (Darwish 2002c). In that unpromising space, what are we to make of the 'lyrical epic'? Does this very modern compound represent an improvement on the classical version, a contradiction in terms, a reconciliation of polar opposites, a powerful poetic synergy, or some combination of these? Certainly, the shift to the lyrical epic constitutes both a poetic project and, to the extent that they can be separated, a cultural and historical project for Darwish.

Darwish is above all a lyric poet—as he said in an interview, if he had not been born into the circumstances of mid-twentieth century Palestine, he would have preferred simply to be a love poet. To that extent, lyricizing other forms—even the epic—is an eminently logical move for him. At the same time, the lyric does not occupy an automatically hegemonic position in relation to other types of poetry: his comment in *La Palestine comme métaphore* regarding his desire for "the liberation of poetic language towards epic horizons" (Darwish 1997: 25) indicates the relatively elevated status of the epic.

Another facet of the poetic project is Darwish's permanent need for development in his poetry. Apart from making him frequently unhappy with, and dismissive of, his earlier work, this contributes to the previously mentioned tendency to offer his readership, and public audiences, new, unlooked-for and challenging forms, and the elaboration of the lyrical epic is very much part of that process. The 'developmental' aspect also generates the perceived need for an appropriate language and form for particular poetic tasks, historical conjunctures or political circumstances, though the distance travelled to reach the 'appropriate' may appear considerable. For instance, the epic is (according to Bakhtin) characterized by sustained, unitary or closed form; Darwish, on the other hand, gives us in *State of Siege* an epic in fragments—sometimes tiny ones—though there are a variety of reasons for that fragmentation, as we will see later.

In relation to the epic, Darwish seemingly does everything differently, though there is space here to indicate briefly just a few of the ways in which he reworks key elements of the genre.

The first of these is *the epic and national identity*. Typically, one of the roles of the epic is to articulate national identity, or at the very least to offer itself for appropriation in the construction of such an identity, particularly in relation to the foundational myths of nation, or what Beissinger et al. (1999) term the epic as tale of origins. For Darwish, however, these are precisely the problem, especially Israeli myths of origin:

> With the disappearance of our country, we found ourselves relegated to a pre-Genesis state. As a result, our poets have had to write our own Genesis, beginning from the Other's mythical one. For you have to be aware that Palestine has already been written. The Other has done it in

his own way, through the narrative of a birth which no one dreams of denying. (Darwish 1997: 27)

In a manner which echoes Said, Darwish simultaneously resolutely defends the rights of his people to an independent (national) existence and is unhappy with prevailing modes of nationalism. In this he also positions himself (postcolonially) close to Fanon's view that the national is a necessary, but insufficient, stage on the road to true or full internationalism. The national nevertheless retains its importance, as indicated by his comment in an interview: "We have to invent new ways of fighting which will serve the greater national interest" (Darwish 2006: 68). Similarly, the Saidian preference for universalizing the particular is something which Darwish shares, and his epics promote universal human issues rather than exclusive national concerns.

> The main thing is that I was able to find a greater lyrical capacity, and a transition from the relative to the absolute; an opening allowing me to write the national in the universal, so that Palestine does not limit itself to Palestine, but grounds its aesthetic legitimacy in a vaster human space. (Darwish 1997: 25–26)

The epic and the hero: The epic is preeminently the story of the individual hero. Again, Darwish is not interested: for him, the move to the epic is precisely the move to the collective (in different guises: a collective consciousness, a collective perspective, and—if you must have a hero—a collective hero). The sense of unease with the category of the heroic also emerges in Darwish's preference for an unheroic hero: "Perhaps we are bored of heroism, though it is a daring thing to say, perhaps. The real hero is the one who doesn't know he is a hero" (Darwish 2002c); which is in turn part of his desire to produce an 'epic of the ordinary.' Set against that, however, "Exile #4: Counterpoint" contradictorily, but appropriately for Darwish, figures Edward Said as "the last epic hero / defending the right of Troy / to its place in the narrative" (Darwish 2007: 132).

The epic and lament: As mentioned, epics frequently operate as celebrations of national greatness, glory or triumph, but there is in some, possibly in many, a counter-element of lament:

> Lamentation threatens to undermine the *kleos-*[i.e. praise]conferring function of the epic because it stresses the suffering caused by heroic death rather than the glory won by it; lamentation calls into question the glorification of death sponsored by martial societies and the epics that celebrate them. (Murnaghan 1999: 204)

Although Darwish's epics deal with what in *Entretiens sur la Poésie* he calls the 'cosmic themes' of loss and mourning, he is not concerned with the public male discourse of revenge which often accompanies them in the classical epic. Loss and mourning are figured most poignantly in a generalized way in "Eleven Stars in the Last Andalusian Sky" and "The Speech of the Red Indian," both of which are discussed below, though "Exile #4: Counterpoint" once again goes against Darwish's usual practice, containing as it does a remarkable example, perhaps unique in his oeuvre, of an extended lament for an individual —in this case Edward Said.

The epic and distance: As far as Bakhtin is concerned, one of the many problems of the epic is its remoteness:

> The epic world is an utterly finished thing, not only as an aesthetic event of the distant past but also on its own terms and by its own standards; it is impossible to change, to re-think, to re-evaluate anything in it. It is completed, closed and immutable, as a fact, an idea and a value. This defines absolute epic distance. (Bakhtin 1983: 17)

Again, Darwish rejects this: he wants an appropriate relational distance. Poetry in general must have some distance, to rescue it from the negative effects of conjunctural or political immediacy, about which he has a lot to say, but it does this in order to establish the correct relation to its subject and to achieve proper perspective. A poem which is not in close contact with its human dimension is a dead text for Darwish. There is an additional parallel with Said here, on the need for critical distance which the exilic position or perspective can provide. Other types of distance, related, but different, which Darwish makes use of, include ironic distance, which he feels he owes to a clearer understanding of the workings of history, and spectatorial distance, where a clear sight of events may be accompanied by the inability to influence them. Although the latter is not necessarily tied to questions of history, Darwish illustrates what he means by it with an image drawing upon history: "The poet who watches the succession of imperial armies—Roman, Assyrian, Persian—has no recourse other than to behave like a child who observes the scene through a keyhole" (Darwish 1997: 45).

The epic and open-endedness: For Bakhtin, one of the great achievements of the novel was the breaking down of formal and generic boundaries, the kind of things which completely constrain the epic: "There is no place in the epic world for any open-endedness, indecision, indeterminacy. There are no loopholes in it through which we glimpse the future . . . " (Bakhtin 1983: 16). As we will see in due course, however, the 'novelization' of the epic genre is precisely what Darwish is doing, both in terms of introducing something more approximating a Bakhtinian polyphony, and in producing epics which at least glimpse the future—however uncertain, or in some cases utterly bleak, its particular manifestations may be.

The epic and hybridity: As we have seen, the epic for Bakhtin is the ultimate non-hybrid form: fixed, unitary, monoglot. For Darwish, hybridizing it has, once again, both a poetic and a cultural and political point. In a way which recalls Said's important formulation "Overlapping territories / Intertwined histories" in *Culture and Imperialism* (1993), the lyrical epic's radical hybridity mirrors the historical facts of—in Darwish's term—"crossbreeding" in Palestine and the region beyond, which rigid essentialized Israeli conceptions of cultural and ethnic identity strenuously deny. Although Darwish's hybridizing may look radical and innovative, there is also a sense in which he may be doing nothing more than staying true to the nature of the (misrepresented) epic, as well as contemporary reality: "We find ourselves today in a hybrid place, at a median point between the historical and the mythic. Our situation, our very existence, contain both of these" (Darwish 1997: 27–28).

The epic and the Other: Epic has little to say about the Other, apart from negatively and ideologically, as the necessary antithesis of the hero or his community. One of Darwish's most radical moves is therefore to write the epic *of* the Other. Several examples of this will be discussed later, but for the moment it is important to note that writing about and on behalf of the Other aligns what Darwish is doing with one of the fundamental aspects of postcolonial studies.

The epic and the postcolonial: At one level, this may appear not to be an obvious pairing, partly because of the disparity between the supposed irredeemable ancientness of the epic and the modernity of postcolonialism, but more for various well-rehearsed reasons about the relation of postcolonial culture to 'difficult' and exclusionary Western canonical forms. At the same time, there is always the possibility of 'writing back' via the epic, thereby transforming it into another anti-colonial or post-colonial mode, though this process often highlights those elements of exclusive national or cultural identity and heroic masculinity which typify the originals, marking their oppositional stance, but also thereby potentially making them problematic in terms of more positive or progressive formulations of postcoloniality. Affirming the existence of 'colonized' epics—"You have your *Odyssey*; we have our *Soundiata*"—is also a claim to high-status cultural production. Major postcolonial epics such as *Omeros* do exist—and Walcott happens to be Darwish's favourite Anglophone poet. Nevertheless, Walcott's Caribbean rewriting of Homer is still a long way away from Darwish's approach to the epic.

Within postcolonial studies, there is a set of problems which we might categorize as 'resistance to resistance': on the one hand, there is the idea that postcolonial studies has for far too long focused on the theme of resistance, and that it should move on to other topics with greater contemporary relevance. On the other, there is the sort of dismissal of resistance as 'part of the triumphalist narrative of postcolonialism' offered by Robert Young in a paper given at EACLALS 2008. In the case of Darwish, there is the added complication of his own resistance to resistance, because it is the one topic he is automatically connected with. The fact that he is still routinely referred to as 'the poet of the Palestinian resistance' is not something which pleases him, since he feels it pigeon-holes him far too much, and restricts his ability to be simply a poet. As he comments tersely: "I do not want to be a poet with a label" (Darwish 1997: 135).

Regardless of his personal situation, however, Darwish is very clear that for the Palestinians, resistance remains essential:

> Resistance to the occupation is not only a right, it is also a duty. It can take several forms, including the rejection of any Israeli strategy which aims at the annihilation of Palestinians. We have to invent new ways of fighting . . . (Darwish 2006: 68)

Beyond rights and duty, however, there is the perpetual question of the means of resistance: how do you resist; what might the "new ways of fighting" look like? Darwish has offered a possible answer for a cultural producer such as himself in the collection of recent interviews, *Entretiens sur la Poésie*. There, he argues for fighting war with its opposite as the only (ethical) possibility for the weaker party, which the Palestinians self-evidently are. In this approach, the clamour of war is to be resisted through silence or softly spoken speech (rather than screams or slogans); the dehumanization caused by war is to be resisted through highlighting the human and the humane; and the brutality of war resisted through the gentleness and fragility of human beings and nature. In this context, he says, "Love poetry is the personal, intimate dimension of cultural resistance" (Darwish 2006: 92).

An alternative strategy, apparently more robust, is resistance through narration, in the shape of the epic of the Other. The fact that these are the narratives of the defeated and the downtrodden; history's victims not its victors; those silenced, and erased from the archive; might appear to compromise the idea of robustness, but for Darwish, writing what he calls the "poetry of Troy," taking the side of the defeated, is the very opposite of surrender. In addition, his understanding of the cultural need for an historical narrative, as well as the power politics linked to that, echo Said's better-known comments on the subject:

> I have chosen to be the poet of Troy because Troy did not tell its history. And up till now we have not told ours [. . .] That is what I wanted to say when I wrote "He who succeeds in imposing his story will inherit the Land of the Story." (Darwish 1997: 30)

Questions regarding the many and varied forms of loss: whether of the land, or identity, of culture or language; as well as the problematic role of history and its denial (precisely whose history or narrative is remembered, and whose disavowed?) are all familiar in the context of colonialism. The struggle for them in relation to Palestine is, however, less familiar in a postcolonial frame. There are obvious parallels between Palestinians and others of the (colonial) defeated, but the poetry of Troy includes more, such as Native Americans (or 'Red Indians' as Darwish persists in calling them) and fifteenth century Arabs. These groups are dealt with in the lyrical epics "The Speech of the Red Indian," and "Eleven Stars in the Last Andalusian Sky," both from the 1992 collection *Eleven Planets*. Both poems are the result of extensive periods of research lasting several years, in order to produce—in Darwish's terms—as honest and accurate a narrative of the Other as can be achieved. Both represent the destruction of cultures unfortunate enough to be standing in the path of a ruthlessly expansionist West, "Eleven Stars in the Last Andalusian Sky" in a manner one could call historical, in so far as it deals with the fall of Granada in 1492 (though it is more than just historical), while "The Speech of the Red Indian" has a somewhat more epochal feel, dealing as it does with the passing of a whole continent's way of life.

In addition, both poems chronicle the destruction of quasi-utopian spaces and cultures. In the case of Andalusia, its utopian dimension may not be hard to find, in the rich, diverse, multi-cultural and multi-faith communities, the remarkable scholarly activity, and the glories of the Alhambra, the great mosque of Cordoba, the Giralda and the Alcazar in Seville. For Darwish, this is "the perfect time, the golden age that is past" (Darwish 2000: 165), and the speaker of part of "Eleven Stars in the Last Andalusian Sky" says: "I am the Adam of two Edens / Lost to me twice" (Darwish 2000: 154). On the other hand, while 'utopian' might appear less obvious in relation to the 'Red Indians,' it is nevertheless carefully argued for by Darwish, particularly in terms of an ethical existence, life respecting life, respecting Nature, and respecting others—in stark contrast to the way in which the White invaders behave:

> We lived and flourished before the onslaught of
> English guns, French wine and influenza,
> living in harmony side-by-side with the Deer People,
> learning our oral history by heart.
> We brought you tidings of innocence and daisies.
> But you have your god and we have ours.
> You have your past and we have ours.
> Time is a river
> blurred by the tears we gaze through.
>
> But don't you ever
> memorise a few lines of poetry, perhaps,
> to restrain yourself from massacre?
> (Darwish 2000: 139–140)

The utopian here is very much an Other space (not least in its Edenic dimension). It is also Other to the contemporary world, and to what different modernities have made of the older, Other spaces. As such, it constitutes a space of resistance to the values and practices of the expansionist West, though such is the power of the latter that resistance may be hard to spot. Certainly, there is nothing resembling physical resistance in "The Speech of the Red Indian"—quite the opposite: the speaker appears stunned, reduced to a state of shocked immobility by the unexpected brutality of the Europeans. Not meeting violence with violence is, at the same time, part of the culture as Darwish represents it, and constitutes at least an ethical resistance to the very physical attack of its enemy. That ethical dimension is strengthened by the refusal to surrender: "I refuse to sign a treaty between victim and killer. / I refuse to sign a bill of sale / that takes possession / of so much as one inch of my weed patch" (Darwish 2000: 140–141). In "Eleven Stars in the Last Andalusian Sky," there is no armed resistance either: the long siege is over, Granada has been captured, and in the new, dystopian space of surrender, "Who will take down our flags, us or them? / Who will read out the *Peace Accord* to us, O King of Fall?" (Darwish 2000: 159).

As mentioned earlier, one of the less recognized aspects of the epic is mourning, though as Thomas M. Greene's title "The Natural Tears of Epic" (1999) suggests, it is one which deserves greater recognition. Appropriately enough for exemplars of 'the poetry of Troy,' Darwish's lyrical epics have their quota of lamentation, and, like the great classical epics, "Eleven Stars in the Last Andalusian Sky" ends with tears, though in this case, rather than tears shed for the death of the individual hero, the mourning is collective: "Violins weep with Arabs leaving Andalusia" (Darwish 2000: 169). The fall of Granada is, of course, most famously associated with the lamentations of its last king, Abu Abdallah Mohammed (Boabdil), looking back at his lost city, as well as his mother's crushing rebuke: "You weep like a woman for what you could not hold as a man," and in keeping with that unheroic status and Darwish's reservations about the category of hero mentioned earlier, the poem eschews classical lament for the dead or departed leader. Instead it offers both the leader's own shame-filled lament in section 4, "I'm one of the last kings of the decay," and the biting, ironic attack on him in section 6, "Reality is two-faced; snow is black." More extensively, in its different ways and different parts, the poem mourns the loss of the good life in the paradise of Granada, the loss of the land, the culture which it bred, and the identity grounded in all of these: "I know who I was yesterday / but who will I be tomorrow / under the Atlantic flags of Columbus?" (Darwish 2000: 163).

"The speech of the Red Indian" is both more and less of a lament than its companion epic: more, in so far as it laments more consistently, and the loss to be lamented is greater; less, in so far as it also functions as an appeal, an admonition, and statement of unpalatable truths—all of these directed at the European audience. While the speaker mourns his people, their lives, their culture and their relation to nature, nature in turn weeps for those who loved and respected it. Sheila Murnaghan comments: "the unsettling experience of loss generates a description of the social structure as seen by its most vulnerable members" (Darwish 1999: 208), and though her remarks concern the classical epics, they are highly relevant to Darwish's works. In this way, lament rather surprisingly manages to combine a number of important features: through the 'unsettled' gaze of society's vulnerable, it operates as a form of ideology critique, identifying and challenging the mystifications perpetrated by the dominant order; it offers a space for the often occluded speech of the Other; it also instantiates what, in *Entretiens sur la Poésie*, Darwish suggests as poetry's best mode of resistance to violence—the restrained statement, the highlighting of human fragility, the quiet courage of the victim. All of these also occur in the last of the lyrical epics to be examined here.

Given Darwish's stated aims, what could better constitute 'writing the poetry of Troy' than a first-hand account of life under siege—even if the siege, and the living through it, was a completely unlooked-for event? Just such an account is what Darwish offers in his anti-epic epic *State of Siege*, written under the conditions of siege imposed by the preposterously-named Israeli invasion of West Bank towns, Operation Defensive Shield, in 2002. As a work of astonishing immediacy—especially from the pen of a writer who has become so deeply distrustful of poetry which responds too quickly to the pressure of events—*State of Siege* stands as a powerful refutation of Bakhtin's claim that: "The epic was never a poem about the present, about its own time . . . " (Bakhtin 1983: 13). Writing about the present may not be the poet's ideal first choice, but it may be the only one:

> Poetry requires a margin, a siesta [. . .] The situation in Ramallah does not give me this luxury. To be under occupation, to be under siege, is not a good inspiration for poetry. Still, I can't choose my reality. And this is the whole problem of Palestinian literature: we can't free ourselves of the historical moment. (Darwish 2001: npn)

At the same time, this response to the unavoidable fact of the Israeli attack is also the story of a people under perpetual siege for more than half a century—an important generalizing, if not quite universalizing, of the situation.

As an epic, *State of Siege* is highly transgressive—or, at the very least, pushes the boundaries of the genre: it is non-nationalist, non-heroic, non-triumphalist; it is not closed, unitary, distant, or monologic; it is also, as previously mentioned, composed of a multitude of fragments. In case it would seem thereby to have removed itself entirely from the realms of the epic, especially as categorized by Bakhtin, it remains, nevertheless, "a poetic narrative of length and complexity that centres around deeds of significance to the community," as Beissinger and her colleagues define the epic, though some might query whether it manages to produce anything like a narrative (Beissinger et al. 1999: 2). If the poem challenges its epic nature, its fragmentary structure also puts its lyricism under pressure, and at the opposite extreme to the presumed expansiveness of a lyrical epic, Darwish here more frequently offers the reader lyrical aphorisms as the most that fragmented life under siege allows. In particular, the idea that the epic is monologic is firmly refuted by all three examples here, though none more so than *State of Siege*. In addition to the general [non-] narrative, there are sections where the speaker addresses particular groups: Israelis (as ordinary soldiers, but also in categorized, capitalized forms: "To a Killer," "To a Guard"), or individuals: "To a Critic," "To a Quasi-Orientalist," as well as non-human entities: "To Death," "To Love." In turn, the speaker is addressed (harangued, warned, 'besieged') by others, especially the paradigmatic martyr: "The martyr teaches me: no aesthetics outside my freedom" (Darwish 2002a: npn). In addition, there are dialogues and monologues, and through them the various, and varied, voices of the besieged are heard.

One thing which the voices achieve is a modified form of resistance. Die, disappear, surrender: these would be the options preferred by the Israelis (the second above all, perhaps); the voices, however, are a testament to the fact that none of these has been taken, that the Palestinians are still there. The power of resistance through '*summud*,' simply staying put, is something that both Said and Darwish have commented on, and in *State of Siege* the speaker (with a slight edge of humorous realism) says: "We stand here. We sit here. We are here. We're always here. / With one aim in life: just to be! / Apart from that, we disagree about everything . . . " (Darwish 2004: 19). In addition to the voice, other corporeal elements are needed if one is to stay put:

> To resist means—to be confident of the health
> of the heart, and of the testicles; to be confident of your incurable malady,
> The malady of hope. (Darwish 2002a: npn)

The idea of hope as an incurable disease was one which Darwish retained in the increasingly hope-less conditions for Palestinians in the last fifteen years.

The speaker of *State of Siege* somehow finds time among the bombs to reflect on culture, its resistant power as well as its seeming powerlessness. Sometimes—unsurprisingly no doubt, in the face of a massive military onslaught, as well as the despair engendered by a relentless siege—writing can appear to lack the kind of power one might wish it to have: "Writing is a small puppy biting nothingness / Writing wounds without blood" (Darwish 2002a). Powerless, or pointless in the face of suffering: "Rhyme is redundant / when the tune can't be tuned / and pain is beyond measure" (Darwish 2004: 14). Pointless, too, because reality overtakes art; even satire can't cope: "A satirist told me: / 'Had I known how this would end from the very beginning, / I'd never have written a word'" (Darwish 2004: 11). Certainly, the material conditions of the siege impact on art as much as on other areas of life:

Our losses: Between two and eight martyrs a day.
And ten wounded.
And twenty houses.
And fifty olive trees.
In addition to the structural faults that damage
the poem, the play and the unfinished painting. (Darwish 2002a: npn)

In this context, formal fragmentation would be the appropriate structural correlate for the general conditions of existence.

More often, however, culture appears to embody the possibility of resistance, not least in such profoundly optimistic pieces as: "When I write twenty lines about love / I imagine this siege / has gone back twenty metres" (Darwish 2004: 22) and "To poetry: / Besiege / your siege" (Darwish 2004: 22). The latter fragment encapsulates an interesting history: "Besiege your siege" is a fairly well-known quotation from a poem of Darwish's written during an earlier and much bloodier Israeli siege—Beirut in 1982. On the one hand, then, it draws attention to the relentlessness of Israeli oppression, the siege as permanent danger for the Palestinians—even becoming, in this poem, the very condition of existence for its victims. At the same time, its appearance here carries an air of self-contradiction, given that Darwish had subsequently repudiated most of what he wrote at the time of the siege of Beirut on the grounds of—in his terms—its strident over-politicization. Whether its inclusion marks another example of poetry reluctantly acknowledging the pressures of the political moment remains a matter of conjecture.

As well as providing a means of resistance, culture's power under siege can be both pedagogical and potentially reconciliatory, as the speaker says: "This siege will endure / until we can teach our enemies / odes of our Canaanite poetry" (Darwish 2004: 9). The Canaanites are another 'Trojan' people: defeated, neglected, lacking a narrative and a proper historical presence. Acceptance of their poetry by their conquerors would indeed represent a breakthrough, not just in the world of the siege, but also in twenty-first century Palestine/Israel, given the widespread Israeli reluctance to acknowledge, still less accord appropriate value to, Palestinian culture. Darwish has often remarked that although he is open to, and appreciative of, Israeli culture, the reverse is simply not the case. In the absence of mutual recognition, particularly at the level of basic humanity, peace remains unlikely. *State of Siege* contains a number of examples of the besieged making unreciprocated attempts to interact with the besiegers as humans. The most interesting of these is probably the following, where the Israeli fear of peace is only exceeded by their fear of the literally disarming effect of Palestinian music:

A truce! A truce! So we can see if it's really true
that fighter planes can be beaten into ploughshares!

We begged for a truce—just to test the waters,
just to see if peace could seep back into the bloodstream,
just so we could fight our battles with poetry for once.
But they told us: Haven't you heard that peace begins at home?
What happens if your music brings our high walls tumbling down?
And we answered: So what's wrong with that? Why not? (Darwish
2004: 30–31)

Why not, indeed?

Asked in an interview in 2002, "So when will the great Palestinian epic be
written?" Darwish replied:

> Perhaps after the victory. Perhaps after independence, when the story is
> finished, when we've known the beginning and the end. We are now in
> an obscure chapter of the epic, a chapter that has fled from the text, it is
> not under the control of the author, the witnesses or the protagonists. It
> is a chapter that has been written as if it were the last but it is not. We are
> all playing roles in the not-last chapter. (Darwish 2002c)

Despite his feeling that the conditions of Palestinian life were increasingly
unsuitable for the epic, Darwish remained confident of its relevance for articulating his people's story. It is a cause for sadness that he did not live to write
"the great Palestinian epic," though in the face of current Israeli policies
(including the latest siege, the illegal three year blockade of Gaza), it is hard
to imagine when the conditions he set—"after independence," even more so
"after the victory"—might come about. In the meantime, resistance, whether
figured in poetry or embodied in the 'incurable malady of hope,' continues
to be a necessity. "I believe that the unwavering commitment to resistance
and defence is not some sort of nostalgia, but the saturation of the present
and future with the past, without which neither present nor future will come
to be." (Darwish 1999: 8)

Notes

1. All translations from Darwish (1997) *La Palestine comme métaphore*, (2006)*Ent-
    retiens sur la Poésie*, and (2007) *Comme des fleurs d'amandier, ou plus loin*, are my
    own. Thanks are due to Syracuse University Press for granting permission
    to quote from *The Adam of Two Edens* by Mahmoud Darwish (Syracuse Uni-
    versity Press, Syracuse, NY 2000), to Amina Elbendary and *Al Ahram Weekly*
    for granting permission to use her translation of *State of Siege* by Mahmoud
    Darwish, *Al Ahram Weekly*, 11–17 April as well as to *MPT* for approval to
    quote from Mahmoud Darwish, *State of Siege*, trans. S. Maguire and S. Hafez,
    Modern Poetry in Translation, 3/1 (2004): 4–33. An extract from the poem can
    be found at www.mptmagazine.com.

Works Cited

Adonis (1990) *An Introduction to Arab Poetics*, trans. C. Cobham, London: Saqi Books.

Bakhtin, M. (1983) *The Dialogic Imagination*, Austin: University of Texas Press.

Beissinger, M., Tylus, J., and S. Wofford (eds) (1999) *Epic Traditions in the Contemporary World*, Berkeley: University of California Press.

Benjamin, W. (1982) *Illuminations*, trans. H. Zohn, Glasgow: Collins.

Darwish, M. (1997) *La Palestine Comme Métaphore*, Paris: Actes Sud.

———. (1999) 'There Is No Meaning to My Life Outside Poetry', *Banipal*, 4, Spring.

———. (2000) *The Adam of Two Edens*, Syracuse, NY: Syracuse University Press.

———. (2001) "Poet's Palestine as a Metaphor", Interview with Adam Shatz, *New York Times*, December 22.

———. (2002a) *State of Siege*, trans. A. Elbendary, *Al Ahram Weekly*, 11–17 April, (online version: http://weekly.ahram.org.eg/2002/581/bo7.htm. Accessed: July 20, 2009).

———. (2002b) Interview with Maya Jaggi, *Guardian*, June 2002.

———. (2002c) Interview with A. Elbendary, *Al Ahram Weekly*, 19–25 December, (online version http://weekly.ahram.org.eg/2002/617/cu1.htm. Accessed: July 20, 2009).

———. (2004) *State of Siege*, trans. S. Maguire and S. Hafez, *Modern Poetry in Translation*, 3/1: 4–33.

———. (2006) *Entretiens sur la Poésie*, Paris: Actes Sud.

———. (2007) *Comme des Fleurs d'Amandier, ou Plus Loin*, Paris: Actes Sud.

———. (2009) *A River Dies of Thirst*, London: Saqi Books.

Farrell, J. (1999) 'Walcott's *Omeros*: The Classical Epic in a Postmodern World', in Beissinger et al. (eds) *Epic Traditions in the Contemporary World*, Berkeley: University of California Press, 270–296.

Fantham, E. (1999) 'The Role of Lament in the Growth and Eclipse of the Roman Epic', in Beissinger et al. (eds) *Epic Traditions in the Contemporary World*, Berkeley: University of California Press, 221–235.

Gregory, D. (2004) *The Colonial Present*, Oxford: Blackwell.

Greene, T.M. (1999) 'The Natural Tears of Epic' in Beissinger et al. (eds) *Epic Traditions in the Contemporary World*, Berkeley: University of California Press, 189–202.

Murnaghan, S. (1999) 'The Poetics of Loss in Greek Epic', in Beissinger et al. (eds) *Epic Traditions in the Contemporary World*, Berkeley: University of California Press, 203–220.

Mill, J.S. (1981 [1833]) 'Thoughts on Poetry and its Varieties', in J.M. Robson and J. Stillinger (eds) *Autobiography and Literary Essays: John Stuart Mill*, Toronto: Toronto University Press, 341–366.

Said, E. (1993) *Culture and Imperialism*, London: Chatto.

Trotsky, L. (1967) *History of the Russian Revolution*, vol. 1, London: Sphere Books.

5　Genre

Fidelity and Transgression in the Post-colonial African Novel

Mpalive-Hangson Msiska

Introduction

This chapter considers the question of genre in the post-colonial African novel, exploring, among others, the following questions: what is the nature of the African novel? Given that it is a product of the colonial ideological intention of cultural incorporation, to what extent has it really been able to escape the political determination of the moment of its genesis and proceeded to function as a form of counter-hegemony? If so, what is the specificity of the location of that resistance? As one investigates these questions, it becomes clear that the African novel throws enormous light on issues pertinent to the contemporary formations of genre not only in Africa, but generally.

Evidently, the post-colonial African novel is primarily marked by a structure of fidelity and transgression in which genre practice is expressed as a dynamic contingent production and sublation of the settled dominant of a given instance, a dialogic tension between the Self and the Other, as it were. The nature of post-colonial cultural formation itself poses particular problems for the production and elaboration of post-colonial genre practice in that the concern with genre is often related to the very foundational normative values of the post-colonial formation itself. Thus, to speak of genre is also necessarily to comment on the nature of society, its politics, its beliefs, and most importantly, its varied and complex power relations at given historical moments.

It is impossible to grasp the particular character of novelistic genre practice in post-colonial Africa without a full appreciation of the ways in which the literary aesthetic norms that constitute the contemporary post-colonial aesthetic bear within them the imprint of cultural colonization. As Okwui Enwezor notes "[t]he current history of modern art sits at the intersection between imperial and postcolonial discourses" (Enwezor 2003: 59). Indeed, the history of genre practice in Africa today, to be amply cognizant of the totality of the cultural field and the contingency of its formation has to be located in the meeting point between the colonial production of a specifically colonial culture and the anti-colonial opposition to that culture and its attempt to create a new post-colonial sensibility.

Genre and the Colonial Formation

Indeed, as Gauri Viswanathan has shown, literature was at the heart of the project of cultural colonization, the emblematic and defining centre of the "civilising mission" (Viswanathan 1987: 95). That was also true of the history of literary education in Africa, where literature was regarded not only as having a civilizing import, but also a theological redemptive capacity. Writing in 1882, Duff Macdonald, a Scottish missionary at the Blantyre Mission in Malawi asserted that: "Literature is likely to be an important means of elevating and purifying the native" (Macdonald 1862: 261). From this perspective, literature was the means by which the colonized would enter the new social, economic, and cultural hierarchy and signifying system instituted by colonial rule.

So, by means of colonial ideological intention and indoctrination, for the first products of the mission schools, defined by Simon Gikandi as "the Catechist class" (Gikandi 2000), identification with the civilizing values of the hegemonic colonial order would become a way of achieving status and value within the colonial social structure and forming a new, but modernizing elite whose power did not emanate from the indigenous traditional system.[1] Thus, literary values were generally part of the privileged culture in which the aspiring colonized subject would need to be steeped, if he or she were ever able to achieve any meaningful cultural and economic advancement.

It was the colonial novel, among others, with the specific aim of representing the colonial experience that offered ideal models of subjectivity to the colonized within a structure in which anything closely resembling indigenous value would be represented as the negation of progress and civilization. Ngugi, decrying this state of affairs, notes:

> Orature (oral literature) in Kenyan languages stopped. In primary school I now read simplified Dickens and Stevenson alongside Rider Haggard, Jim Hawkins, Oliver Twist, Tom Brown—not Hare, Leopard and Lion—were now my daily companions in the world of imagination. (Ngugi 1981: 12)

It was not only the language of literature or the fact that it was English that was alienating: according to Abdul JanMohamed (1985), there was something in the generic character of the texts that undermined the identity of the colonized reader. Whether it was Graham Greene's *The Heart of the Matter* (1971 [1948]), Joseph Conrad's *Heart of Darkness* (1973 [1899]) or Joyce Cary's *Mister Johnson* (1939), they all exemplified the privileged values of the colonial formation, in the process engendering what JanMohamed has aptly defined as the genre of "racial romance." In other words, what was being read, as Ngugi suggests in the notion of "a simplified Dickens," was not in fact mainstream literature, but a particular kind of text.

For JanMohamed (1985: 71–72), the colonial desire to produce a generic normative aesthetic ends up undercutting the very ideal aesthetic norms of the novel, since what is produced is more of a popular genre than the intended privileged high culture.

If one takes Fanon's (1991) and JanMohamed's idea of the immanence of the Manichean dichotomy in the structure of the colonial formation seriously, then it becomes abundantly clear that *it is impossible for the colonial settlement as a formation to produce a novel, for the primary requirement of traditional novelistic practice, that is, vraisemblance, being true to life, cannot be achieved* under such cultural conditions, since the colonial writer is unable to produce the image of a 'real native,' but rather one of his or her own imagination. Moreover, there is the suggestion here that *mimesis* is undermined by the overriding power and authority of the Manichean principle inherent in colonialist fiction, with the result that the colonized space and its subjects are reified into figments of the colonial imagination. It needs to be noted, however, that what is indicated here is a conflict of two models of reality, that of the colonialist and of the colonized. The distorted character of Mr Johnson in Cary's novel, for instance, is mimetically probable within the world of the colonialist, but improbable in that of the colonized. Thus, the alienation Ngugi and other colonized subjects felt was largely because a different reality from the one they were familiar with was being imposed upon them through the literature they read.

The romance genre is used to *interpellate*, to use Louis Althusser's term, the colonized into an ideal subject of the colonial Sovereign (Althusser 1968: 115). What is also fascinating about this genre is that while it targets the colonized, it simultaneously excludes him. It clearly does not include the colonized as its ideal reader—he or she is not considered part of its target audience, its presumed community of readers, so to speak, for the intended comic dismemberment, as in the case of Mr Johnson, is predicated on an insider's joke, a shared sense of what is funny, and that community is clearly the metropolitan community at home as well as their representatives in the colony (JanMohamed 1985: 65–66). As JanMohamed observes, this genre is based on an implicit set of values in which the constructed alterity of the colonized is presented as unquestionably true. It is such a quality that limits the universality of colonialist fiction.

Indeed, even where it is adopted by the Catechist class, it functions as a form of mimicry, not so much in Homi Bhabha's sense (Bhabha 1994: 825–892), as immanently subversive, but rather in that of absolute imitation. Samuel Ntara's *Man of Africa* (1934) illustrates how this class imbibed the forms of the romance genre and adapted them to the needs of creating an indigenous written literature.[2] In this instance, the Manichean dichotomy is presented as the difference between Christianity and urban secularism, with the latter being seen as inherently destructive and continuous with the supposed heathenism of indigenous culture. It is this drive to *interpellate* the colonized in a genre of self-denigration that produces a crisis in the reading of the colonial novel, but, one that also foregrounds its character as more of a 'racial romance' than the conventional novel.[3]

Writing as the Critique of the Colonial Norm

The cultural ideals proffered by the colonial novel as the popular form of the novel, which may have appealed to the first generation of the colonized, came under increasing pressure with the rise of nationalism and decolonization from the 1920s onwards. Chinua Achebe's case best illustrates how the post-colonial African novelistic genre emerged from the *interpellative* limitations of the colonial novel. If the rise of the novel in Europe was prompted by the need to represent new forms of social subjectivity produced by changes in the social and economic structures of the eighteenth century, fuelled by the shift from Feudalism and Mercantilism to Capitalism, the post-colonial novel emerged in response to changes wrought by the Second World War, characterized by an increased political consciousness among the colonized and a desire for greater representation in cultural forms. It is in this context that the alienating effects of the colonial novel as 'racial romance' become even more obvious. Recalling his undergraduate days at the University of Ibadan, Achebe observes:

> I read lots of English books [. . .] I did not see myself as an African to begin with. I took sides with the white men against the savages [. . .] But a time came when I realised [. . .] I was not on Marlowe's boat steaming up the Congo in the *Heart of Darkness*. I was one of those strange beings jumping up and down on the river bank, making horrid faces. [. . .] That is when I realised that stories are not innocent. (Achebe 1990: 7)

Achebe gives us a sense of the ontological performance of *interpellated* subjectivity and its palpable effects on the formation of the identity of the African youth brought up during colonial occupation and, significantly, he also foregrounds the process of political awakening. He represents the colonized as "the bad subject" (Althusser 1968: 115–124), that is, the subject who sees through the *interpellative* function of ideology and begins to counter-identify with it, undermining the intended ideological and historical determination of his or her identity. In this way, "the bad subject" evinces the limitations of dominant ideology to *interpellate* absolutely, for the very process of cultural *interpellation* also involves the unveiling of the real terms by which colonial truth is constituted. It is not by coincidence that Achebe's insights are engendered at a colonial British University based in Africa, since University College Ibadan, founded as part of the University of London, like its counterpart in East Africa, Makerere University College which Ngugi attended, was intended to produce a local intellectual elite that would underpin the modernizing colonial enterprise.

It was also part of an *emergent class* which, in Raymond Williams's sense of the term (Williams 1977: 121–127), was the new dominant in the process of formation and, as such, its members were working both inside and outside the dominant ideology, constituting an oppositional bloc. If the European novel had been invented to represent the *emergent* European bourgeoisie of the eighteenth century, the new African elite of the twentieth century, such as Achebe, who could not see themselves in the image reflected back from Joyce Cary's *Mr Johnson*, were perhaps, in a sort of Pirandelloan way, new subjects in search of an author.[4] In this manner, the rise of the post-colonial African novel was a function of a profound conflict over the politics of representation. As Stuart Hall (1996: 442) suggests, this is a form of political articulation where a marginalized group demands visibility of institutional representation as well as contesting the dominant discursive forms of meaning production.

In some ways, Cyprian Ekwensi's racy novels published in the early Fifties, such as *People of the City* (1954), were attempts to register the African urban experience which had emerged as a consequence of colonial modernity. The new literature sought to capture the lived experience of African subjects, but in a way that was meaningful and understandable to an African audience. Although, seen as imitative of Euro-American popular writing, there was an abundant originality in this form of writing, primarily in terms of its creation of new models of African subjectivity. That might also be said to be true of the popular genres churned out by Onitsha Market writers from the 1940s onwards (Obiechina 1973: 18–19). Moreover, unlike the 'racial romances' produced by colonial writers, the new writing included the colonized African as the target audience. This mode of writing would resolve the fundamental contradictions in the aesthetics of reception of colonialist fiction in which the ideal reader was conceived of within reception norms that more or less constituted a *discursive idiolect*, in that the presumed *community of readers* (Fish 1980) excluded the colonized.

It is intriguing that the response of Chinua Achebe, widely regarded as the founding father of modern post-colonial African writing, did not follow the popular genres established by his compatriot, Ekwensi, but rather the tradition of European realism. Perhaps Achebe did not want to respond in the form of the modernizing ethos embraced by African writers of popular fiction because of its 'mimicry' which could be mistaken for a legitimation of the colonial project, even the colonial 'racial romance.' Ekwensi and the Onitsha Market writers were to a large extent uncritical of the idea of colonial modernity, seeing it as the highest form of progress, a view that in effect unwittingly played into the colonial denigration of African indigenous culture (Appiah 1991: 348). Thus, radical as it may have been in some respects, African popular literature did not offer a sufficient distance from the dominant aesthetic forms of the colonial formation to serve as the space of a genuinely new and profoundly transformative *post-colonial counter discourse*.

To counteract the 'racial romances' of the colonial era, Achebe appealed to the norms of *verisimilitude* and *mimesis* offered by the traditional novel, employing the novel to present a life-like image of an Africa before Europe had intervened. So, his first novel *Things Fall Apart* (1958) attempted to recover the full humanity of the African. In his own words:

> It is inconceivable to me that a serious writer could stand aside from this debate, or be indifferent to this argument which calls his full humanity into question. [. . .] This theme [. . .] is that African peoples did not hear of culture for the first time from Europeans; that their societies were not mindless but frequently had a philosophy of great depth and value and beauty, that they had poetry and, above all, they had dignity. [. . .] In Africa he cannot perform this task unless he has a proper sense of history. (Achebe 1973: 8)

Thus, for Achebe, the post-colonial African novel should employ the mode of realism, but particularly historical realism, to uncover the moment when colonial culture and values entered the historical consciousness of the colonized African subject. This kind of writing is unashamedly nationalistic, as Appiah has observed:

> These novels seem to belong to the world of eighteenth- and nineteenth-century literary nationalism; they are theorised as the imaginative recreation of a common cultural past that is crafted into a shared tradition by the writer. They are in the tradition of Sir Walter Scott. (Appiah 1991: 349)

Undoubtedly, Scottish literary nationalism, which had sought to defend a national culture against that of its dominant neighbour, England, may have contributed to the emergence of a practice of post-colonial nationalist resistance to Anglo-acculturation and also of a particular poetics. Scott's novels, as, indeed, later Scottish writing, such as Grassic Gibbon's *A Scott's Quair* (1935), may have offered exemplary literary models of an oppositional aesthetic. That would also be true of Irish writers, especially John Middleton Synge (1907) and W.B. Yeats (1933), with whom writers such as Achebe were familiar, who sought to found an Irish National Theatre and literature. Besides, there were examples of a poetics of cultural nationalism within the English tradition itself, for example, Thomas Hardy's Wessex novels which would have shown that even in England there was a mode of realism that attempted to defend tradition against the relentless pursuit of modernity, especially its corrosive effect on the local beliefs and lore.[5] This anti-modernist realism may also have provided an aesthetic legitimation for the new practice of writing.[6]

Thus, Achebe's privileging of realism over the colonial 'racial romance' may be seen as grounding the authentic African novel within the scope of the English literary tradition itself, a subversive occupation of the dominant tradition in order to point out the weaknesses of novels such as Conrad's *Heart of Darkness* and Joyce Cary's *Mister Johnson*, which did not explore African cultures which, like traditional cultures in Europe, were equally being threatened by a relentless modernity. It is also true that the colonial location of the writers explains the extent to which they enacted both fidelity to and transgression of the dominant European aesthetic forms. As Gikandi notes:

> the theoretical questions that have haunted Achebe's writing career—the writer's relationship with his dual tradition, the value of history, and the possibilities of an African literature in a colonial language—are all prompted by the desire to initiate a discourse of resistance and to re-present Africans other than they have been presented in colonialist discourse. (Gikandi 1991: 24)

Another way of specifying its distinctiveness was for this literature to posit itself as a multiplicity of sub-genres. If historical and social realism defined the new novelistic practice in Africa, they also coexisted with other forms, such as modernism and indigenous African *oraturial* practices. The ideological significance of Achebe taking the title of his first novel from W.B. Yeats' poem 'The Second Coming' (1933), has often been remarked upon by critics, but what has not been sufficiently underlined is its import as a generic marker of the text. Here, Achebe affiliates himself to modernism, especially that aspect of it that sought to go beyond realism. Yeats's mysticism and his interest in Irish oral tradition were very much akin to Achebe's concerns in his first novel, just as the former's commitment to the cause of Irish Independence would have offered a template for the latter's *literary nationalist political commitment* (Innes 1994: 1–114).

There is also a sense in which modernism modifies Achebe's realism, making the new literature palpably part of *avant garde* aesthetics. In Virginia Woolf's view, the role of modernism was to recover the reality beyond the quotidian, the surface experience that formed the staple of nineteenth-century realism (Woolf 1925: 4–5). Modernism offered Achebe freedom from the constraints of realism, providing an opportunity to produce a particular form of realism, a sort of modernist-realism, that would, on the one hand, avail itself of realism's emphasis on *vraisemblance* to produce a literature of social comment and, on the other, of modernism's critique of the straight-jacket of the traditional realist narrative, constituting a formal eclecticism that would be ample enough to mix unobtrusively with indigenous African aesthetic forms. Modernism demonstrated that what was considered strange and unconventional could be part and parcel of a new literary sensibility and that established literary conventions could be violated in the name of a new mode of writing, especially, if it claimed, as modernism had done, to apprehend reality much more profoundly.

So, modernism became an important marker of the *avant garde* quality of the *emergent post-colonial African novel*, as it distanced itself from a 'romance-realism' that had developed during colonialism. In this way, *Things Fall Apart* and novels such as Ngugi wa Thiong'o's *The River Between* (1965) and *Weep Not Child* (1964) are a formal hybridity of realism and modernism. In that space of experimentation opened up by modernism, Achebe and his colleagues inserted an indigenous aesthetic that modified significantly the received novelistic practice, starting the process of decolonizing the novel as a genre in Africa, adapting it to the specificity, both cultural and political, of the African post-colonial formation.

Genre and the Pitfalls of a Teleological Post-Modernist Critique

It is in this respect that critics such as Appiah who have castigated the first generation of novelists for being realists have misrepresented the complex relationship these writers had with the received tradition. Appiah informs us that:

> The generation of Chinua Achebe's *Things Fall Apart* [. . .] were written in the context of notions of politics and culture dominant in the French and British University and publishing in the 1950s and 1960s. [. . .] Part of what was held to be obvious both by these writers and by the high culture of Europe of the day was that new literatures in new nations should be anticolonial and nationalist [. . .] These novels of the first stage are thus realist legitimations of nationalism: they authorise 'a return to traditions' while at the same time recognising the demands of a Weberian rationalised modernity. (Appiah 1991: 348–349)

In a bid to construct a linear genealogy of the development of African genre practice, Appiah seems to have glossed over the essential transgressive nature of the first stage of the post-colonial novel in English. In fact, that is surprisingly close to the wholesale dismissal of 1950s writing that one finds in Chinweizu's *Decolonizing African Literature* (1985).

Clearly, Okonkwo, the protagonist of Chinua Achebe's novel, cannot be regarded as an affirmation of Weberian rationalization, a man likely to react with his fist to such an accusation! Achebe and his colleagues simply endorsed neither Weber nor Western realism to shore up African nationalism. On the contrary, they were responding from a position suspicious of such discourses, just as they were of uncritical 'nativism.' The destruction of Okonkwo, a man who holds onto tradition inflexibly in *Things Fall Apart,* bespeaks a much more complex approach to both the West and Africa in Achebe's novel. Indeed, as F. Odun Balogun has observed, Achebe deliberately eschewed what might be described as 'nativism' by opting for a more hybrid form of novelistic practice. As he puts it: "[i]n order for the message [. . .] to remain clear and unambiguous [. . .], Achebe rejected the folklore-informed and necessarily complex novelistic style of his predecessor, Amos Tutuola" (Balogun 1997: vii). Perhaps Jonathan Dollimore's notion of "transgressive mimesis" (Dollimore 1984: 70–82) best defines the novelistic practice fashioned by Chinua Achebe and his colleagues. They modelled themselves on European cultural practices, but also sought to create a new signifying practice that would represent the world as they knew it. It was an imitation that exceeded the bounds of the object of imitation.

A closer look at Appiah's dismissal of this genre as simply an extension of Euro-American ideology and style reveals the extent to which his position exhibits the very ailment he ascribes to Achebe and others. There is a teleological reading of the history of genre in Africa in Appiah's conception, in which the African novel is seen as evolving from its colonial phase, through the anti-colonial realist or nativist one to the supposedly more progressive post-realist and post-nativist stage. He describes the latter as follows:

> Far from being a celebration of the nation, then the novels of the second, postcolonial, stage are novels of delegitimation: they reject not only the Western Imperium but also the nationalist project of the postcolonial national bourgeoisie. (Appiah 1991: 352)

It is evident that the post-realism Appiah approves of transcends the idea of the nation and becomes palpably transnational. While the transnational, as a corrective to the excesses of nationalism, is to be welcomed, yet a transnationalism that does not recognize the reality of the national space as one of historical struggle, particularly in Africa, is a disembodied construct that is a negation of the national rather than a genuine sublation of the national into a meaningful cosmopolitanism.

Additionally, Appiah's disapproval of the first generation of writers and his preference for the so-called post-nativist and post-realist ones betrays a rather overenthusiastic privileging of postmodernist narratives. In this respect, he reproduces the same uncritical Western determination he ascribes to the first generation of African writers. Indeed, it is such dismissals of cultural and political processes that have in their time served as conduits of important freedoms that has made some African critics wary of some aspects of contemporary critical theory. Femi Osofisan, for instance, has argued that "[m]any aspects of postcolonialist theorising have made the humanization of discourse impossible as a result of their fetishisation of the text and its theory" (Osofisan 1996: 1).

The mistake Appiah makes is that he assumes that because the first generation of writers was ideologically determined in terms of collective subjectivity and cultural practices by the colonial dominant, its claim to a decolonizing impulse is false and unfounded. That argument is also aligned with another one which asserts that, because the discourse of nationalism failed to deliver the promised liberal democracy and a functioning modernity to post-colonial Africa, the idea itself could not have had any validity whatsoever. It is true, as a number of writers, including—as Appiah himself acknowledges—those of the first generation, have decried the failure of the post-colonial governments to translate the idealism of nationalism into reality. However, to take the disenchantment with such failures as a total rejection of the entire nationalist project and its contribution to the process of decolonization is to underestimate grossly the value of African nationalism as a counter-hegemonic ideology and practice that achieved much in getting rid of blatant colonial oppression and bringing into existence new national spaces, which, imperfect as they may be, have given post-colonial Africans a national sense of belonging, which was greatly lacking in colonial times. In that process of decolonization, literature played an important part. However, that is not to say that, as the writers of the first generation themselves admit, the nationalist mode of novelistic practice had answered all the demands of aesthetic decolonization in Africa or addressed all the relevant political issues of the time.

It is certainly the case, that Achebe's novelistic practice became the dominant form of African literature and that there have since then been several attempts to evolve new practices, and what Appiah terms "post-realism" is one example among many. What unifies these experiments is not the quest for a transnational non-otherness as Appiah (1991: 352) suggests, but rather an attempt to continue the labour of self-representation that earlier writers, such as Chinua Achebe, had begun and continue to contribute to actively. The transnational or cosmopolitan may be desirable and necessary, but they are certainly not the starting point for these new writers. My sense is that in their genre practice, they exhibit the kind of "self-apprehension" that Wole Soyinka enjoins African intellectuals to adopt. As he contends, genuine "self-apprehension" opens out to the Other, but not to negate the Self or the Other (Soyinka 1976: xii).

Thus, it is possible to see the development of the African novelistic practice as a gradual process of indigenization, with different writers employing varying strategies for doing so. This is the opposite of regarding the writers as facing outward constantly, either in support of colonialism or the transnational and cosmopolitanism. What particular writers adopt as strategies of novelistic adaptation will always be a function of the aesthetic and ideological horizon that constitutes their lived reality. As Balogun puts it:

> The nationalist anti-colonial novel, epitomised by Chinua Achebe's *Things Fall Apart*, was consciously ethnographic in cultural detail and realistic in artistic execution because its aim was to show that, in spite of certain limitations [. . .] pre-colonial African culture was well-organised and humane [. . .] In order for the message [. . .] to remain clear and

unambiguous [. . .], Achebe rejected the folklore-informed and necessarily complex novelistic style of his predecessor, Amos Tutuola, and
adopted [. . .] the methods of the English realistic novel. *Things Fall
Apart* became the thematic and artistic model for African nationalist
prose [. . .], including Ngugi's first two novels. (Balogun 1997: vii)

Rather than simply dismissing the genre out of hand because of its association with the West, Balogun profitably focuses on its ideological function in
relation to surrounding genre formations.

This approach complicates the historical trajectory of African genre,
by not solely opposing the nationalist novel against the so-called post-na-
tionalist type, but also by including earlier writers such as Tutuola who
were equally engaged, perhaps, in a slightly different way, with the process
of indigenizing the novel in Africa.[7] In Balogun's view, compared with
Tutuola's, Chinua Achebe's version was perhaps less traditionally African
than it could have been, though the reasons for opting for a lighter form of
indigenization are understandable in terms of the nationalists' desire for a
literature that also served as political pedagogy. This is a radically different
calibration of the history of genre development in Africa from that offered
by Appiah.

Genre and the Concept of Literature

Moreover, when discussing the concept of genre or literary taxonomy, it is
often forgotten that underlying particular notions of genre are ideas about
the nature of literature itself. Literary practice may be universal, but the
categories of form and literary value vary from culture to culture. It is not
surprising that one of the first people to raise the question about the nature
of African literature in Africa is Ngugi wa Thiong'o, a member of the first
generation of African novelists. The hybridity of the first generation of novels was fine in terms of addressing the specific historical challenges posed
by colonialism and the period of decolonization. However, though the writers had questioned the received literary values, the aesthetic practices they
adopted had not resolved all the underlying contradictions.

It was particularly the continued use of the English language by African
writers that Ngugi saw as symptomatic of cultural neo-colonial relations. In
his view: "The choice of language and the use to which language is put is
central to a people's definition of themselves in relation to their natural and
social environment" (Ngugi 1981: 4). In this way, the adoption of English
as the language of creative expression is seen as having constrained the
effort of self-apprehension and self-representation—the language in which
the resistance of colonial cultural domination was being conducted during
the period of decolonization and after was itself one in which the African
was Othered. Thus, the aesthetic hybridity of the African novel of the first

generation had concealed profound unequal power relations. Language as a signifying practice will always articulate existing relations of power. True, as Bakhtin argues, it can also express the struggle over signs and their meaning (Bakhtin 1981: 273)—evident in the first generation of writers. Nevertheless, without the total discursive terrain of power being addressed, language by itself cannot be an adequate site of resistance.

It is that insight that must have led Ngugi and others to argue that the term literature needed to be replaced by a more suitable one. For Ngugi, the term "literature" itself, as a classificatory designation for verbal creative practice, betrays a certain arbitrary cathectation of the field. It privileges the chirographic over the perceived alterity, the oral text. Hence, he proposed the term "orature" (Ngugi 1981: 12), which echoes the Derridian notion of *supplementarity*, erasing the dichotomy between literature and oral literature, positing the conceptual possibility of 'texts' that partake of both, which truly most African novels do regardless of the period in which they were written. In that way, oral tradition is removed from the sometimes denigrated domain of folklore into a post-colonial aesthetic that is located in a cultural universe in which orality and chirography coexist amicably rather than as absolute binary opposites.[8]

Ngugi's subsequent creative practice has sought to continue the earlier effort, finding more ways of indigenizing the African novel. According to Balogun:

> Ngugi has become the first among the foremost African novelists to make the novel truly African. [. . .] [H]is experimentation has transformed the novel into an artistic multiform within which several genres co-exist. (Balogun 1997: ix–x)

Indeed, Ngugi has transformed African novelistic practice radically. His novel *Matigari* (1987), for instance, is a textualized oral performance that aspires to the condition of an oral text, even as it presents itself in the written form of a conventional novel. The preface to the novel is aptly illustrative in this regard:

TO THE READER/LISTENER

This story is imaginary.
The actions are imaginary.
The characters are imaginary.
The country is imaginary—it has no name even.
Reader/listener: may your story take place in the country of your choice. [. . .]
Reader/listener: may it take place in the time of your choice. (Ngugi 1987: ix)

The narrative is framed in terms of the open-endedness of a traditional folk-tale, whilst at the same time, self-reflexively highlighting the *duality of textual ontology*, that it is both an oral as well as a written text.

Yet, it is also noticeable that Balogun locates Ngugi's authenticity within Bakhtin's definition of the novel, saying:

> According to Bakhtin, these are the characteristics that give the novel its capacity to incorporate other genres. As already pointed out, they are the same characteristics that Ngugi has capitalised on to create the equivalently multigenre novel. (Balogun 1997: 19)

Balogun shows how the African novel at its most authentic is in fact similar to the European idea of the novel. In other words, at its most particular it is also most universal. The post-colonial African novel is both itself and Other, as a function of the contingent history and politics of its formation. Fundamentally, the location of the African novelistic practice has not changed, whether it is in its phase of African realism or post-realism—it is still defined in terms of its degree of indigenization or its affiliation to the received tradition. That applies to the literatures in African languages as well, especially the experiments by Ngugi wa Thiong'o in Kikuyu, which despite their radical difference from the European novel display a similar generic inheritance to those in the English language.[9] As Karin Barber (Barber 1995) has argued, we need to set the study of the appropriation of European literary practices in Africa in a context that includes African-language literatures, which have, in some respects, transformed radically the received forms, making them very much part and parcel of the modern lived experience of particular language communities. Ngugi exemplifies the fact that the African writer in English cannot be regarded as hermetically sealed off from the living oral culture and written local-language literatures around him or her.

Conclusion

It is for this reason that what we need to foreground in the study of the African novelistic practice is not so much a tradition in which Europe and Africa are dichotomous, but one in which there has been a constant attempt to indigenize the novel. However, those efforts also continually reveal the extent to which the idea of the novel is not entirely indigenous, always alluding to a referential nexus outside the universe of post-colonial African cultural practice.

It is also here that the practice of the novel in Africa can be said to follow the model proposed by Jacques Derrida (1980: 55–81). The attempts to transcend the generic structures of the European novel ultimately lead to the very affirmation of the universal idea of the novel. The new genre depends for its identity and legitimation on that very arch-genre, with which it counter-identifies and whose regulatory parameters it breaches. Derrida contends that in genre: "all the sophisticated transgressions, all the infinitesimal subversions that may captivate you are not possible except within the enclosure for which these transgressions and subversions moreover maintain an essential need in order to take place" (Derrida 1980: 72).

In this sense, the African novel is a sub-species of the European genre of the novel as well as an autonomous practice that is a subset of the totality of African indigenous aesthetic taxonomy, reflecting the entire discursive formation of its African and international conditions of production.

It is thus, both a distinct as well as a derived practice that appropriates the cosmopolitan and the indigenous literary resources, contributing to the stabilization of the novel as a genre, even as it disturbs its core identity. That is a law of fidelity and transgression that Tzvetan Todorov describes as follows: "One might say that every great book establishes the existence of two genres [. . .] that of the genre it transgresses [. . .] and that of which it creates" (Todorov 1988: 158–159). Thus, Achebe affirms the validity of the European traditions as much as he offers something really new, an African novelistic practice.

In this way, it can be argued that there is an authentic African novelistic practice, but it is transcultural—its authenticity lies in the fact that it is both a specific elaboration of the law of genre as well as the affirmation of its universality. It is this contingent existence that sublates the universal to a particular formation of the Self-Other dialectic. If, on the one hand, the African novel were totally Other, it would not be perceived as a species of the international novelistic practice and would thus not receive institutional recognition, but, if on the other, it were simply a replica of the European novel, it would be redundant and therefore lacking in any distinctive worth. Represented thus, the *textual duality* of the African novelistic practice in English is illuminated and shown to occupy the intersection between two universes of discourse. Additionally highlighted is its coexistence with the written and oral literatures in African languages. In this respect, the varied expressions of a counter-aesthetic in the work of the first and later generations of novelists writing in English are different, but particular formations of this dialectical synthesis of the received universal norms and local ones. It is the ideological ground and even intention that marks each group of writers and texts.

Notes

1. However, as the emergence of African-led churches in the early part of the twentieth century shows, there might have been conformity in terms of cultural value, but that the overall place of European Christianity within Africa was being contested—see for instance, John McCracken (1977).
2. Some of the missionary-sponsored narratives by the first generation of African educated elites tended to follow the narrative structure of the colonial novel, for example, Samuel Ntara's *Man of Africa* (1934).

3. The term 'interpellate' is employed here in the sense used in Althusser (1968).
4. I am referring here to Pirandello's play *Six Characters in Search of an Author* (1995 [1925]), in which characters abandoned by an author go about looking for someone to complete their characterization.
5. These would include, for instance, Hardy's novel *The Woodlanders* (1896).
6. A comparative approach to post-colonial African nationalist realism, on the one hand and Irish and English writing of the nineteenth and early twentieth centuries, on the other, does also undermine Fredric Jameson's notion that Third World literatures have a monopoly on the 'allegorical' articulation of the national—see Jameson (1986).
7. Amos Tutuola started publishing his anglicized oral tales from the late forties, which were modelled on those written in Yoruba by such writers as D.O. Fagunwa (1903–1963).
8. For the relationship between orality and chirography, see Walter Ong (1982).
9. On indigenization and hybridity in local language literatures, see Barber (1995: 3–30).

Works Cited

Achebe, C. (1958) *Things Fall Apart*, London: Heinemann.
———. (1973) 'The Role of the Writer in a New Nation', in G.D. Killam (ed.) *African Writers on African Writing*, London: Heinemann, 7–13.
———. (1990) 'African Literature as Restoration of Celebration', in K. Holst Petersen and A. Rutherford (eds) *Chinua Achebe: A Celebration*, Oxford: Heinemann, 1–10.
Althusser, L. (1968) *Lenin, Philosophy and Other Essays*, London: New Left Review.
Appiah, K.A. (1991) 'Is the Post—in Postmodernism the Post—in Postcolonial?', *Critical Inquiry*, 17/2: 336–357.
Balogun, F.O. (1997) *Ngugi and African Postcolonial Narrative*, Quebec QC: World Heritage Press.
Barber, K. (1995) 'African-Language Literature and Postcolonial Criticism', *Research in African Literatures*, 26/4: 3–30.
Bakhtin, M. (1981) *The Dialogic Imagination*, Austin TX: University of Texas Press.
Bhabha, H.K. (1994) *The Location of Culture*, London and New York: Routledge.
Cary, J. (1939) *Mister Johnson*, London: Gollancz.
Chinweizu, O. Jemie and Madubuike I. (1985) *Toward the Decolonization of African Literature*, London: Routledge and Kegan Paul.
Conrad, J. (1973 [1899]) *Heart of Darkness*, London: Penguin.
Derrida, J. (1974) *Of Grammatology*, Baltimore and London: Johns Hopkins University Press.
———. (1980) 'The Law of Genre', *Critical Inquiry*, 7/1: 55–81.
Dollimore, J. (1984) *Radical Tragedy*, Chicago: Chicago University Press.
Ekwensi, C. (1954) *People of the City*, London: Andrew Daker.
Enwezor, O. (2003) 'The Postcolonial Contemporary Art in a State of Permanent Transition', *Research in African Literatures*, 34/4: 57–82.
Fanon, F. (1991) *Black Skin, White Masks*, London: Pluto Press.
Fish, S. (1980) *Is There a Text in This Class? The Authority of Interpretive Communities*, Cambridge, MA: Harvard University Press.
Gibbon, L.G. (1935) *A Scot's Quair*, London: Penguin.
Gikandi, S. (1991) *Reading Chinua Achebe*, London: James Currey.

————. (2000) 'The Embarrassment of Victorianism: Colonial Subjects and the Lure of Englishness', in J. Kucich and D.F. Sadoff (eds) *Victorian Afterlife*, Minneapolis and London: University of Minnesota Press, 157–185.

Greene, G. (1971 [1948]) *The Heart of the Matter*, London: Penguin.

Hall, S. (1996) 'New Ethnicities', in D. Morley and K.-H. Chen (eds) *Stuart Hall*, London: Routledge, 441–449.

Hardy, T. (1896) *The Woodlanders*, London: Penguin.

Innes, C.L. (1994) 'Virgin Territories and Motherlands: Colonial and Nationalist Representations of Africa and Ireland', *Feminist Review*, 47: 1–14.

Jameson, F. (1986) 'Third-World Literature in the Era of Multinational Capitalism', *Social Text*, 15: 65–88.

JanMohamed, A.R. (1985) 'The Economy of Manichean Allegory: The Function of Racial Difference in Colonialist Literature', *Critical Inquiry*, 12/1: 59–87.

McCracken, J. (1977) *Politics and Christianity in Malawi*, Cambridge: Cambridge University Press.

Macdonald, D. (1969 [1862]) *Africana or the Heart of Heathen Africa*, London: Dawsons of Pall Mall.

Ngugi wa Thiong'o (1964) *Weep Not Child*, London: Heinemann.

————. (1965) *The River Between*, London: Heinemann.

————. (1987) *Matigari*, trans. Wangui wa Goro, Nairobi, Kenya: Heinemann [rpt. London: Heinemann 1989].

————. (1981) *Decolonising the Mind*, London: James Currey.

Ntara, S. (1934) *Man of Africa*, London: Religious Tract Society.

Obiechina, O. (1973) *An African Popular Literature*, Cambridge: Cambridge University Press.

Ong, W. (1982) *Orality and Literacy*, London: Methuen.

Osofisan, F. (1996) 'Warriors of a Failed Utopia? Writers since 70s', *Leeds African Studies Bulletin*, 61: 1–10.

Pirandello, L. (1995 [1923]) *Six Characters in Search of an Author and Other Plays*, London: Penguin.

Soyinka, W. (1976) *Myth, Literature and the African World*, Cambridge: Cambridge University Press.

Synge, J.M. (1907) *The Aran Islands*, London: Elkin Matthews.

Todorov, T. (1976) 'The Origin of Genres', *New Literary History*, 6/1: 159–179.

————. (1988) 'The Typology of Detective Fiction', in D. Lodge (ed.) *Modern Criticism and Theory*, London: Longman, 158–165.

Viswanathan, G. (1987) 'Currying Favor: The Politics of British Educational and Cultural Policy in India, 1813–1854', *Social Text*, 19–20: 85–104.

Williams, R. (1977) *Marxism and Literature*, Oxford: Oxford University Press.

Woolf, V. (1925) *The Common Reader*, London: Hogarth Press.

Yeats, W.B. (1933) *The Collected Poems*, London: Macmillan.

6 "De-Formed Narrators"

Postcolonial Genre and Peripheral Modernity in Mabanckou and Pepetela

Sharae Deckard

Given that the orientation of many novels from so-called 'post' colonial nations is increasingly towards a critique of globalization rather than the former imperial metropolis, a reconstitution of the field of postcolonial literary studies seems ever more urgent. One possible reorientation would be to develop a globalized postcolonial comparativism that critically engages the aesthetics of literatures of capitalist peripheries, in order to theorize the uneven relations of global capitalism and new and ongoing forms of military and economic imperialism. As such, Franco Moretti has provided a useful starting point in his conceptualization of "world literature" as neither a *canon* of masterworks, nor merely as a *mode* of reading, but rather as literature of the capitalist world-system:

> I will borrow . . . [my] initial hypothesis from the world-system school of economic history, for which international capitalism is a system that is simultaneously *one*, and *unequal*; with a core, and a periphery (and a semi-periphery) that are bound together in a relationship of growing inequality. One, and unequal: *one* literature (*Weltliteratur*, singular, as in Goethe and Marx), or, perhaps better, one world literary system (of inter-related literatures); but a system which is different from what Goethe and Marx had hoped for, because it's profoundly *unequal*. (Moretti 2000: par 6)

In particular, Moretti's emphasis on "one, and unequal" system calls for a new consideration of the aesthetics of world literatures in light of the Marxist theory of combined and uneven development.

Moretti proposes what he calls *distant reading* supported by the work of nationalist specialists as a way of addressing the methodological problems of language and cultural specificity raised by the sheer scale and amount of texts that would be implicated in such a comparativist envisioning of world literature (Moretti 2000: par 8). However, his provocative rejection of close reading and interpretation in its entirety in favour of a "distant" graphing of the movement and reproduction of larger formal structures and elements— his proposed morphology of form—is dissatisfying to those who would like to preserve the role of close textual analysis in investigating the precise literary ways in which peripheral aesthetics through their generic formal innovations self-consciously encode and engender critique of both local conditions within the nation but also of the larger processes of globalization through which the local is mediated. It is here that Pascale Casanova's call in *The World Republic of Letters* for the restoration of the lost transnational dimension of literature which understands literary fields as produced in a Braudelian economy-world also proves useful, despite its overly Franco-centric insistence on Paris as the literary Greenwich Meridian and its ambitiously generalizing argument. Casanova asserts that literary revolutions are produced on the peripheries in response to dependency and marginalization. As with Moretti, the term *periphery* is not intended as a value judgment, merely as a statement of a structural economic and political relation. Far from privileging the cultural production of economic cores as somehow more authentic, original, or aesthetically valuable, Casanova's formulation suggests that the production of the peripheries is more original in its formal innovations and that the relationship between core and periphery's cultural production should not be examined in terms of foreign debt, influence, or mono-directional movement of forms, but rather in terms of structural codetermination.

Nicholas Brown makes a similar point in the introduction to his study of African and European modernisms, *Utopian Generations*. He argues for "establishing the interpretive horizon of twentieth-century literature at capitalism's internal limit," analyzing the displacements of the rift between capital and labour, particularly the division of labour in the globe "between wealthy nations and a much larger and poor economic periphery" (Brown 2005: 1). In particular, he contends that neither "British modernism between the world wars nor African literature during the period of the national independence struggles" can be understood in isolation; rather, "the full meaning of each only emerges in relation to the other and to the rift, both internal and external, which they each try in different ways to represent" (Brown 2005: 1). Brown emphasizes his aim is not genetic criticism and offers Ayi Kwei Armah's rejoinder to a monograph tracing the "influence" of Joyce on *The Beautyful Ones Are Not Yet Born* as a refutation of such a project: "the language of borrowing and influence is usually a none too subtle way Western commentators have of saying Africa lacks original creativity" (qtd. in Brown 2005: 2). Instead, while being careful not to do violence to either body of work by applying methodological norms for one literature to the other, Brown aims "to reconstellate modernism and African literature in such a way as to make them both comprehensible within a single framework within which neither will look the same" (Brown 2005: 3). Brown wisely cautions the impossibility of applying methodological norms for one literature to another because "capitalism as a global economic system is also predicated on an uneven development that produces uncountable eddies and swirls in historical time, the literary unthinkable complexity of contemporary history that thwarts any overhasty universalizing gesture" (Brown 2005: 3).

However, the shared nature of this process of uneven development might again be understood as providing a baseline of comparison, the experience of an uneven space-time sensorium with its radical mixtures of residual, and new cultures and economic formations—the Krupp factories alongside peasant huts observed by Trotsky, or the mobile phones and Internet cafes alongside shanty towns to be observed in the megacities of Kinshasa, Lagos, or Rio—all producing pressures on aesthetics to register the shock of the new, the eddies and swirls of uneven development encoded as formal incongruity, and poetic innovation. A globalized postcolonial comparativism, therefore, would be a mode of reading which would seek to track formal and generic innovations across literatures of the periphery throughout the capitalist world-system and generate *not only* an understanding of the political, cultural, and aesthetic *differences* across multiple *local* traditions, but *also* to detect structural homologies, particularly in those ways in which literatures respond to the uneven development projects of global capital and their impact on local environments and subjects, thus registering what Ernst Bloch called *Gleichzeitigkeit des Ungleichzeitigen*, the "synchronism of nonsynchronism" (Bloch 1977: 22). Such homologies of form might appear simultaneously in multiple temporal and geographical contexts but would always be different in their configurations, reflecting the irreducible specificity of their social contents.

This chapter will attempt to demonstrate a case study of a comparativism of formal (in)congruities by considering two contemporary fictions from the periphery and the ways in which their self-conscious parody and transformation of genre conventions obliges the reader to engage in a dialectical hermeneutics. Congolese Alain Mabanckou's *African Psycho* (first published 2003) and Angolan Pepetela's *Jaime Bunda Secret Agent: Stories of Various Mysteries* (first published 2001) both employ comically 'deformed' or 'imperfect' narrators, self-consciously appropriating and transforming innovations in the form of narration from earlier writers in the periphery, including Machado and Dostoevsky. These narratological innovations are welded to hybridized postcolonial aesthetics that combine elements of crime, detective, and thriller fiction. The formal conventions of these genres could be seen as particularly suited to the registration of unevenness; indeed, crime as literary trope and psychopathology as a subject of metaphysical and literary interrogation in relation to the pressures of peripheral modernity harks back to Dostoevsky.

In contrast to Franco Moretti's argument that bourgeois European detective fiction resolves social anxieties by exploring criminality but ultimately reaffirming "that society is still a great *organism*; a unitary and knowable body" (Moretti 2005: 145), recent critics such as Nels Pearson and Marc Singer have argued that "transnational" detective fictions from postcolonial or economic peripheries are more prone to exposing and destabilizing epistemological and ideological tensions, replacing closure with ambivalence and fragmentation (Pearson and Singer 2009: 1–4). Yumna Siddiqi argues that postcolonial literature like Ondaatje's *Anil's Ghost* and Amitav Ghosh's *The Circle of Reason* adapt aspects of genre fiction

> but tweak it or turn it inside out in what becomes a narrative of "social detection," to borrow a phrase from Fredric Jameson, a "vehicle for judgments on society and revelations of its hidden nature." These novels identify social and state practices as invidious, even vicious. (Siddiqi 2002: 177)

The genre conventions revolving around ratiocination and objective detection are held in tension with unreliable narratologies that reflect the contradictions at the heart of social and legal orders. I will argue that the 'failed narrator' device prominent in the fictions of Pepetela and Mabanckou could be understood as a structural homology registering the social deformations of uneven development across multiple socio-temporal contexts and I will interpret its contemporary use in these two different linguistic sites of postcolonial African nations in light of earlier peripheral sites and times of literary production. Pepetela's Luanda and Mabanckou's Brazzaville will thus be considered together with Dostoevsky's St Petersburg, Herman Ungar's Prague-Boskovice and Machado's Rio de Janeiro.

"Swollen-Headed" Individualism

I will begin by ruminating on Brazilian critic Roberto Schwarz's observation of a structural homology in the relation between form and ideology in the aesthetics of nineteenth-century Brazilian novelist Machado and Russian authors Dostoevsky and Gogol:

> Perhaps this is comparable to what happened in Russian literature. Faced with the latter, even the greatest novels of French realism seem naïve. And why? In spite of their claims to universality, the physiology of rational egoism and the ethics of Enlightenment appeared in the Russian Empire as 'foreign' ideology, and therefore as a localized and relative one. Sustained by its historical backwardness, Russia forced the bourgeois novel to face a more complex reality. (Schwarz 1992: 29)

Machado's posthumous narrator Brás Cubas famously claims to have adopted an "unequal philosophy, now austere, now playful, something that neither builds nor destroys, neither inflames nor cools," and a peculiar aesthetic:

> It's a question of a scattered work where I, Brás Cubas, have adopted the free-form of a Sterne or a Xavier de Maistre. [. . .] The work of a dead man. I wrote it with a playful pen and melancholy ink and it isn't

hard to foresee what can come out of that marriage. (Machado de Assis 1997: 11, 5)

The tensions between the imported bourgeois ideology of the realist novel and the immediate social context of nineteenth century Brazil's illiberal, socially stagnated Rio slavocracy produce what John Gledson has called Machado's "deceptive realism," a proto-modernist, self-conscious aesthetics which predates the "cannibal realism" of Oswald and Mario de Andrade's Brazilian modernism by more than three decades. For Schwarz, Brás Cubas's narration is characterized by a peculiar "volubility" and impudence, and self-conscious parody becomes the inherent form of the narration, articulating the contradiction between a Brazilian social reality characterized by paternalistic relations and the false ideology of the striving individual specific to bourgeois realist fiction.

Schwarz cites the passage in Georg Lukács's 1949 essay "Dostoevsky" which heralds the psychological pathologies of *Crime and Punishment*'s Raskolnikov as "the literary embodiment of a new human type" which incarnated the tensions of semi-peripheral modernity in St Petersburg:

> The psychic organization of Dostoevsky's characters, the deformations of their moral ideals grow out of the social misery of the modern metropolis. The insulting and injuring of men in the city is the basis of their morbid individualism, their morbid desire for power over themselves and their neighbours [...] Dostoevsky's characters go to the end of the socially necessary self-distortion unafraid, and their self-dissolution, their self-execution, is the most violent protest that could have been made against the organization of life in that time. (Lukács 1973: 156)

What Lukács refers to politically incorrectly as the "backwardness" of Russia is its semi-peripheral relation to Western Europe: previously underdeveloped but now in a period of accelerated modernization from above. Lukács emphasizes semi-peripheral modernity and the experience of uneven development as giving rise to formal innovations in narrative, characterization, and aesthetic and moral philosophy:

> 'Suddenly' there appeared from an underdeveloped country [...] works that stated—imaginatively—all the problems of human culture at its highest points, stirred up ultimate depths and presented a totality hitherto never achieved and never since surpassed, embracing the spiritual, moral, and philosophical questions of the age. (Lukács 1973: 146)

The social deformations of St Petersburg's experience of uneven modernization are reflected in the moral and psychological deformations of the central protagonist and in the form of the novel's narration, with Raskolnikov's hallucinatory dreams and deliriums straining the limits of realism. As Mikhail Bakhtin famously noted in his essay on Dostoevsky's poetics, the novel is not only polyphonic, positioned in multiple consciousnesses, amongst which the narrator is only one of many, equal to the other characters, but generically hybrid, absorbing elements of gothic, the thriller and the crime novel into Dostoevsky's "fantastic realism" (cf. Bakhtin 1984).

In Mabanckou's *African Psycho*, systemic violence and social deformation are similarly embodied in the morbid desires and quite literal deformation of the "block-headed" protagonist. "Square-headed" Gregoire, like one of Ungar's orphans, is a "picked-up child," abandoned in Congo-Brazzaville after the civil war, raised briefly by a bourgeois family, but soon expelled onto the streets after blinding a sexually abusive step-sibling. He is no genteel student fallen on hard times, but rather a boastful, autodidactic car mechanic, patriotically proud of his slum neighbourhood, "He-Who-Drinks-Water-is-An-Idiot," who loudly proclaims his love of "vulgarity" and announces from the first line, "I have decided to kill" (Mabanckou 2008: 1). Gregoire's failed will to power is a parody of rampant individualism and the second-hand ideology of 'free market' democratization from outside. The novel is set in Brazzaville, the capital of the Republic of Congo, part of a megacity-conurbation with its sister-city Kinshasa across the Congo River. The city is home to more than a third of the country's population, awash with an army of refugees, homeless and unemployed, many of them children. The nation is rich in oil reserves; however, over-mortgaging of petroleum revenues and drastic inflation after the 1994 devaluation of Franc Zone currencies led to the state's acceptance of neoliberal economic reforms, which were interrupted by the 1997 civil war, leading to the evacuation of foreign capital. Despite record-high oil prices since 2003, Congo-Brazzaville is now a candidate for the Heavily Indebted Poor Countries Initiative, with 70% of its population living below the poverty threshold. The vicious cycle of foreign debt, structural adjustment policies, privatization of state enterprises, and withdrawal of state aid and crony capitalism has produced ever-increasing pauperization in rural agricultural areas, mass unemployment in urban areas, and sharp increases in sex trafficking and child prostitution.

Alain Mabanckou is one of Africa's foremost francophone writers, born in the Congo but currently resident in Los Angeles, where he is a professor of literature at UCLA. His novel self-consciously references a genealogy of murderers and "psychos" in the context of systemic capitalist violence, explicitly alluding to *American Psycho*, Brett Easton Ellis's savage satire of 1980s Reagan-era consumerism, in its title, and choosing its epigraph from Prague German-Jewish writer Hermann Ungar's collection, *Boys and Murderers*. Heralded as the "Moravian Dostoevsky," Ungar occupied a peripheral space in the crumbling Austro-Hungarian empire similar to that of Kafka, and his short fictions demonstrated a similar aesthetic mixture of the grotesque, sado-masochistic, and the comical in their portrayal of travelling salesmen, bankers, and file clerks from Boskovice and Prague, all of them maimed, marginalized, and socially deformed in some way, their murderous and self-mutilating inclinations symptomatic not only of their individual alienation but of their decaying social contexts and experience of economic rationalization.

However, Mabanckou's Gregoire Nakobomayo—whose surname cheekily translates as "I'm going to kill you"—crucially differs from these previous archetypal murderers in his impotence, unreliability, and vulgarity, narrative characteristics which reflect the different social content of Mabanckou's twenty-first century Congo-Brazzaville setting. Gregoire extols the will to power and envisions committing a "beautiful crime" which would purify the slum:

> I was going to clean it up real good, give it back some dignity, rid it of its refuse, of its detritus, of its filth [. . .] of its bitches who came from the country over there, its bitches who disloyally compete with our own girls [. . .] I hate these bitches because they sell off their attributes like secondhand chewing gum. (Mabanckou 2008: 88)

Here the sexual gaze is conflated with commodity fetishism: in Gregoire's misogynist, xenophobic vision, women's bodies are fetishized as abject emblems of the penetrations of foreign capital and the privatization/prostitution of the country: "these whores who arrive in our city in their canoes as if we were still in the time of the Gold Rush, for them this is Peru, this is Eldorado" (Mabanckou 2008: 90). Yet he repeatedly fails to execute his planned acts of violence, losing his erection when he tries to rape a nurse in white, falling asleep when he lies in wait with a hammer for his prostitute girlfriend, Germaine, waking to discover she's been murdered by another client. In contrast to Raskolnikov or Bateman, Gregoire is all talk, no action; his great envisioned act of erotic, *lumpen* revenge—"my large hands were made to kill [. . .] those whose social position I envied"—never comes off (Mabanckou 2008: 31).

In contrast to Raskolnikov's grandiose Napoleonic delusions, Gregoire self-consciously summarizes his own psychic deformation in comically bathetic terms, as "mayonnaise gone bad" (Mabanckou 2008: 10). His narrative hallmark is a profuse loquacity, an endless narratorial chattering: first-person, confessional, present-tense, factually and emotionally unreliable, only partially linear, repetitive, doubling back and forwards, characterized by gaps and transitional leaps between narrative fragments and torrential monologues, alternating between linguistic registers—allusions to Rousseau, Voltaire, Dostoevsky, and Ungar mixed with comic strips, pulp detective fiction, street songs, popular music, and radio talk shows, all in French suffused with street dialect. This volubility is self-conscious:

> I have been talking in a choppy, almost winded manner since then, and without stopping. I talk to myself as I usually do, which is to say

confusedly and with this vulgarity that contrary to the education I received here and there in the wealthy families, attests to my street culture. (Mabanckou 2008: 87)

Gregoire is obsessed with drunkenness, sex, and excrement, the waste of society. He seeks to emulate the ghost of his idol, a dead serial killer named Angoualima whose scatological performance art motto becomes a mantra of resistance in popular culture:

The entire city knows that before committing suicide, my idol Angoualima, had sent the national press and the press of the country over there an audio tape on which he spent 120 minutes repeating, "I shit on society," the very words that the neighborhood's most popular band, the Brothers The-Same-People-Always-Get-To-Eat-in-This-Shitty-Country, later used in their hit song. (Mabanckou 2008: 6)

Angoualima is a cult celebrity figure, whose penis is as big as his arm and whose feet point backwards. At the end of the novel, his ghost is not exorcized, but rather achieves ascension: He is the spectre of a social conscience which is deformed, a carnivalesque manifestation of a corrupt popular discourse that blindly celebrates banditry and macho violence as the only mode of resistance against poverty and public hypocrisy.

Zimbabwean writer Dambudzo Marechera has written about the scatological aesthetic of his fiction as embodying a critique of "the life of blind poverty, blind impulse" (Marechera 1987: 102). Marechera's novels portray poverty as experienced physically in the body, as gut-rot, as defecation, with the body representing both the individual, immiserated postcolonial subject, and the larger nation, corrupt, rotting from within. The spectral apparitions of Mabanckou's Angoulaima enact a similar critique, interrupting and replacing the 'serious' deliriums of the gothic with a profane bodily humour which carnivalizes the state and highlights its corruption: a Bakhtinian "grotesque realism" whose very degradation demands the need for something better. It is shit, not petroleum-revenues, which Gregoire describes flowing free through the Brazzaville slums, "excrement wrapped in little baggies arriving" from the "Right Bank" of the Congo-"Seine" (Mabanckou 2008: 80). Gregoire himself is a mechanic doomed to repair the black Mercedes of the neocolonial elite without owning a car himself; indeed, his first attempt at a violent act of protest, the rape and murder of the nurse, is thwarted by the spectral appearance of one of these luxury automobiles. The failed "magic" of commodity fetishism, the witchdoctor's sorcery of capital which distributes revenues only to the elites, is countered by Gregoire's advice for the poor and indebted: "you should always have a few magic words, like 'oh shit'" (Mabanckou 2008: 70).

The novel is driven by a humour derived from impotence, improbability, and incongruity, whose comic elements are discursively disruptive of

Afropessimism. Gregoire's scatological loquacity contrasts the poetic deliriums of Dostoevsky's "soulful murderer" and the formal radicalism of the
blankly impersonal narration of Easton Ellis's psychotic Bateman, whose total
lack of psychological depth behind his façade of face moisture and designer
clothes is meant to embody the slick, shallow psychopathology of corporate
American capitalism and late commodity fetishism. His comic garrulous-
ness shares more with the volubility of Machado's Brás Cubas, but lacks the
polished insouciance of that dead narrator, whose audacity in speaking from
beyond the grave is an expression of his elite status as a member of the slave-
owning class and their moribund society. In fact, it is the contrast between
Gregoire's verbal bravado and his complete inability to follow through with
his premeditated crimes that forms the central irony of the novel's narration;
the doubling back of his speech mimics the narrative's inhibited progression,
his inability to "conjugate" his worshipped verb "to kill," despite so much
breathless chatter (Mabanckou 2008: 37).

In a riff on French cultural imperialism, Gregoire disparages European
criminology and epistemology, proclaiming this is "no time to act like a philosopher of the Enlightenment;" yet, at the conclusion he wistfully reflects on
the lack of resolution, his failure to commit the crime and be caught according
to generic conventions of the *roman noir*: "I tell myself that in a normal situation there would have been a detective like in the movies or in crime novels"
(Mabanckou 2008: 77, 156). Gregoire's judgment on society cannot lead to the
subsequent exposure and suturing of social wounds; it is a failure of "social
detection," the generic progression from murder to investigation to judgment
in crime and thriller fiction, whose function is to enact social judgment and
reclaim society's hidden nature. The suspense mechanism of the crime novel
is inverted, so that the awaited event is not murder or detection but rather the
event of failure, the anticlimax. Gregoire's narrative of confession (with its
shadow-text of Rousseau) is revealed as fundamentally unreliable, a confession
of the wrong causes and events, a faecal narrative of the scatological and the
incongruous couched in prevarication and false consciousness.

Dragon Kujundzic argues that Dostoevsky's Raskolnikov, "heavily in
debt to his landlady," is an incarnation of "phantasmatic production and
phantomatic economy" and that his cleaving of the pawnbroker's skull is
both revenge for and re-enactment of the "primordial crime of modernization" in St Petersburg, staging the self-mutilation of identity imposed from
above (Kujundzic 2000: 903). Gregoire's desire to commit a violent "act,"
like Raskolnikov's wielding of the axe, is a parody of morbid individualism
and rational egoism, as previously noted by Schwarz, and a desire for protest
against the asymmetries of his society, as suggested by Lukács's reading of
Dostoevsky's psychopathologies. However, his inability to take up the hammer (with its blunt political symbolism) emphasizes the hollowness of his
belief in the power of individual will to escape structured poverty, as when
he ruefully reflects: "Could it really be that my willpower has no part in what

I undertake? That my entire life has been drawn in advance so that I am only following a path established by a force above me?" (Mabanckou 2008: 31). Gregoire is no captain of industry, like Bateman, with the power of multinational capital behind his actions, rather he is a "lost mollusk [. . .] no more than an empty shell, an ordinary being [. . .] on the margin of society" (Mabanckou 2008: 37). His impotence expresses the political unconscious of IMF-dependency, of abortive neoliberalization, reforms half-carried out but never carried to fruition, of the country's failure to achieve a free market economy or install a secure middle class befitting the borrowed ideologies which Gregoire mockingly professes: "I believe in paper money, in Santa Claus [. . .] and all that stuff . . . " (Mabanckou 2008: 107).

Hence the irony of the novel's epigraph from Ungar's *Boys and Murderers*: "Besides, am I truly a murderer? I have killed a human being, but it seems to me I haven't done it myself . . . " (Mabanckou 2008: i). Gregoire's impotence is a reversal of Ungar's protagonist. He yearns to be a murderer and at the end of the narrative, when he discovers that Germaine is dead, even fantasizes that he might have killed her unconsciously. However, his hands are ironically clean, unable to commit the kind of protest which Lukács heralds Dostoevsky's characters as performing. With his swollen-headed individualism, his mangled belief in the violence of sexual purgation, and his inability to diagnose the structural causes of social immiseration, he is literally a "rectangular head," a "blockhead," with no clear sense of political or moral responsibility. What he does share with Ungar's protagonist is a characteristic lack of awareness, a failure of perception, which forces onto the reader the responsibility of the actively critical perspective that the narrator is unable to assume.

Fat Arses and Imperfect Investigators

Corporal tumescence similarly acts as a figuration of neoliberal turpitude in Angolan writer Pepetela's *Jaime Bunda*, signalled from the opening sentence of the novel:

> Jaime Bunda was seated in the big room set aside for detectives. [He] settled his abundant arse, out of all proportion to the rest of his body, [whose] physical characteristic had led to his name. His real name was long—two surnames of illustrious families in Luanda circles. (Pepetela 2001: 11)

The protagonist has been branded a loser since childhood, when he was nicknamed "bunda"—abundant-arse, or "arsehole"—due to his hindquarters, so prodigious that he toppled over when playing basketball. Here, it is the buttocks, not the head, which are swollen and literally unbalanced, signifying the debasement of the former revolutionary vanguard, the creole elites of the once-Marxist MPLA who abandoned their utopian ideology in the 1990s for the cronyistic-petroleum and diamond-based capitalism, enriching their own incestuously interrelated Luanda-based networks while leaving the rest of Angola more impoverished than before.

Callow, gluttonous, and easily distracted by his pursuit of flesh, food, and profit, Bunda is an incompetent apprentice detective for the government's secret investigative branch who retains his low-paid job only through nepotism: his distant relation to the "two families" of creole elites. Plunged into the underbelly of criminal Lunda when he is sent to investigate the rape and murder of an Island girl by a mysterious high-placed man in a luxury car, he proves himself the opposite of the glamorous noir private eye or secret agent. Despite his voracious consumption of crime novels, he is hermeneutically challenged, making absurd inferences and inductions, unlike his heroes Sherlock Holmes and Raymond Chandler. He soon loses sight of solving the original crime, caught up in the labyrinthine webs of corruption and strategic battles for political influence spreading out from the initial event, which he proves finally unable to decode. The girl's body remains nameless, her government attacker unidentified, secure in his cocoon of privilege and wealth. Here, as in *African Psycho*, the anticipated climax of detection, judgment, and closure is denied, as "preoccupations with questions of globalization, strategic alliances and national identity deflect the action away from its original course" (Henighan 2006: 148).

Pepetela is a pseudonym meaning "eyelash" and was Artur Carlos Maurício Pestana's guerilla codename during the 1960s when he fought with the MPLA in the seven-year guerrilla war against the colonial Portuguese. The sobriquet, in its bathetic demystification of the revolutionary hero, but also its suggestion of an irritant that provokes new perception, encapsulates his sensibility. In the grand tradition of anticolonial liberation activists such as Fanon, he also trained as a sociologist in Algeria. After independence, he became regional commander against South African invasion in 1975 and served as the deputy minister of education from 1976 to 1982. However, deeply disillusioned with the growing corruption and authoritarianism of the party and its betrayal of revolutionary promises to redistribute wealth and land, he resigned and became a lecturer in sociology at Agostinho Neto University. He has confessed in interviews to conceiving the Bunda series because he wanted to make money but also to be read more widely—commercial thriller and crime genre fiction is popular across Southern Africa and more likely to be read by the middle-class. Indeed, the comic Bunda series has proved to be more popular within Angola than his previous fictions, which were most heartily endorsed in Portugal and amongst a postcolonial critical audience in Euro-America.

Pepetela's previous novels chart Angola's progression from colonialism to independence in changing aesthetic modes whose generic shifts correspond to political-social content. The political revolutionary agenda of his earlier fictions is accompanied by aesthetics, which while hybridized, are more realist in their tendencies. However, in later novels he increasingly turned away from realism towards satire and magical realism, as in *The Return of the Water Spirit* (first published and titled in Portuguese "The Desire of Kianda,") where the betrayals of independence are scathingly satirized and the rekindling of utopian desire can only be imagined in magical realist terms as a supernatural flood unleashed by a water spirit which washes away the colonial foundations of the capital and makes way for a new people's movement. By the time of his Jaime Bunda novels, Pepetela cannot even offer utopian possibility couched in the supernatural. Instead, his formal turn to genre fiction, after the didacticism and magical realist satire of his previous novels, uses the irony generated by the disruption of the formal conventions of the crime novel and the thriller to illustrate the impossibility of justice in a country riddled with the junk capitalism of mafia smuggling, sex trafficking, and currency falsification, heightened by the policies of dollarization and export-heavy SAPs enforced by the IMF and the World Bank.

Jaime Bunda's anti-police procedural carnivalizes crime and detective to illustrate the widespread corruption of institutions under neoliberalization (Ribeiro Secco 2003). As Bunda himself reflects, there is a gap between the metaphysical certainties of the police procedural and the reality of crime detection in contemporary Angola, which he attributes to the hermeneutical failures of real-life detectives:

> There's no such thing as a perfect crime, justice always triumphs, evil will be conquered, he had learnt these absolute truths in those books. Well, he was going to prove his idols Spillane, Chandler or Stanley Gardner were absolutely right and there are no perfect crimes, there are imperfect investigators. (Pepetela 2001: 24)

Ironically, Bunda himself is one of these "imperfect investigators," unable either to overcome his own greed or to properly decode the networks of organized crime connected to the girl's murder. In contrast, Jaime's "subversive" cousin, Gégé notes the hollowness of Angola's newly democratic status in light of the profoundly asymmetrical accumulation and control of capital and land:

> [In a country run by a dictator] whoever apportions and reapportions and is not left with the largest portion is either an ass or has no artistry. Whereas here, in the country of greed, whoever apportions never reapportions because they are left with everything. (Pepetela 2001: 181)

Formally, the novel registers Angola's profoundly uneven development and distribution of wealth on multiple levels: in its "insistently asymmetrical plotting mimetic of the warped structures of Angolan society" (Henighan 2006: 146), in the body and discourse of Bunda, who reflects that he is '*um James*

Bond subdesenvolvido', "an underdeveloped James Bond" (Pepetela 2001: 115), and in the discursive polyphony between the alternating voices of four narrators and one pseudo-author.

The novel is subdivided into four books, titled after their individual narrators, from "Book of the First Narrator" to "Book of the Fourth Narrator." Each narrator has his or her own sensibility and epigraph, three are masculine and unnamed, and one is female. However, throughout the novel, an italicized, bracketed, metafictional *voz de autor* caustically interrupts the other narrators, criticizing their tone, excessive use of adjectives, inconsistent point-of-view, and uneven pacing. This metafictional narrator eventually fires the first narrator for plodding recklessness and a frivolity of tone too akin to Bunda's—a case of free, indirect discourse gone too far and overwhelming the narrator's authority—and deposes the rest in quick succession. The fourth narrator, "invented" to be "economic[al]" and "closer to the classic canons of this genre" nonetheless proves unable to unravel the crime or collate the novel's previous three parts into a classic exposition, dissection, and conviction (Pepetela 2001: 233). Jaime's ideological task as a detective, then, becomes, as Stephen Henighan argues,

> not to re-establish a social order disrupted by crime, but [rather] to understand the structures of a disordered society. In this sense, the novels are about Jaime's education and by extension that of the generation to which he belongs, immersed in a corrupt present and an ahistorical popular culture that prevents them from comprehending how this world came into being. (Henighan 2006: 148)

Because Jaime and his generation are "imperfect investigators," the narrative's metatextual mechanics displace the hermeneutical responsibility to the reader.

The novel's staged erosion of narrative authority employs "author-as-outsider" distancing strategies and playful scepticism which can be traced back through the Lusophone (post)colonial literary tradition to Machado de Assis, who places an obligation on the reader to become slyly cosmopolitan and act out the very reverse of Brás Cubas's parochial technique of "staring down the tip of his nose" in order to avoid social verities:

> As the reader knows, a fakir spends long hours looking at the tip of his nose with his only aim that of seeing the celestial light. When he fixes his eyes on the tip of his nose he loses his sense of outside things, becomes enraptured with the invisible, learns the intangible, becomes detached from the world, dissolves, is aetherialized. (Machado 1997: 82)

A homology can be drawn to Pepetela and Mabanckou's novels, whose protagonists and narrators are similarly enraptured nose-gazers, and whose readers are thus placed in an analogous obligation to reject the pleasures of cultural and class-based solipsism that efface worldly consciousness.

Bunda and Gregoire lack the distance to interpret their situations accurately or critically, but the reader is granted that crucial distance from parochial ideologies and allegiances, what Paul Ricoeur calls the "disappropriation of the self" which can thus lead to the "critique of false consciousness" which Ricoeur sees as the "integral part of hermeneutics" (Ricoeur 1981: 84–85). As readers, we are left to collate the evidence from Jaime's peregrinations through the uneven geographies of Angolan society—mapping the elite creole districts of the Luandan capital alongside its slums and markets and villages—not in order "to deduce solutions to particular crimes (which, in any event, are predetermined by societal power-structures)" (Henighan 2006: 148), but rather in order to interpret his position as a critique of the local conditions under the Angolan regime and as symbolic of the periphery's structural relation to global capitalism. Similarly, the gothic elements of witchcraft, shamanism, and spectrality in this novel—"forest-buffalo *funje and* flying sorcerers"—signal the recalibration of residual cultures as a negotiation with the seeming "sorcery" of uneven development in the periphery and offer the reader a flickering apprehension of the social totality which cannot be grasped by its incompetent narrators.

Opening Out Detection

In conclusion, the comic deformations and failures of both novels' grotesque narrators—Mabanckou's "macrocephalic" Gregoire, and Pepetela's "fat-arsed," "underdeveloped" Bunda—could be read as a structural homology for the incongruity and violence of the "secondhand" ideologies of neoliberalism implemented by neocolonial elites. Both writers subvert conventions of genre fiction and recalibrate the materials of earlier peripheral modernist texts to register the contemporary conditions of ongoing uneven development and social immiseration specific to their post-colonial nations. Mabanckou transcribes aspects of Dostoevsky's delirious axe-murderer and of Hermann Ungar's maimed boy-murderers to form his impotent, would-be murderer narrator; the manipulation of multiple levels of narration and free indirect discourse in Pepetela is shot through with the sensibility of the narrative voice in *Posthumous Memoirs of Brás Cubas*, what Machado calls the marriage of "the ink of melancholy" and the "playful pen" (Machado 1997: 5).

Jaime Bunda concludes with an epilogue and a telling epigraph: "In which the author dispenses with narrators and takes up the pen again. To close circles. Or to open new ones" (Pepetela 2001: 293). The epilogue also reintroduces Jaime's younger brother, the "irreverent and subversive Gégé," who despite Jaime's admonitions to let "uncomfortable truths remain discreetly under seven veils," insists on writing for a local political paper in order "to make the world hear and see everything which the eternally marginalised population feel and want" (Pepetela 2001: 294). The epigraph's circles could be interpreted as an ode to poststructuralist relativism, the *aporias* that perpetually open before any detective, and indeed, the novel's narrative techniques have been read by some critics as quintessentially postmodernist. However, it is not language itself that is the object of Pepetela's critique, but rather those social structures and ideologies that obscure perception and prevent interpretation. In light of Gégé's commitment to writing the truth of the *local* township in order for the *world* to become aware, it is impossible to conceive of those circles as anything else but the opening out of consciousness, in which it is not closure of but a widening out of the *detection* attempt from the particulars of the local which offers any hope of apprehension of the totality and thus of local or international resistance.

Works Cited

Bakhtin, M. (1984) *Problems of Dostoevsky's Poetics*, trans. C. Emerson (ed.) Minneapolis: University of Minnesota Press.

Bloch, E. (1977) 'Nonsynchronism and the Obligation to its Dialectics', trans. M. Ritter, *New German Critique*, 11: 22–38.

Brown, N. (2005) *Utopian Generations: The Political Horizon of Twentieth-Century Literature*, Princeton: Princeton University Press.

Casanova, P. (2004) *The World Republic of Letters*, trans. M.B. DeBevoise, Cambridge, MA: Harvard University Press.

Gledson, J. (1984) *The Deceptive Realism of Machado de Assis: A Dissenting Interpretation of* Dom Casmurro, Liverpool: Francis Cairns.

Henighan, S. (2006) '"Um James Bond Subdesenvolvido": The Ideological Work of the Angolan Detective in Pepetela's Jaime Bunda Novels', Portuguese Studies, 22/1: 135–152.

Kujundzic, D. (2000) '"After" Russian Post-Colonial Identity', *MLN*, 115/5: 892–908.

Lukács, G. (1973) *Marxism and Human Liberation: Essays on History, Culture and Revolution by Georg Lukács*, trans. R. Wellek, New York: Dell.

Mabanckou, A. (2008 [2003]) *African Psycho*, trans. C. Schwartz Hartley, London: Serpent's Tail.

Machado de Assis, J.M. (1997) *The Posthumous Memoirs of Brás Cubas*, trans. G. Rabassa, Oxford: Oxford University Press.

Marechera, D. (1987) 'The Writer's Experience of African Literature', *Zambezia*, 14/2: 99–111.

Moretti, F. (2000) 'Conjectures on World Literature', *New Left Review*, 1. http://www.newleftreview.org/A2094. Accessed: Feb. 10, 2012.

———. (2005) *Signs Taken for Wonders*, London: Verso.

Pearson, N. and Singer, M. (eds) (2009) *Detective Fiction in a Postcolonial and Transnational World*, Farnham: Ashgate.

Pepetela (2001) *Jaime Bunda, Secret Agent: Story of Various Mysteries*, trans. R. Bartlett, Wiltshire: Aflame.

———. (2005) *The Return of the Water Spirit*, trans. L.R. Mitras, Oxford: Heinemann.

Ricoeur, P. (1981) 'What is a Text? Explanation and Understanding', in J.B. Thompson (ed.) *Hermeneutics and the Human Sciences: Essays on Language and Interpretation*, Cambridge: Cambridge University Press, 145–164.

Ribeiro Secco, C.L.T. (2003) 'Entre Crimes, Detetives e Mistérios ... (Pepetela e Mia Couto: Riso, Melancolia e o Desvendamento da História Pela Ficção)', *Revista Eletrônica do Instituto de Humanidades*, 2/5: http://publicacoes.unigranrio.com.br/index.php/reihm/issue/view/5. Accessed: 15 June 2012.

Schwarz, R. (1992) *Misplaced Ideas: Essays on Brazilian Culture*, J. Gledson (ed.) London: Verso.

Siddiqi, Y. (2002) 'Police and Postcolonial Rationality in Amitav Ghosh's *The Circle of Reason*', *Cultural Critique*, 50: 175–211.

Ungar, H. (2006) *Boys and Murderers*, trans. I. Fargo Cole, Prague: Twisted Spoon.

7 V.S. Naipaul's Heterobiographical Fictions or Postcolonial Melancholia Reinterpreted

Walter Goebel

In his *Theorie des Romans*, Georg Lukács contrasted epic and novel as belonging to different worlds: the epic to a more homogenous and evidently meaningful world, in which the epic hero can exhibit an unchallenged code of conduct, while the novel belongs to a world in which meaning and teleology have become problematic, a world without transcendental signposts, in which the individual strives to regain some form of meaning and coherence and where homelessness and the search for a form of totality are characteristic (Lukács 1971: 51, 52). The paradigmatic models for the emerging novel were the biography and the autobiography, the latter, like the novel, a new genre in the seventeenth century, the century of the British enlightenment. Autobiography and novel joined forces as aesthetic templates for the formation of enlightenment individuality, both striving for a containment of secular arbitrariness and chance in an expanding world, characterized by new horizontal and vertical—or geographical and social—dynamics, in which—besides the loss of epic certainties—the correspondence between station and character could also no longer be taken for granted.[1]

Biography, autobiography, and autobiographical novel were the forms within which enlightened man sought for meaningful teleologies, for a coherent narrative with a beginning, a middle, and an end in the form of the attainment of a goal, with definable initiations and tribulations and some form of social or spiritual elevation—whether in straightforward auto/biographies[2] or in novels of character, novels of adventure, epistolary novels, novels of education, or in the bildungsroman. With the spiritual auto/biography, originally modelled upon the lives of saints and martyrs, and the secular auto/biography or success story the two main subgenres of Western autobiographical texts are identified. Both can be interpreted as presenting exemplary lives of eminent men or women, and in both the authors have traditionally to defend themselves against the accusation of pride or hubris in presenting their lives as worthy of imitation. Thus the auto/biography and the auto/biographic novel are the exemplary genres in which Western hubris is made acceptable. And the anti-novel, for example Laurence Sterne's *Tristram Shandy*, is the form in which modern hubris is questioned, in this case from a medieval *miseria hominis* point of view.[3]

As paradigmatic expressions of enlightened individualism, auto/bio-graphical texts are also products of imperialist and capitalist tendencies, which thrived equally on spiritual and materialist aspirations, as Max Weber has demonstrated. From modern imperialistic biographical dramas like Mar-lowe's *Tamburlaine the Great*, via novels of adventure like *Robinson Crusoe*, auto-biographical fictions like *Moll Flanders*, Benjamin Franklin's *Autobiography* or Jane Austen's novels of education, then to biographical fictions like Theodore Dreiser's Cowperwood-Trilogy, the imperialist and materialist subtexts have been pervasive, while, on the other hand, the deification of Western spiritual models has inspired the associated tradition—from the life of St. Theresa to *The Vicar of Wakefield*, including Rousseau's *Confessions*, Wordsworth's *Pre-lude* and novels of devotion and suffering like George Eliot's *Middlemarch*. But even in the spiritual tradition—which is often typologically patterned in imitation of the life of Jesus, of Job, of St. Theresa—the exaltation of the indi-vidual for his or her visionary powers or his or her capacity to suffer is cen-tral. In both forms the evolution of an enlightened auto/biographical focus accompanies the movement from what the sociologist Ferdinand Tönnies called *Gemeinschaft* to *Gesellschaft*, that is, from a unified organic community to the contractual unity of individual free wills in a society (Tönnies 1963). Only in the latter is what James Olney has called an "isolate uniqueness" possible, as central category and aim within the autobiographical tradition (Olney 1972: 21).

According to Roy Pascal, the autobiography generally attempts to make sense of life, to order it, and to achieve a balance between the past and the present (Pascal 1963: 76). Its main aims are a clearly visible pattern and a form of coherence in the life of an eminent person (Pascal 1963: 21). The battle for its ascendency as a model literary form in Western letters is visible in its formal negations: in the systematic denial of teleology in *Tristram Shandy* and in the general anti-enlightenment world view presented in this novel. According to the Russian Formalists, such parodies most clearly delineate the laws of the genre in question, in this case elucidating the autobiographical formula—which is also called in question by some aspects of picaresque novels.

In order to achieve coherence, the autobiographer usually works retro-spectively, selecting and excising consciously or unconsciously from a store of memories. Autobiographies are generally composed quite late in life, and as they attempt to present an official version of the life of an individual, they aim to be unique in spite of typological patterning, which slowly recedes after the enlightenment. Coherence is all the more easily achieved if the media-tion between individual and social interests is to some extent successful, and if some form of equilibrium can be established, from which a casual glance back is possible. In other cases, e.g., when an uncomfortable outsider-per-spective prevails, autobiographical texts (a more appropriate term, perhaps, as it includes autobiographical novels) can be multiple, as with Frederick Douglass or V.S. Naipaul. Naipaul's case is remarkable, however, in that there are so many autobiographical texts or examples of life-writing—the more modern and comprehensive term—and most of his not overtly auto-biographical novels and travelogues are also coloured by autobiographical elements. It appears that Naipaul has never achieved the singularity of an 'official version,' which most autobiographers aim at. And it is also remark-able that Naipaul's autobiographical obsession began quite early in life with the collection of stories *Miguel Street* (1959) and with the autobiographical novel *A House for Mr Biswas* (1961), that is, before he was 30 years of age. Dislocation, alienation, marginalization, self-hatred, and scapegoating seem to be some of the enabling conditions for an "autobiographical obsession," which spills over into proliferating travelogues, novels, short stories, memoirs and truncated autobiographies in Naipaul's case.

In this chapter I am not going to address epistemological questions, but, focusing on genre, I shall concentrate on the translations of the classical auto-biographical form in Naipaul's works without any reference to philosophical questions of authenticity, which, I believe, are for my more formal approach unnecessary and in the now prevailing poststructuralist readings are often oversimplified. The death of the author has meantime been revoked by the "autobiographical turn" (Huddart 2008: 9), and the importance of what Donna Haraway has called "situated knowledge" (Haraway 1991: 191) has been generally acknowledged, so that we can observe the slow revocation of poststructuralist epistemological premises in the postcolonial field.[4] Never-theless, this chapter is to some extent influenced by poststructuralist ideas, because it makes no clear distinction between autobiographies and autobio-graphical fictions, both forms sharing a number of common features—autobi-ographies as retrospective constructs generally partake of the fictional.

Naipaul's Inconclusive Autobiographical Gestures

It is remarkable that V.S. Naipaul should have repeatedly adopted and adapted the traditional model of the novel in his autobiographical fictions, while at the same time so deftly opposing any kind of closure and contain-ment or even teleology—all the more remarkable because his own life to quite some extent follows the 'self-made man' formula, leading to finan-cial success and international fame. Naipaul is fascinated—or perhaps even obsessed—by the autobiographical form and by his own autobiography, but if read as autobiographical texts his fictions follow neither of the two main formulas, neither are they quite spiritual autobiographies nor success stories. The autobiographical gestures, as it were, appear generally incomplete and provisional, a balance between individual and communal interests, the main aim of the bildungsroman, is not even marginally visible. His autobiographi-cal fragments, which have also been called "deflected autobiographies" (Levy 1995: xi), usually deconstruct the traditional Western model and move towards the inconclusively episodic as "travel undermines the possibility of locatedness" (Anderson 2007: 119). Even the gains in mother-wit and the questionable material successes of the picaresque hero are largely absent. I would now like to comment on some main differences between Naipaul's somewhat inconclusive autobiographical gestures and the classic Western autobiographical models. Naipaul's texts can be characterised as follows:

- Autobiographical fictions produced from an early age onwards and lacking closure
- Often more than one point of view (first and third person mixed)
- No linear plot or clear coherence of episodic parts
- Multiple plot-lines
- Proliferation of autobiographical gestures and fascination for alternative life-stories (heterobiography)
- Melancholia as governing temperament

Let me begin with "Prologue to an Autobiography," as Naipaul tells us, "not an autobiography, a story of a life or deeds done" (*FTC* 9).[5] As a 'prologue,' this short text is mainly concerned with Naipaul's father and his own search for inspiration as an author, as he has it in the "Author's Foreword"—characteristically speaking of himself in the third person, e.g., about "the writer's beginnings" (*FTC* 10). And a few paragraphs later, concerning his travelogues, he reports in the first person:

> When it came to writing, I was uncertain about the value I should give to the traveller's 'I'. This kind of direct participation came awkwardly to me, and the literary problem was also partly a personal one. (*FTC* 11)

The unease with the first person pronoun anticipates the failure of Naipaul's autobiographical efforts from the very beginning and conveys a pervasive feeling of alienation and inauthenticity. This unease with the centring or dominant "I" is, by the way, shared by J.M. Coetzee and may thus be a specific feature of a postcolonial aesthetics of decentring.[6] The "Autobiographical Prologue" is contained in a volume entitled *Finding the Centre* (1984), that is: finding a position to write from, and this positioning depends largely on the discovery of one's past, in Naipaul's case of the, as it were, absent father-figure and the grandparents. Again, characteristically, this search for the past is interlaced with early attempts at fiction. Bogart, a friend of his mother's, is transformed into the hero of a story and also provides a model for the recurring theme of futility and failure in Naipaul's work—and of journeys which seem to offer a new life, but usually end in disappointment or even, as in *A House for Mr Biswas* and *The Enigma of Arrival*, with death. In the "Autobiographical Prologue," we find a number of miscellaneous biographical fragments about Naipaul's grandfather, a man who was quite successful in Trinidad and acquired much property, who, however, finally decided to escape back to India with a new wife, but died on the way there. He provides a first model for the many truncated, incomplete biographies we find in Naipaul's works. Or we learn about former indentured servants who also went back to India, in this case to Calcutta, only to be met by repatriated Indian Trinidadians in despair:

> Seven weeks later the *Ganges* reached Calcutta. And there, to the terror of the passengers, the *Ganges* was stormed by hundreds of derelicts, previously repatriated, who wanted now to be taken back to the other place. India for these people had been a dream of home, a dream of continuity after the illusion of Trinidad. All the India they had found was the area around the Calcutta docks. (*FTC* 53)

In spite of such glimpses of disillusionment, which anticipate the melancholy tone of *The Enigma of Arrival*, Naipaul does learn bits and pieces about his past in this "Prologue," about his father, whom he seldom met as a child, and about his hard life. In a letter from Oxford, he even asks his father to write an autobiography of his own, to help locate the family history, but his father is reluctant: " . . . some deep hurt or shame, something still raw and unresolved in his experience, kept my father from attempting any autobiographical writing" (*FTC* 54). Naipaul finally discovers a possible cause of this shame: After criticizing a Hindu animal sacrifice to the goddess Kali in the *Trinidad Guardian*, his father had been threatened in an anonymous letter and forced to sacrifice a goat for the goddess himself. Such pieces of random knowledge create the impression of a life of failure, fear, vacillation, and shame, in which the father also had to plead for jobs with the white masters. His father's life leaves Naipaul himself with little more than a legacy of fear of failure, hardly the best psychological basis for the autobiographer.

> . . . he so accurately transmitted to me—without saying anything about it—his hysteria from the time when I didn't know him: his fear of extinction. That was his subsidiary gift to me. That fear became mine as well. [. . .] A panic about failing to be what I should be, rather than simple ambition . . . (*FTC* 72)

"Fear of extinction:" Late in life Naipaul recalls a scene with his father after he has suffered a nervous breakdown and, because he is unable to see himself in a mirror, falls into a fit of mad screaming (*FTC* 70). Alienation and effacement dog Mohun Naipaul's life, and how should the inconclusive biographical fragments of such a father-figure be of any help as a guide for the young author in search of a usable past? The earlier fictional version of his father's biography, *A House for Mr Biswas*, had focused on ineffectivity and futility as well, symbolized by the recurrent burning of the family's houses, and by the quite unexpected and untimely ending of his father's life, which is anticipated in the first sentence of the novel: "Ten weeks before he died, Mr Mohun Biswas, a journalist of Sikkim Street, St James, Port of Spain, was sacked" (*HB* 7). This most depressing anticipation of the final anti-climactic ending of an otherwise quite successful life, considering the imperialist context, provides the second pattern for a truncated (auto-)biography. Both father and grandfather are actually successful men, but both end their lives in futility, alienation, and with a sudden and untimely death. However, Naipaul also finds much to admire in his father, his literary talents, his tenacity and endurance, his bouts of good humour. But "success" is found only intermittently, as opposed to the life of his aunt, who feels she has been successful when, after 30 years, he meets her on her deathbed, surrounded by a large family: "She was attended by children and grandchildren, people of varying levels of education and skill [. . .]; my father's sister, at the end of her life, could see success" (*FTC* 55). This aunt is also able to open another window upon the past, providing Naipaul with a version of the story of his ancestors' immigration to Trinidad.

Naipaul is a collector of bits and pieces about his family history, some of which he presents in more detail and in fictionalized form in *A House for Mr Biswas* (1961). The feelings of futility and a makeshift life are similar, also sometimes of despair and shame, culminating finally in remorse, because he was not able to appreciate his father more during his lifetime. The story of the father is retold again and again is various versions, (e.g., in *The Enigma of Arrival*), often accompanied with a feeling of guilt because of the lack of understanding for his endurance and suffering. That the father died in the absence of his son, who hadn't even looked back at the airport when he left for England on a scholarship, seems to be a traumatic part of Naipaul's life which he retells compulsively, somewhat like a modern *Ancient Mariner.*

In a similar way, Naipaul again and again retells his own life-story, searching for autobiographical order but always suspecting final failure and futility. He had apparently failed to find an anchor for his own existence in a past he had perhaps too rashly rejected in his youth, and had thus set out on a life of inconclusive journeys, always searching for models of orderly lives and for some kind of cohesion. In *The Enigma of Arrival* this longing for order, for the fusion of haphazard and hybrid cultural experiences into one single story, is expressed in a key passage:

> Ever since I had begun to identify my subjects I had hoped to arrive, in a book, at a synthesis of the worlds and cultures that had made me. The other way of writing, the separation of one world from the other, was easier, but I felt it false to the nature of my experience. (*EA* 144)

'The Enigma of Arrival' and 'Half a Life'

The Enigma of Arrival is perhaps Naipaul's most complex autobiographic text. It attempts to interweave personal experiences with the closely observed lives of a number of Englishmen, beginning with Jack and Jack's garden, continuing with the life of his slothful landlord, with a number of farm labourers and other country people. "I saw aspects of myself, echoes of my own journey and the yearning at the back of that journey" (*EA* 145), he maintains, wondering about the changes, dislocations, and adaptations to be observed in England as much as in Trinidad and about any human being's resilience in the face of death, decay, and dilapidation. Those who achieve some stability or can create their own blissful little gardens like Voltaire's Candide are envied:

> [Jack] had created his own life, his own world, almost his own continent [. . .] and it was only when he was gone [. . .] that I saw how tenuous, really, the hold of all of these people had been on the land they worked or lived in. Jack himself had disregarded the tenuousness of his hold on the land, just as, not seeing what others saw, he had created a garden on the edge of a swamp and a ruined farmyard. (*EA* 87)

The image presented of Jack displays a veiled longing for stability and simplicity, which Naipaul himself, the great traveller, apparently felt he had never achieved—and which he appears to be looking for in the biographies of others. Jack had apparently found a form of arrival by creating his own small world in an agrarian setting which must follow the laws of nature, whether in England or in Trinidad. The entire first part of the novel/autobiography is entitled "Jack's Garden" and projects an ideal of pastoral enclosure which remains unattainable for the writer as outsider, as the final "Ceremony of Farewell" elucidates; it presents a journey back to Bombay, for the burial of his younger sister. Again the hero recalls his traumatic first departure from his homeland:

> When I had left Trinidad in 1950, when the little Pan American Airways System plane had taken me away, Sati was seven weeks short of her sixteenth birthday. When I next saw her and heard her voice, she was nearly twenty-two, and married. Trinidad had since become almost an imaginary place for me; but she had lived all her life there, apart from short holidays abroad. She had lived through my father's illness in 1952 and death in 1953; the political changes, the racial politics from 1956, the dangers of the street, the near-revolution and anarchy of 1970. She had also lived through the oil boom; she had known ease for many years; she could think of her life as a success. (*EA* 311)

We find a peculiar contradiction here: While talking mainly about disruptive political events and about death, Sati's life is nevertheless associated with success, partly, presumably, because she remained with the father whom Naipaul himself often felt he had abandoned and misunderstood, partly because she never began his life of travel and alienation. His own sister, though now dead, is presented as an object of envy and a focus for self-pity, as it were. That her name, Sati, implicitly refers to the theme of female self-sacrifice, unwittingly unveils the hypocrisy of such a melancholic self-fashioning *ex negativo*: as the pitiful outsider-figure and alienated artist and onlooker, cheated out of the happiness of an alternative stable life which his sister apparently enjoyed.

"I can suck melancholy out of a song, as a weasel can suck eggs . . . " says Jaques in Shakespeare's *As You Like It* (II.5.12)—and Naipaul is surely his match. In his book *Postcolonial Melancholia*, Paul Gilroy speaks of the melancholia of the former imperialists after having lost an empire—in Naipaul's case, the term had initially exactly this meaning, but later in life an entirely different sense predominates. 'Postcolonial melancholia' comes to indicate the sadness of the eternal traveller, for whom the modern world has no more to offer than repeated alienation and homelessness, a kind of reversed middle passage for an ageing and alienated mariner. Melancholia comes here to be wedded with self-pity. *The Enigma of Arrival* is one of the great melancholy works of English Literature, to be set beside *The Anatomy of Melancholy* and *Tristram Shandy*, albeit with a specific postcolonial message.

Compared to the earlier ventures into autobiographic form, which focused on the burden of and the uses of the past, *The Enigma of Arrival* is structurally characterised by a proliferation of lifelines and plots, by a heterogeneity of biographical data and possible lives which the narrator seems to immerse himself in, or to mimically enact and which shape a melancholy mosaic with glimpses and fractions of the narrator's own situation. Naipaul's entire world seems to open up into an egocentric kaleidoscope of lost possibilities and fractured existences, which could be called a heterobiography. The term alludes to the heterogeneity of texts and genres in his autobiographical fictions, then to his fascination with other people's, apparently more coherent, biographies, which he seems to 'try on,' and finally to his obsession with the experience of estrangement and alienation.

Some model Others, like Jack, seem to provide a modicum of hope for a very limited form of closure, which is enabled first of all by a kind of seclusion in a *hortus conclusus* and, as in his sister Sati's case, by immobility and confinement to one's own culture, or more generally by a love of provinciality. In this context, it is significant that in Naipaul's novels the idea of and the very word "success"—usually at the centre of the Western autobiographical template—is applied mainly to women's lives, and then in a somewhat deprecating manner. Of his aunt, mentioned above, whom, after 30 years, he meets on her deathbed, he says:

> She was dying in a daughter's house on the traffic-choked Eastern Main Road that led out of Port of Spain, in a cool, airy room made neat both for her death and for visitors. She was attended by children and grandchildren, people of varying levels of education and skill; some had been to Canada. [. . .] my father's sister, at the end of her life, could see success. (*FTC* 55)

Women seem to find fulfilment in traditionally circumscribed roles, while the male figures venture out into the world and learn to philosophize on homelessness, suffering, and alienation, bearing the burden of a marginalized existence much more extensively. Such an opposition of exploratory male and secure female worlds might recall the contrasts established in Joseph Conrad's *Heart of Darkness*, though the localities are definitely inverted; for Naipaul the causes for the suffering of the male traveller are the experience of modernization and continued dislocation in the West itself. Is there, however, not perhaps a common patriarchal subtext which also becomes apparent in the peculiar absence, even silencing, of Naipaul's wife—and wives—in all his autobiographical narratives?[7]

Another example for the truncated auto- and also heterobiographical model is *Half a Life* (2001), declared to be a novel. Again elements from former stories surface like hidden palimpsests of traumatic experiences. The hero, Willie Chandran, another well-veiled alter ego, is ashamed of his parents, finds little to admire in the melancholy life of his grandfather, which forms the first part of the short novel, and, having received his father's lifestory, upbraids him with the words: "I despise you. [. . .] What is there for me in what you have said? You offer me nothing" (*HL* 35). He entirely rejects his parents and invents stories about an alternative family for himself, pretends he is a Canadian with "parents who were called 'Mom' and 'Pop'" (*HL* 39). Deep-seated feelings of shame and the denial of one's family and heritage are at the very root of the alternative autobiographies he—and like him Naipaul himself—plots out and 'tries on.' Dogged by feelings of futility, Willie Chandran escapes to a college education in England in the second part of the novel, feels even more alienated and not at all respected there (his father's former acquaintances, among them the author William Somerset Maugham, after whom he was named, keep him at a safe distance), but does discover some of the dizzying possibilities of how to model his own life, his own past according to his imagination and to literary patterns. He turns his father into a 'courtier,' his mother into a member of an old Christian faith, and thus can apparently overcome his shame by again creating an idealized family in an imagined homeland. Having learnt to know a girl from a Portuguese African colony, who admires some of his published essays, he decides to move to this unnamed former colony and again, quite naturally perhaps, feels homeless on the very first day of arrival:

> 'I don't know where I am. I don't think I can pick my way back. I don't even want this view to become familiar. I must not unpack. I must never behave as though I am staying.' He stayed for eighteen years. (*HL* 135)

The laconic last sentence symbolizes failure again: the failure to make one's own decisions or to live up to them. Finally, Willie must face the fact that our lives are the products of chances and of stultifying accommodations to habits and routines, eighteen years passing in a moment without much to recollect. A prolonged flashback does, however, fill in some of this life of uselessness and indulgence in sexual adventures, until in the end Willie finds he has achieved nothing:

> 'I have been hiding from myself. I have risked nothing. And now the best part of my life is over.' [and to his wife he remarks:] 'I've given you eighteen years. I can't give you any more. I can't live your life any more. I want to live my own.' (*HL* 138, 136)

Whether this wish is ever fulfilled is beyond the scope of the novel, which ends on a twice-melancholy tone: of only having lived half a life, and that half in a state of alienation and mere makeshift accommodation to the quotidian. However, the final words are given to his wife Ana: 'Perhaps it wasn't really my life either' (*HL* 228).

What but a form of postcolonial melancholia should emerge from such a life of denial, futility, and exposure to chance? There is little difference in this respect between Willie's and his father's life, pursued by shame and the ensuing melancholia: "I began [. . .] to take refuge in my melancholy. I courted it, and lost myself in it. Melancholy became so much a part of my character that for long periods I could forget the cause" (*HL* 33).

Autobiographic Form and Postcolonial Melancholia

A Way in the World is similarly mosaic and inconclusive, as indicated by the searching title, though here history is added to auto/hetero/biography. The apparently haphazard history of Central America and the Caribbean, from Sir Walter Raleigh to Simon Bolivar, which "confounds the quest to ground Caribbean identity" (Moore-Gilbert 2009: 74), can finally provide no sense of purpose and order; instead the narrator finds

> . . . a sense of the absurd, the idea of comedy, which hid from us our true position [. . .] perfectibility—made sense only when people were more truly responsible for themselves. We weren't responsible in that way. [. . .] We didn't have a past. For most of us the past stopped with our grandparents; beyond that was a blank. If you could look down at us from the sky you would see us living in our little houses between the sea and the bush; and that was a kind of truth about us, who had been transplanted to that place. We were just there, floating. (*WW* 79)

The perspective emphasizes the idea of a *comedie humaine*. History, biography, autobiography, travelogue, and fiction vie for precedence in *A Way in the World*, but offer little more than a carnivalesque mosaic without dominant genre. The mixture of genres and modes mirrors the comic and absurd qualities of a decentred life. Even the publishers seem confused about its genre, as it was published by Heinemann in London with the subtitle "A Sequence," but in the U.S. with the subtitle "A Novel." As Bart Moore-Gilbert remarks: "inter-generic traffic and experimentation characterises postcolonial life-writing" (Moore-Gilbert 2009: xxii).

Let me end with a few remarks on the possible meanings of the truncated, haphazard, and melancholy heterobiographical form. If we grant that Western autobiographies traditionally aimed at closure and at the presentation of exemplary lives of men and women, of a form of fulfilled or successful individuation, Naipaul's truncated and melancholy texts can first of all act as parodies of Western autobiographical traditions and formal conventions. The suffering and futility that marginalized existences often experience, due to frequent dislocation and to forms of discrimination, disallow closure and coherence. Instead of a chronological presentation of genealogy and achievements, we have in Naipaul's autobiographical texts fractions of the undocumented past emerging erratically, and mainly causing shame in the descendants, to which are added many biographical patterns of Others which are partly mimicked. Blotting out the past is for Naipaul's figures often the only means to ensure some modicum of self-respect. Such experiences of early shameful dissociation pattern a course of footloose multiple emigration and nomadism, leading to fractured heterobiographical texts, in which a melancholy yearning for a lost homeland or lost homelands dominates— whether with aspects of a final and entire rejection of the worldly, as is a Hindu ideal, will remain beyond the scope of my investigation. The yearning for a homeland of some kind leads to projections of more communal forms of life, which are apparently especially accessible to women who have travelled less or have accumulated a large family. In their lives a non-individualist, communitarian ideal surfaces nostalgically, if only in a few fleeting scenes.[8]

Naipaul's truncated heterobiographical texts question aspects of Western individualism, while at the same time offering stories of transatlantic suffering as inversions of tales of successful passages to the West—the latter presented, for example, by Bharati Mukherjee—or of tales of euphoric hybridization, as told by M.G. Vassanji. Vassanji, in contrast to Naipaul, constructs a multilocational identity for himself and some of his characters. In an interview he has maintained: "Once I came to the United States I had a fear of losing my link with Tanzania. Then I feared going back because if I went back I feared losing the new world one had discovered" (cf. Carey 1999: 3). While Vassanji is thus in a win-win situation, Naipaul sees only the double loss brought about by travelling. Vassanji's concept of identity is multilocational and transnational. The gunny sack is, much like Salman Rushdie's concept of the chutneyfication of history in *Midnight's Children*, a symbol for the bricolage, for the mosaic, and multilocational quality of the lives he presents. In his novels and stories, memories from confusing intercultural pasts are stored, pasts which cannot be comprised within the scope of a single self-image, pasts

which include the construction of imagined homelands. Even more radical is
Hélène Cixous's celebration of exile. Huddart speaks of "the desirability of a
kind of exiled self" and of the fact that "she exults in being in this continual
state of non-arrival," gladly escaping both the constrictions of identity politics and of predefined textualities. And Edward Said presents a similar concept of "privileged exile" (Huddart 2008: 40). In *Out of Place*, he sees himself
as a "cluster of flowing currents. I prefer this to the idea of a solid self" (Said
1999: 295). Such self-conscious hybrid positionings of what has been called
members of the "upwardly mobile diasporic academic community" (Huddart 2008: 41), are definitely called in question by V.S. Naipaul. In his case,
suffering seems to outbalance the feeling of nomadic liberation, and what is
entirely missing in his self-fashioning is the success story of the author who
finally won the Nobel prize. As Harish Trivedi sums up: "Few writers even in
modern times of widespread migrancy have inherited a sensibility so widely
dislocated and so deeply disjointed as V. S. Naipaul" (Trivedi 2008: 19).

The interpretation of Naipaul's truncated heterobiographical texts as not
only melancholic self-fashionings but also, to some extent, parodies indicating an unease with Western modernization and enlightenment, is only
acceptable, however, if we see the autobiography—at least in the form of
the success story—as an essentially Western form. Recent investigations into
the extremely complex Arabic and Chinese autobiographical traditions
have tended to call this in doubt (Reynolds 2001 and Wu 1990). Reynolds
examines more than 140 examples of Arabic life-writing from the ninth to
the nineteenth centuries and speaks of "the fallacy of Western origins" for
the autobiographical genre (Reynolds 2001: 17–35). His examples mainly
concern a variety of autobiographical forms—such as conversion narratives,
spiritual autobiographies, parts of a family history, reports of historical
events etc.,—which often appear to be, as it were, less individualized than
the European models—or which were influenced by the latter since the nineteenth century. But much research remains still to be expected in the field.
It may transpire, finally, that Naipaul is reacting more against a concept of
what we have long—especially since Burkhardt's studies in the Renaissance—
regarded to be the essentially Western autobiographical form than to an
actually homogenous generic tradition.

To return to Lukács and move a step further: from the epic to the autobiographic novel to decentred and melancholic heterobiographical fictions and
fractions, in which location is no longer possible. Naipaul, and even more so
Coetzee, who equally plays with multiple masks, has apparently revolution-
ized the autobiographic form, the most obvious formal features being the
use of the third person personal pronoun and the proliferation of fractions of
alter egos which are used as models for self-fashioning. In this revolution of
the paradigmatic Western enlightenment genre, we can observe the conjunction of postcolonial and postmodern/poststructuralist elements. In both cases
we have multiple projections of the self and complex forms of self-doubt, as

well as a lack of linearity and closure. But contrary to postmodern autobiographical experiments, such as, for example, John Barth's "Autobiography," which decentres the hero because of epistemological doubt and questions the very process of enunciation and writing, the postcolonial auto/hetero/biography usually arises from forms of existential decentring, whether caused by racism, scapegoating, or other experiences of victimization, leading in Naipaul's case to self-denial or shame and to an incessant outpour of auto- and heterobiographical fictions, to a sort of vicious autobiographical circle, which only on the surface has postmodern formal features. And racism or scapegoating—quite contrary to postmodern and poststructuralist epistemological conundrums—depends on the construction of stable narratives and clear-cut binary oppositions.[9] In Naipaul's works, a deeply felt melancholia is added, originating in successive experiences of alienation and homelessness. Naipaul has himself interpreted the experiences of alienation and disassociation and the movement from a communal to an individualist culture in Lukácsian terms in one of his travelogues:

> [With modernization] the ties of clan and family are loosened [. . .] and perception has to become 'an individual rather than a social function'. This threatens everything; it unbalances people [. . .] Caste and clan and security and faith all go together. [. . .] How can men learn to presume? When caste and family simplify relationships, and the sanctity of laws cannot be doubted, when magic buttresses the laws, and the epics and legends satisfy the imagination, and astrologers know the future anyway, men can easily begin to observe and analyse. (Naipaul 1979: 112)

What is described here are, however, merely some effects of modernization, without the postcolonial aspects which complicate the picture. But the passage does explain some elements of a deep-seated melancholy longing for a more coherent past and a more unified self-image in Lukácsian terms. The passage also recalls Ferdinand Tönnies's description of the move from *Gemeinschaft* to *Gesellschaft*: For Naipaul, this move away from communal roots is interpreted negatively, as it finally leads to melancholia and disorientation. Other postcolonial writers have offered a more balanced view. George Lamming's *In the Castle of My Skin* (1953), for example, also presents the move from a compassionate and supportive *Gemeinschaft* in Barbados to its dissolution through capitalist greed and egoism as a tragedy, but he balances this tragedy with the story of the artist-narrator as a young man who can escape. Thus the traditional linearity of the bildungsroman formula and of the story of initiation can to some extent be preserved.

In Naipaul's case, however, the formal observations made so far add up to a variety of the de-personalized, mosaic, and melancholy postcolonial heterobiography, reflecting alternative and somewhat negative experiences of modernization. If Paul Gilroy has described the confluence of deportation, suffering, and alienation as the dark side of the Black Atlantic, Naipaul's melancholy and somewhat haphazard autobiographical texts may be an aesthetic correlative. Part of the picture is that these auto-and heterobiographical gestures begin to proliferate at quite a young age, in Naipaul's case before he was thirty years old. This early predominance of the autobiographic genre indicates a deeply seated obsession with one's own identity and position in society and also a prolonged suffering from alienation and self-denial. A young man's autobiography is necessarily incomplete and opposed to the traditional Western formula, which is usually told from a vantage point of success or at least of well-earned leisure. Such early autobiographical gestures and the lifelong tracing of a vicious autobiographical circle of repetition appear to originate, to some extent, in traumatic childhood experiences of alienation and self-doubt, born from the ostracizing of the father/mother, the family, the race, or the gender. One of Naipaul's traumatic experiences of dissociation, which possibly helped to trigger the proliferation of truncated autobiographical gestures, seems to have been the first leave-taking from his family, which, counter to the usual feeling of loss, was experienced as a liberation, until England, India, and the world began to disappoint him. The collapse of the idealized centre and the early estrangement from his origins seem to have stimulated continual feelings of a form of postcolonial melancholia—in spite of his eminent worldly successes.

In J.M. Coetzee's case, the feeling of exclusion—from both Afrikaans and British cultures, as it were—was not as dramatic as for Naipaul, but the principle of disassociation and the lack of a stable identity seem to have been experienced in a similar way, leading to less pessimistic, but just as repetitive explorations in the form of autobiographical fictions and fractions. A more extreme case would be Bharati Mukherjee, who rejected her heritage absolutely and in her novels returned again and again to aspects of her personal history of alienation and estrangement, as well as to euphoric celebrations of assimilation—first to Canada, then to the U.S.—to only in her later works revise her dark presentations of the rejected homeland India. In *The Holder of the World* (1993) and in *Desirable Daughters* (2002), she apparently wants to balance early experiences of disaffection and exploitation of the female with more positive and perhaps even partly utopian images of a more intercultural past (in which an American could translate herself into the lover of an Indian raja) and of an intercultural present, in which Hindu culture in Calcutta is just as syncretic and tolerant as life in New York appears to be. Such harmonizing and somewhat cosmopolitan gestures are also to some extent products of postcolonial melancholia and of a passionate longing for a lost homeland that must be partly imagined or invented. However, Mukherjee's intercultural optimism differs markedly from Naipaul's deeply melancholic and pessimistic acknowledgement of continual alienation as the only postcolonial condition in a globalized and individualist world, which is haunted by the spectre of a lost commonality. Here, perhaps, Naipaul's melancholia reverberates with a deep-seated longing for a more communitarian vision, which can be felt in his early cycle of stories *Miguel Street* and in the village sketches Dirk Wiemann interprets in this volume, as well as in Harish Trivedi's discussion of pre-colonial Indian narratives.

Notes

1. As it was by the character-writers (Hall, Overbury). With the incipient enlightenment, character-writing in its typological form comes to be generally restricted to the flat characters or minor figures in novels, especially in comic novels.
2. This spelling, which is not adopted throughout, wishes to indicate that both forms are closely related genres and that much that is said about the autobiography applies equally to the biography.
3. Cf. W. Göbel (1988).
4. This has been excellently demonstrated by Huddart, who expands on the "native informant in postcolonial theory" (Huddart 2008: 122–154).
5. The following abbreviations are used for Naipaul's works: *FTC* for *Finding the Centre*, *HB* for *A House for Mr Biswas*, *EA* for *The Enigma of Arrival* and *HL* for *Half a Life*.
6. Even in Coetzee's first autobiographical "Memoir" (*Boyhood: A Memoir* (1997)), the family is presented as "they," his alter ego as "he," emphasizing the hero's estrangement from Afrikaans as from English culture and to some extent also from his own family. The third person pronoun stresses the outsider status, whether for Coetzee or for Naipaul. When, in his most recent autobiographical fiction, *Diary of a Bad Year* (2007), Coetzee does use the first person pronoun, he nevertheless maintains distance by presenting the writer as a persona, as Señor C, an ageing author. The unmediated enunciation of the "I" or the 'mastery' of the self seem impossible.
7. It would also be far-fetched to look for decentring strategies similar to those found in feminist autobiographies in Naipaul's case (a main interest of Moore-Gilbert 2009), as they usually wilfully reject forms of unified selfhood for which Naipaul craves.
8. As it does, by the way, in Naipaul's early collection of stories/novel *Miguel Street*, which could well support Dirk Wiemann's argument in this volume.
9. Here I would like to differ from Judith Levy, who sees both postmodern and postcolonial formal strategies merging easily in Naipaul's fiction (Levy 1995: 120f).

Works Cited

Anderson, L. (2007) *Autobiography*, London and New York: Routledge.
Carey, G. (1999), 'Ramji's Amrika', 3. http://www.rediff.com/news/1999/dec/08us. html. Accessed: Nov. 21, 2011.
Coetzee, J.M. (1997) *Boyhood: Scenes from Provincial Life*, London: Vintage.
———. (2007) *Diary of a Bad Year*, New York: Viking.
Gilroy, P. (2006) *Postcolonial Melancholia*, New York: Columbia University Press.
Göbel, W. (1988) 'The Suppositional Structure: *Tristram Shandy* as a Playful Inquiry into Human Nature', *Arbeiten aus Anglistik und Amerikanistik* 13/2: 155–181.

Haraway, D. (1991) *Symians, Cyborgs and Women: The Reinvention of Nature*, London: Free Association Books.

Huddart, D. (2008) *Postcolonial Theory and Autobiography*, Routledge Research in Post-colonial Literatures, vol. 20, London and New York: Routledge.

Lamming, G. (1994 [1953]) *In the Castle of My Skin*, Harlow: Longman.

Levy, J. (1995) *V.S.Naipaul: Displacement and Autobiography*, New York and London: Garland.

Lukács, G. (1971 [1920]) *Die Theorie des Romans: Ein geschichtsphilosophischer Versuch über die Formen der großen Epik*, Berlin: Luchterhand.

Moore-Gilbert, B. (2009) *Postcolonial Life-Writing: Culture, Politics and Self-Representation*, Routledge Research in Postcolonial Literatures, London and New York: Routledge.

Mukherjee, B. (1993) *The Holder of the World*, New York: Fawcett Columbine.

———. (2002) *Desirable Daughters*, New York: Wheeler Publishing.

Naipaul, V.S. (1970 [1959]) *Miguel Street*, London: Andre Deutsch.

———. (1981 [1961]) *A House for Mr Biswas*, Harmondsworth: Penguin.

———. (1979) *India: A Wounded Civilization*, Harmondsworth: Penguin.

———. (1985) *Finding the Centre*, Harmondsworth: Penguin.

———. (1987) *The Enigma of Arrival: A Novel in Five Sections*, Harmondsworth: Penguin.

———. (2001) *Half a Life: A Novel*, London: Picador.

Olney, J. (1972) *Metaphors of Self: The Meaning of Autobiography*, Princeton, N.J.: Princeton University Press.

Pascal, R. (1963) *Design and Truth in Autobiography*, Cambridge, MA: Harvard University Press.

Reynolds, D.F. (ed., 2001) *Interpreting the Self: Autobiography and the Arabic Literary Tradition*, Berkeley: University of California Press.

Said, E. (1999) *Out of Place: A Memoir*, London: Granta.

Tönnies, F. (1963) *Gemeinschaft und Gesellschaft: Grundbegriffe der Reinen Soziologie*, Repr. of 8th ed. 1935, Darmstadt: Wissenschaftliche Buchgesellschaft.

Trivedi, H. (2008) 'Locating Naipaul: "Not English, Not Indian, Not Trinidadian"', *Journal of Caribbean Literatures*, 5/2: 19–32.

Vassanji, M.G. (1989) *The Gunny Sack*, Oxford and Ibadan: Heinemann.

Wu, P.-Y. (1990) *The Confucian's Progress: Autobiographical Writings in Traditional China*, Princeton: Princeton University Press.

Part III
Longue Durée Perspectives and Orature

8 Folktales In(to) Postcolonial Narratives and Aesthetics

Ferial Ghazoul

In postcolonial studies, the emphasis has been on deconstructing colonial historiography and Orientalist aesthetics by writing back. What has been less studied is how postcolonial literature re-uses indigenous traditional genres—oral and written—to address contemporary issues. Literature of formerly colonized people is concerned with decolonization, but it is equally concerned with its own legacy and how to recycle its heritage, incorporating a modern and humanistic vision.

Within the discourse of postcolonialism, the question of nation and trans-nationalism has been a major concern. Whether Jameson dubbing all Third World literature as a national allegory or Said reading Third World literature as resisting imperial hegemony, the overall view of such literature has been situated on the horizontal axis, in terms of space and geography, the Self and the Other. Without denying the importance of the impact of colonial experience on the colonized, it is reductive to see all literature coming from the three continents, formerly or presently colonized, as simply preoccupied with the Other. Part of the preoccupation is with the Self, with one's history—literary and non-literary—and how to perform effectively in a contemporary and changing world while maintaining a cultural identity.

Aijaz Ahmad has persuasively shown that there are additional aspects of social life that surface in Third World literary representations, including class and social injustice (Ahmad 1992: 95–122). But there are a myriad of other concerns that postcolonial writers address in their writing. In the Arab world, for example, the question of modernity versus authenticity (*al-hadatha vs. al-asala*) is constantly posed. There is almost a phobic concern about what is called 'cultural conquest,' *ghazu thaqafi*, that is the penetration of the Other into the collective identity via culture, something akin to 'cultural occupation.' This phobia of cultural hegemony of the Other, and its subtle appropriation of one's heritage, is on the mind of many Arab intellectuals from the nineteenth-century liberals to today's fiction writers. This, in itself, shows a lack of cultural confidence and an underlying admission of the fragility of one's aesthetic traditions and cultural legacy. In the light of these concerns, writers in the Third World in general have tried to investigate their own cultural patrimony and re-shape it to speak to the present. In doing so, they have called on their folk heritage and their classical legacy, works of the people—mostly oral and fluid—and works of the elite and the establishment, considered canonical literature, *adab rafi'*.

By examining the re-cycling of such genres, of folk or originally related to folk literature, and observing how genres have been modified or used for new aesthetic and social functions, the postcolonial field looks vertically into post-colonial genres, rather than the usual horizontal perspective. In other words, the history of genres and their transformation need to be examined. Folklore and folktales, as we know, have been used also to draw the contours of the nation, whether in Europe or elsewhere. In Germany, for example, the folk-tales and fairy tales of the Brothers Grimm were both instrumental in shaping the German nation as well as an interest triggered by the idea of a German nation. Romantic nationalism based the idea of the nation as an "imagined community"—to use the terminology of Benedict Anderson—on the Volk/the people/*al-sha'b* and their lore as human vehicles of the so-called spirit of the nation. But the interest in folklore is more than an interest in nation building; it is also an interest in marginalized voices, in oral traditions, and in local mem-ory. Thus it functions as an expression of the subaltern majority in the Third World and by extension its coverage and centrality work towards democrati-zation.[1] In the context of cultural and identitarian concerns, folklore is a touch-stone, as it represents what has been preserved through popular memory. Thus resorting to folktales is both a literary strategy in contemporary writing and a form of cultural resistance both to imperial hegemony and its racism, on one hand, and to national repression and class hierarchy on the other hand. It is only by looking closely into the works of postcolonial literature that we can figure out the significance of such use of folk traditions.

In "Problems in Current Theories of Colonial Discourse," Benita Parry contrasts the positions of Spivak and Bhabha to that of Fanon:

> For Spivak, imperialism's epistemic bellicosity decimated the old culture and left the colonized without the ground from which they could utter confrontational words; for Bhabha, the stratagems and subterfuges to which the native retorted, destabilized the effectivity of the English book but did not write an alternative text—with whose constitution Bhabha declines to engage. (Parry 1995: 43)

Parry clearly sides with the progressive text of the native, even though that text is difficult to define at this stage:

> While conceding the necessity of defending the past in a move away from unqualified assimilation of the occupying power's culture, Fanon recog-nizes the limitations on the writer and intellectual who utilize "techniques and language which are borrowed from the stranger in his country." Such

transitional writing, reinterpreting old legends "in the light of a borrowed aestheticism and of a conception of the world which was discovered under other skies," is for Fanon but a prelude to a literature of combat which "will disrupt literary styles and themes [. . .], create a completely new public," and mould the national consciousness, "giving it horizons." [. . .] This is a move which colonial discourse theory has not taken on board, and for such a process to be investigated, a cartography of imperialist ideology, more extensive than its address in the colonialist space, as well as a conception of the native as historical subject and agent of an oppositional discourse is needed. (Parry 1995: 44)

The need to make use of genres that developed in the culture seems to be both an aesthetic and a political necessity. As Ella Shohat states in *Taboo Memories, Diasporic Voices*:

While avoiding any nostalgia for a prelapsarian community or for any unitary and transparent identity predating the fall, we must also ask whether it is possible to forge a collective resistance without inscribing a communal past [. . .]. For communities that have undergone brutal ruptures and are now in the process of forging a collective identity, no matter how hybrid that identity has been before, during, and after colonialism, the retrieval and reinscription of a fragmented past becomes a crucial contemporary site for forging a resistant collective identity. (Shohat 2006: 244–245)

She adds:

The de facto acceptance of hybridity as a product of colonial conquest and post-independence dislocations, as well as the recognition of the impossibility of return to an authentic past, do not mean that the politico-cultural movements of various racial-ethnic communities should stop researching and recycling their precolonial languages and cultures. (Shohat 2006: 245)

In the line of Fanon, and the need to reconsider the precolonial legacy as articulated by Parry and Shohat, this article examines how postcolonial writers have incorporated the literary traditions of their own in their works. The article is not only concerned with the oppositional discourse aimed at colonial erasure of the native foundations of the culture, but also with the tyranny within that erases the potential for innovation and creativity. The oppositional stance in postcolonial writing sees the repressive character in all its myriad masks, white and black, foreign and native.

* * * * *

Chinua Achebe in *Things Fall Apart* (1958) writes back but also attempts to preserve the coherence of Ibo culture in its many uses of folk proverbs and tales. While not idealizing his own culture, Achebe shows its coherence and its aesthetics.

Barbara Harlow, in the Preface to her *Resistance Literature*, opens up with Achebe's folktale that explains why the tortoise's shell is not smooth. She sees in it "political significance and [. . .] an allegory for an African strategy of independence" (Harlow 1987: xv). The tortoise, who had convinced the birds to take him flying in the sky by borrowing a feather from each, ends up calling itself "All of you" for the occasion:

> through this linguistic manipulation [he] succeeds in getting for himself the best part of food and palm wine served at the feast in the sky. The angry birds then took back their feathers, leaving the tortoise stranded high above the earth. (Harlow 1987: xiv)

However, the parrot delivered a message from the tortoise to his wife to prepare a soft landing, but the parrot modified the message so he landed on a pile of sharp objects that were in his house, including spears and guns. His shell was broken and the medicine man had to piece the shell together and that is why the shell looks as it does, made up of small pieces (cf. Harlow 1987: xiv). Harlow sees in the tortoise colonial power that uses verbal manipulations to subjugate and exploit the others. This takes place

> because the parrot, legendary for his proclivity to repeat just what he has heard, has overcome this stereotypical image and learned to use language to his and the birds' own ends. He has altered the tortoise's message to his wife. The folk wisdom in this fable turns out in fact to be ideologically sophisticated and Achebe's message is clear: the language skills of rhetoric together with armed struggle are essential to an oppressed people's resistance to domination and oppression and to an organized liberation movement. (Harlow 1987: xv)

Things Fall Apart is an ethnographic novel par excellence: Its very fabric, dialogue, themes, and style partake of Ibo oral culture. It has often been read by critics as a response to Conrad's *Heart of Darkness* in the sense that it writes back to the empire and shows the sophistication of the culture dubbed 'primitive.' The novel contrasts the view of the protagonist Okonkwo, as a tragic figure, to his presentation by the colonial District Officer, as no more than a curious figure, as a passing curiosity, to be mentioned in imperial historiography in a paragraph. Thus, Achebe presents a novel centred around Okonkwo as a hero, albeit with tragic flaws, fighting against impossible odds, unlike the book which the District Officer would write and would classify as "history," giving it the title *Pacification of the Primitive Tribes of the Lower Niger*, devoting only a few lines to the 'exotic' character Okonkwo.

But what has been less noted perhaps is the way Achebe subverts the underlying depiction of Africans in Conrad's work vis-à-vis language and literature. Racism often presents the Other as less articulate or inarticulate. The word "barbarian" from Greek *barbaros*, meaning non-Greek or foreign, also carries in the repetitive syllable an indication of an incomprehensible language. Achebe himself points to how Conrad characterizes the Africans as either silent (and thus lacking articulation) or babbling in a frenzied way— frenzy being the negative face of articulation. Achebe, in a lecture he delivered that was published in the *Massachusetts Review*, stated it clearly:

> I am not going to waste your time with examples of Conrad's famed evocation of the African atmosphere in *Heart of Darkness*. In the final consideration it amounts to no more than a steady, ponderous, fake-ritualistic repetition of two sentences, one about silence and the other about frenzy. [. . .] 1. *It was the stillness of an implacable force brooding over an inscrutable intention*, and 2. *The steamer toiled along slowly on the edge of a black and incomprehensible frenzy*. (Achebe 1977: 3)

What Achebe achieves, besides humanizing his people in *Things Fall Apart*, is a response to Conrad by highlighting the ability of the characters to speak and argue as Akunna did with Mr Brown, the missionary. In other words, the Ibo not only use arguments, but can also beat their adversary in debates. Achebe does more than present his people as rational beings; he also points out the poetry of Ibo language in everyday life. Even when some Ibo, such as Nwoye, Okonkwo's son, are attracted to Christianity, it is not the dogma and not the trinity, but the poetry of the Bible. It is precisely their sensibility to the language and to the parables, with their appeal to the outcasts that made Christian converts of Africans.

The negative influence of Conrad on Achebe goes beyond the themes and the content to affect the style. Instead of the complexity and ambiguity of the Conradian sentence, that reflect Conrad's French education and Franco-phone sensibility, Achebe writes in simple but no less poetic language, appro-priating the idiom of the colonizer syntactically and embellishing it with Ibo words and rhythms. Achebe writes about his own culture:

> African people did not hear of culture for the first time from Europeans [. . .], their societies were not mindless but frequently had a philosophy of great depth and value and beauty [. . .], they had poetry and above all, they had dignity. It is this dignity that many African people all but lost during the colonial period and it is this they must regain. (qtd. in JanMohamed 1983: 154)

The novel then is a project of literary decolonization in which what is inscrutable about African culture is elucidated, in which Ibo cultural logic is laid bare, and in which the poetic aspect of the culture is highlighted. In a scene in the opening of the novel, Achebe depicts the art of conversation in an African village:

> Having spoken plainly so far, Okoye said the next half a dozen sentences in proverbs. Among the Ibo the art of conversation is regarded very highly, and proverbs are the palm-oil with which words are eaten. Okoye was a great talker and he spoke for a long time, skirting round the subject and then hitting finally. (Achebe 1958: 6)

And again in a passage:

> Everybody laughed heartily except Okonkwo, who laughed uneasily because, as the saying goes, an old woman is always uneasy when dry bones are mentioned in a proverb. (Achebe 1958: 19)

The novel is punctuated by songs in the transliterated native language of Ibo or in English: There are children's songs welcoming the rain (cf. Achebe 1958: 32), as well as praise songs celebrating the winner in a wrestling match (cf. Achebe 1958: 46), and dirges to lament the death of dear ones (cf. Achebe 1958: 122). The motif of poetic lyric is also depicted: "The musicians with their wood, clay and metal instruments went from song to song. [. . .] They sang the latest songs in the village" (Achebe 1958: 107–108). Some of these songs are provocative, such as the anticolonial one sung by the prisoners, who were often incarcerated because they had offended the English and were tried after sending the court messengers to get them. As the court messengers, named locally *kotmas* (corruption of court messenger), wore ash-coloured shorts they were known pejoratively as Ashy-Buttocks. The prisoners who had to cut the grass in their prison compound composed a work song to go along with their grass-cutting:

Kotma of the ash buttocks,
He is fit to be a slave.
The white man has no sense,
He is fit to be a slave. (Achebe 1958: 158)

And despite the anger of the court messengers for being called "ash buttocks," culminating in beating the men who pronounce such pejorative terms for the English, the song spread all over the village.

Songs are not the only genre that taps the verbal and artistic energies of the Ibos. There is also the tortoise story (to which Harlow referred), told by Okonkwo's wife, Ekwefi, to her daughter Ezinma (Achebe 1958: 87–90).

There is also an example of an eloquent speech delivered by Umunna to thank Okonkwo (Achebe 1958: 152).

Apart from the verbal artistry of the Ibos, Achebe shows the rational discourse and the underlying logic of their faith in the conversation between a villager, Akunna, and the missionary Mr Brown. Akunna tries to see analogies between the Ibo animist beliefs and Christianity, while Mr Brown can see only differences: "You say that there is one supreme God who made heaven and earth [. . .]. We also believe in Him and call Him Chukwu. He made all the world and the other gods" (Achebe 1958: 162). When Mr Brown protests that there is but one God and the other gods are carved pieces of wood, Akunna answers like a pantheist, reminiscent of the Andalusian philosopher and mystic, Ibn 'Arabi, who believed in the Unity of Being. Akunna responds: "It is indeed a piece of wood. The tree of which it came was made by Chukwu" (Achebe 1958: 162). Akunna goes on to give Mr Brown an extended simile to make the analogy clear: Just as the Queen of England sends messengers such as the District Officers to represent her and just as the District Officers appoint *kotmas* (court messengers) to help them, so do the minor gods help the supreme God.

Finally, anger and humiliation get Africans to express themselves in strongly worded language and when they are silent, it is not a sign of inarticulateness, but a sign of emotional crescendo. When Obierika sees the body of his friend Okonkwo dangling from a tree, he addresses the District Commissioner, saying: "That man was one of the greatest men in Umuofia. You drove him to kill himself and now he will be buried like a dog." He could not say any more. His voice "trembled and choked his words," only to be told unnecessarily to shut up by one of the court messengers (Achebe 1958: 187). Here, his silence is a sign of an emotional turmoil that cannot be expressed in words, an inexpressible feeling of injustice that comes after an outburst of indignation. Silence, here, is pregnant with meaning.

Although Achebe responds to the accusation of inarticulateness by his own powerful prose and by stressing the verbal prowess of his people, by no means does he present an idealized version of his culture. The masculine pressures on the protagonist to excel economically and physically, the practice of infanticide of twins etc., are also part of the weaknesses of the social system that made outcasts of some of its members, thus constituting a vulnerable stratum through which the colonial order could penetrate the society.

*   *   *   *   *

If Achebe is out to revise the image of the African as an inarticulate savage, and in the process develops his own English and poetics, Salman Rushdie, in his novel *Haroun and the Sea of Stories* (1990), admits to inarticulateness and impotence when faced with repression and censorship. It is only through a child-like story with a child protagonist, evoking the folk traditions and narrative lore, that the gift of speech is regained.

Rushdie's novel, *Haroun*, is linked intertextually to *One Thousand and One Nights* as well as the genre of Indian storytelling known as the ocean of stories. Salman Rushdie reproduces the spirit of the *Arabian Nights*, its emphasis on the role of creativity, and its embodiment of taboo transgressions, articulated in a contemporary mode that touches on his own predicament, that of the freedom of expression. Condemned by the *fatwa* of Ayatollah Khomeini in 1989 for his novel *Satanic Verses*, Rushdie wrote *Haroun*, a story for children, albeit it speaks to adults.

Haroun and the Sea of Stories explores the significance of stories and fiction in our world. Haroun is a child whose father is named Rashid Khalifa (thus alluding to the cycle of Haroun al-Rashid in the *Arabian Nights* as well as the author's name Rushdie). Rashid, like Rushdie, is known for his fertile imagination and ability to create stories. Haroun's mother, however, runs away with another man (recalling the conjugal infidelity of the *Nights'* frame story), who convinces her that there is no use for fiction and storytellers like her husband. Haroun repeats this doubt about storytelling; he asks: "What is the use of stories that aren't even true?" (Rushdie 1990: 22), which in turn becomes the trigger of the fiction showing the necessity of stories and their types. The creative story is seen as redemptive, just as in the *Arabian Nights*.

Rashid loses his ability to tell stories and relates this to the stopping of narrative waters, to be understood as creative juices. This metaphor relates to the genre of *kathasaritsagara*, the ocean of stories. The frequent references to the number 1001 underline the literary kinship between the author, Rushdie, and Shahrazad. The creative waters come back, however, to the silenced storyteller through a djinn called Iff and a hoopoe called Butt (alluding through the alliteration to If and But—metonyms of fiction). Those two djinns take Rashid from Chup, the land of silence and silencing, governed by Khattam-Shud to Gup, the land of free speech, governed by General Kitab (literally General Book).

The entire novel is about fiction and the role of fiction in life—as is the *Arabian Nights*—and how it is made up of older narratives rewoven together, just as Rushdie himself is doing and as the *Nights* was constituted. The novel distinguishes between the dogmatic discourse and the creative one, the first used to oust the latter, but this only leads to amnesia and desolation. The storyteller, Rashid Khalifa, in contrast, is a happy man seen in two different ways—by his admirers as an "Ocean of Notions," as an infinity of ideas, and by his detractors as a "Shah of Blah," a master of nothing (Rushdie 1990: 15).

This is a novel written with an eye to oral storytelling and specifically the genre developed in the *Panchatantra* and in the *One Thousand and One Nights*; it addresses an actual dilemma of the author and an issue relevant not only to the freedom of expression in postcolonial societies, but also touches on the role of the imagination and its relation to resisting routine and political propaganda. In the *Arabian Nights*, storytelling was redemptive and saved Shahrazad from being beheaded. In the *Panchatantra*—literally "Five

Lessons"—the stories are instructive, meant to teach lessons of governance. In Salman Rushdie's *Haroun*, redemption and instruction are conjoined.

Again Rushdie appropriates English as Achebe did, providing a glossary of Hindustani words at the end of the book. The author extends the genre called "ocean of stories" (a metaphor for stories within stories, generating other stories) to respond to current issues.

When Haroun Khalifa, the storyteller's son, flies into the night sky on the back of Butt, the Hoopoe, with Iff, the Water Genie as his guide, they end up in a watery country. What was an idiom and a dead metaphor referring to a narrative genre, "ocean of stories," is presented literally as a huge expanse of water:

> Rushing up towards them was a sparkling and seemingly infinite expanse of water. The surface of Kahani appeared—as far as Haroun's eye could see—to be entirely liquid. And what water it was! [. . .] "The Ocean of the Streams of Story," said Iff the Water Genie, his blue whiskers bristling with pride. "Wasn't it worth traveling so far and fast to see?" (Rushdie 1990: 68)

Once again, the issue here is articulating creatively, resisting silence (and by extension censorship), and opposing words that have lost meaning due to their use by politicians for misinformation and manipulation. Only Rushdie is not writing back to the colonial adversary, but to the forces of apathy and censorship. It is a critique of authoritarianism. The very construction of the work—mixing motifs from Rushdie's Indian Muslim heritage with European works such as Lewis Carroll's *Alice in Wonderland* and Frank Baum's *The Wizard of Oz*, among others—presents hybridity. It recycles precolonial literary legacy into postcolonial discourse on imagination and creativity. The commitment to inclusion rather than exclusion, to pluralism rather than monolingualism, is not only postcolonial but is traditionally Indian. Rushdie's *mélange* then embodies his own background and beliefs. He says:

> I come from Bombay, and from a Muslim family [. . .]. "My" India has always been based on ideas of multiplicity, pluralism, hybridity—ideas to which the ideologies of the communalists are diametrically opposed. To my mind, the defining image of India is the crowd, and a crowd is by its very nature superabundant, heterogeneous, many things at once. (Rushdie 1987: 94)

*   *   *   *   *

Radwa Ashour, in her novella *Siraaj: An Arab Tale* (1992), mixes historical events with a fable-like narrative to criticize both colonialism and authoritarianism. Ashour's novel is written as a folk novella and extended fable. It was written in the late 1980s and published in the early 1990s; it combines the imaginary drawn from Arab fictional sources with the realistic details of historical figures, named (Egyptian resistance leader Orabi) or alluded to (British Queen Victoria). It is set on an imaginary island off the coast of Africa, named Ghurrat Bahr al-'Arab ("Jewel of the Arabian Sea"), run by an authoritarian Sultan, who resembles a nineteenth-century composite ruler of Zanzibar and Yemen. The narrative presents the revolt of the people of the island—fishermen, pearl divers, and plantation slaves—against their monarch and their failure to overthrow him, as the colonial power is there to protect him.

Radwa Ashour, who specialized in African American Literature and the Harlem Renaissance in the 1970s and who wrote a book on West African Literature, *Al-Tabi' yanhad: Al-Riwaya fi gharb afriqiya* (The Subaltern Rises: The Novel in West Africa), no doubt was influenced by Achebe's modern classic, *Things Fall Apart*, in her own writing of *Siraaj*.[2] Her novella wavers between a political allegory and an elaborate folktale. The dominant theme is that of oppression and resistance; it is a tragic tale where women play a significant role in the collective struggle. The novella opens and ends with Amina, the Sultan's baker. Awaiting her teenage son, Said, who departed on a sailing ship and did not come back, Amina gazes at the sea and prays for her son's homecoming in a haunting scene. After wandering in Egypt, Said takes part in adventures he does not fully grasp during the British bombardment of Alexandria and the subsequent occupation. Eventually, he comes home. Now a more mature and militant young man, he becomes a member of an underground movement to overthrow the Sultan. The people's uprising is on the verge of success when the forces in the British Base in the island intervene to save the Sultan, the British puppet, disseminating the crowd and violently suppressing the revolt. Said is shot dead and in the finale, Amina is seen holding her son, resembling a painting of the *Pieta,* a peasant Madonna holding her crucified son. Like Achebe's Okonkwo, the young protagonist Said and other rebels were pitted against impossible odds; but unlike *Things Fall Apart*, the oppressed in *Siraaj*—men and women, African slaves and Arab workers—partake in a collective struggle, even though their solidarity proves not enough for liberation. The autocratic ruler is protected by the colonial presence on his island. The alliance of the powerful—local and foreign—against the dispossessed proves fatal for the cause. Folkloric echoes, as there are in the novella, differ radically from Rushdie's djinn and his fantastic episodes. However, like Rushdie, Ashour plays on the metaphoric and the literal, particularly with *Siraaj/siraaj* (which can be both a name—of a male or a female—and also the term for lamp). The organized uprising of the people on the island use *siraaj* as a code to indicate the use of lamps as a sign for gathering, while the Sultan's spies think it is the name of a person plotting against him. The Sultan's soldiers go searching on the island for anyone named Siraaj only to find a very old, decrepit, and senile woman with that name. She is brought to His Majesty, and a comic exchange, in this otherwise sad story, occurs between the Sultan, who suspects her of plotting against him, and the hag, who thinks she is about to be granted her wishes by the Sultan and thus asks for a husband.

As in Rushdie's *Haroun*, the *Arabian Nights* is implicated in Ashour's *Siraaj*. The episode when young Said, the protagonist, leaves his island and ends up stranded in Alexandria while his ship sails without him, is reminiscent of Sindbad the Sailor. This is underlined by Mahmoud, Said's Egyptian friend, who tells him: "You're lucky, man [...], you travel by ship and roam the world [...] like Sindbad the Sailor" (Ashour 2007: 14). Later on in the narrative, Said has a dream of the repressive Captain "riding on his shoulders." He explains that the dream is not strange as it reproduces an episode in one of Sindbad's voyages in which Sindbad meets a crippled man and carries him out of kindness, only to discover that he is a tormenting devil (Ashour 2007: 72). Ammar, the African slave, interprets the dream: The Captain stands for the Sultan and his exploitation. Like Rushdie, Ashour, too, weaves the historical with the imaginary, contextualizing the novella in the late nineteenth-century Middle East with references to General Orabi and Admiral Seymour. The Egyptian uprising, in which Said's friend Mahmoud participated and was killed, was led by Ahmad Orabi, a leader of peasant background, who apostrophized the Khedive, the Ruler of Egypt, with his famous statement: "We are not slaves and you are not our Master" (Ashour 2007: 15).

The resistance on the island is shaped by oral traditions and classical tales. The written and the oral stories are used to mobilize the dispossessed inhabitants and to secretly communicate the plot of the revolt. *Siraaj* traces the role of creative storytelling in raising consciousness, and of writing in strategizing and organizing the revolt. The novella starts with silence and ends with a mass uprising, a sea of people, articulating their wish to be free. In the opening scene of the novella, we are struck by the silence of the sea as Amina awaits her son Said, followed by a reference to the silenced inmates in their detention or in the Palace:

> She walks along the path that leads to the hill, then begins her ascent to the high house. She passes by the dungeon and hears the murmurs of the *muffled voices*. She continues the climb to the women's quarters, which are *wrapped in silence*. (Ashour 2007: 1; my emphases)

From female silence and muffled voices of political prisoners, the novella unfolds towards articulation and action:

> Boys and girls, men and women, [...] plantation slaves, fishermen, sailors, pearl divers, carpenters, blacksmiths, and masons—all released their birds in the direction of the fortress and followed them, the lanterns in their hands. The people kept climbing until they reached the dungeon and applied the keys to the locks, shoulders to the gates, and axes to

the walls. The dungeon opened up. They cheered, advanced. (Ashour 2007: 80)

The importance of breaking the silence as a step forward in political action is foregrounded in the novella. Even the Egyptian peasant Abu Ibrahim, depressed by the failure of Orabi's revolt (1882), is cheered when he hears his own children singing—as Ibo peasants did in *Things Fall Apart*—against the English. Here, too, the children make fun of Admiral Seymour, deputy of the Queen:

Hey, Seymour, you lousy face,
Who told you you could have this place? (Ashour 2007: 26)

In flashbacks, the novella expands on the autobiographical account of one of its principal characters, the elderly slave Ammar. As a personal slave of the Sultan, Ammar was not allowed to get married and have children of his own, yet he enthralled the children of the island with his fables, stories, and kindness—becoming a father figure. The African lore in his stories is highlighted, while the ruptures of Ammar's life are underlined, from taking him away from his mother, to forbidding him from marrying Maliha whom he loved.

When Said is adopted by Umm Ibrahim in the Egyptian village (as Ike-mefuna was adopted by Okonkwo's family), not only paternal and maternal protection is displayed, but also exchange of stories and comparison of life styles in Egypt and Said's island. The Egyptian children in the novella are shocked to learn that Said does not know how to till the soil since slaves do so in the plantations of his island. Using the mode of defamiliarization, Ashour develops this exchange to point to the exploitation of the simple folk on the island. Said explains that his father was a diver for pearls—more expensive than gold—before he suffocated and drowned: yet, he was not a rich man, as the Egyptian children assumed, since he only got a meagre wage for his risky livelihood while the Sultan got the pearls.

The emphasis on writing as a necessary medium for communication in resistance movements is indicated by Ashour, first through Said's learning to write from the Egyptian children, and later through the young girl Tawad-dud who was fascinated by stories she overheard when the island's judge read them to his son from a beautifully bound book. Storytelling in the novella becomes essential for cultural identity and the two traditions of tell-ing stories, orally and in writing, from Africa and from Asia—as represented by the tales of Ammar and by the fables of Ibn al-Muqaffa'—are embedded in the novella.

The story Tawaddud overheard is that of the ringdove, a story which migrated from India to Persia, and then to Iraq, where it was translated into Arabic by Ibn al-Muqaffa' in the collection known as *Kalila wa-Dimna*. Like the story of the tortoise in *Things Fall Apart*, this animal fable has a political layer. The ringdove, leader of the doves, and her small companions were caught in a hunter's net. Each of the doves began to struggle to escape on its own. The ringdove said, "Do not abandon one another in your struggle! Let us cooperate, and then perhaps we can unfasten the net and rescue one another" (Ashour 2007: 37). They did so, and by cooperating, they flew with the net high into the sky until they reached the ringdove's friend, the rat. The ringdove asked the rat to gnaw on the knots, while leaving the ringdove's knot the last. Otherwise, the rat might get tired and stop gnawing once he had freed his friend. The rat follows the instructions and thus frees all.

The point of the fable is twofold: It addresses the colonial situation and also the post-independence issue of leadership. In contrast to the colonial divide-and-rule principle, there is a need for the colonized to work together. Furthermore, leadership is characterized by wisdom and altruism, not self-centred interest. Ashour's embedding of folktales in her novella and the adoption of an oral style for telling a (post)colonial tale is not unusual for Arab women writers in their endeavour to transplant the genre of the novel into the Arab cultural soil (Hawwas 2010: 40–46). The *Arabian Nights* is not simply present intertextually in *Siraaj*; it is also present structurally through the nesting and embedding of one story within another, such as the ringdove fable and the unfinished fable of the rat and the raven.

*   *   *   *   *

Folktales in postcolonial literature serve both as a framework to tell a narrative of our times and also to draw political and social lessons. By calling on the legacy of the past—oral and scripted—these tales usher in a new poetics based on the interconnection of written and oral, of past and present. Their simplicity is deceptive, as it masks a multi-layered discourse with multiple functions. The three works discussed in this article should not be conflated; their use of folk material is specific to each. However, the three show that the dichotomy between nativist and modernist aesthetics is not tenable. They exemplify the use of native traditions and their deployment without romanticizing them or calling for a return to precolonial cultural roots. They fall into Fanon's third stage of periodization of the native intellectual as outlined in *The Wretched of the Earth*—the first in which he imitates the colonized; the second in which he indulges in nativist traditions; and the third in which he combines both in a progressive perspective. In Achebe's work, the conflict is not Manichean and the native culture is not presented nostalgically, but as a culture worth acknowledging. Rushdie conflated Indian, Arab, and European works to tell a story of our time, to expose a private and a public dilemma, and to condemn censorship. Ashour used the cultural treasury to unlock contemporary issues, from dynastic rivalry to theological short-sightedness, and from national concerns to imperial designs. Such works constitute a beginning of a literary discourse that uses the communal heritage to address present issues, balancing both an acknowledgement of the creative and cultural in one's context, and the necessity to merge it with a more global setting and struggles.

Notes

1. No doubt folklore can also be used as a weapon of national self-glorification, occasionally contributing to racist and fascist cultural politics. On the whole its popular and elusive forms have brought about its manipulation in different ideological contexts. But as postcolonial writers tend to revise colonial representations of them, folktales are used to speak of the people and for the people.

2. *Siraaj* also shows the impact of another writer, the Palestinian Ghassan Kanafani, in his children's story entitled, *Al-Qandil al-saghir* ("The Little Lamp"). In this story, composed and illustrated by the author, the King wants to leave his kingdom to his daughter, provided she can bring the sun to the palace; otherwise she will remain locked in a box as punishment. Having failed to achieve this, she overhears an old man who tries to come into the palace to help her, but her guards, taking him for a fool, prevent him and thus he leaves. When she tries to find him, her guards can only describe him as a man with a lamp. She asks her guards to look for every man who has a lamp and bring him to the palace. That night the princess sees thousands of men coming with lamps to her palace but they cannot enter as the doors are too small, so she orders her servants to knock down the walls of the palace. As she goes down to meet the men with lamps, she grasps that these multitudes with lamps are the sun that her father had meant. Without them, she would be locked in her box, in the interior of the palace.

Works Cited

Achebe, C. (1977) 'An Image of Africa', *Massachusetts Review*, 18: 1–15.
———. (1958) *Things Fall Apart*, London: Heinemann.
Ahmad, A. (1992) *In Theory*, London: Verso.
Ashour, R. (2007) *Siraaj: An Arab Tale,* trans. B. Romaine, Austin, TX: Center for Middle Eastern Studies at the University of Texas at Austin.
———. (2008 [1992]) *Siraj: Hikaya 'arabiyya*, Cairo: Dar al-Shurouk.
Fanon, F. (1967) *The Wretched of the Earth*, trans. C. Farrington. Middlesex: Penguin.
Harlow, B. (1987) *Resistance Literature*, New York: Methuen.
Hawwas, A.-H. (2010) 'Al-Thaqafa al-sha'biyya wa-tawtin al-naw' al-riwai: Isham al-riwaiyyat', *Al-Funun al-Sha'biyya*, 86: 40–46.
Kanafani, G. (1975) *Al-Qandil al-saghir*, Beirut: Dar al-Fata al-'Arabi.
JanMohamed, A.R. (1983) *Manichean Aesthetics: The Politics of Literature in Colonial Africa*, Amherst: The University of Massachusetts Press.
Parry, B. (1995) 'Problems in Current Theories of Colonial Discourse', in B. Ashcroft et al. (eds) *The Post-Colonial Studies Reader*, London: Routledge, 36–44.
Rushdie, S. (1987) 'After Midnight', *Vanity Fair*, September: 88–94.
———. (1990) *Haroun and the Sea of Stories*, New Delhi: Granta Books.
Shohat, E. (2006) *Taboo Memories, Diasporic Voices*, Durham: Duke University Press.

9 A House, a Museum, and a Legend

Bait Al-Kretliya

Nadia El Kholy

Introduction

Major Robert Grenville 'John' Gayer-Anderson Pasha (1881–1945), after qualifying as a doctor, joined the Royal Army Medical Corps in 1904, from which he was seconded to the Egyptian Army in 1907. He was promoted to the rank of Major in 1914, and in the same year, became Assistant Adjutant General for Recruiting, Egyptian Army. He retired from the British Army in 1919 to take up the post of Senior Inspector in the Egyptian Ministry of the Interior and was later appointed Oriental Secretary to the British Residency, Cairo. He finally retired on pension in 1924 but continued to reside in Cairo where, among other unofficial activities, he interested himself in Egyptology and Oriental studies, forming a large and valuable collection of Islamic domestic furniture, faience, carpets, and other objects representative of the arts and crafts of the Near East. In 1935 he was, at his own request, authorized by the Egyptian Government to reside in the Bait al-Kretliya, an old Mamluk house in the keeping of the Committee for the Preservation of Arab Monuments, situated at the entrance to the famous ninth-century mosque of Ibn Tulun.

The following is Gayer-Anderson's own account of his first arrival in Cairo:

> Soon after my arrival I set out one day from Shepherd's Hotel with a dragoman to see the sights, and one of the first places we visited was the great ninth century mosque of Ahmed Ibn Tulun, which stands in a very sacred but slummy part of Cairo. As I approached the Mosque I was lost in admiration of a fine stone-built house, a veritable castle, that rose before me and bridged over the passage to the main door of Ibn Tulun. Suddenly my attention was diverted by a pretty unveiled Egyptian girl who leaned out of one of the latticed windows of the first floor and called to me, smiling and beckoning.
>
> 'What does she say?', I enquired of my guide for I then had no word of Arabic.
>
> 'The shameless one invites you to view the old house.'

> 'Is that all?'
> 'So it would seem.'
> 'Shall we go in?'
> 'Be advised by me. Excellency, do not go in to her,' answered my perhaps over-cautious companion and I took his advice. (al-Kretli 1951: 16–17)

He goes on to say:

> As an ardent collector and Orientalist throughout my adult life, I had for long been trying to find an ancient Arab house in Cairo to furnish, embellish and inhabit; a house away from the everyday Europeanized side of Cairo, for I wished to be largely apart from my own kind and in closer touch with the Egyptian people. (al-Kretli 1951: 19)

Said states that "to be a European in the Orient always involves being a consciousness set apart from, and unequal with, its surroundings" (Said 1978: 157). Gayer-Anderson, however, wanted to bridge this gap; he wanted to penetrate into the 'reality' of his surroundings, and it was through the appropriation of Bait al-Kretliya that he was able to create a bridge between himself and the Egyptian people.

> The house, quite obviously, is a privileged entity for a phenomenological study of the intimate values of inside space, provided, of course, that we take it in both its unity and its complexity, and endeavour to integrate all the special values in one fundamental value. For the house furnishes us with dispersed images and a body of images at the same time. (Bachelard 1969: 3)

The house can be considered as an "'object' on which we can make our judgments and daydreams react" (Bachelard 1969: 3).[1] "It therefore makes sense" epistemologically to say that we "'read a house.'" (Bachelard 1969: 14)

> A house constitutes a body of images that give mankind proofs or illusions of stability. We are constantly re-imagining its reality: To distinguish all these images would be to describe the soul of the house; it would mean developing a veritable psychology of the house. (Bachelard 1969: 17)

Like other intellectuals at that time, Gayer-Anderson looked upon Egypt as a country with two contrasting cultures: "an image that corresponded with, and also reflected Europe's common taste for the exotic nature of the Oriental world. This went side by side with its fascination of the antiquities of ancient Egyptian civilization" (Ahmed 1978: 8). Like the travellers' accounts that were meant to re-construct the Oriental picture, and, if reality was disappointing, patched it up from other places in the East like Turkey, Persia, or India, Gayer-Anderson re-constructed the house to emerge as a show place, a museum. He adopted the old idea of presenting the Oriental Image to the European public in the form of an Exhibition:[2] "Living within a world of signs, they took semiosis to be a universal condition, and set about describing the Orient as though it were an exhibition" (Mitchell 1988: 14). Walking about the Exhibition, the spectator consumes history as a commodity (McClintock 1995: 57). In the middle of the nineteenth century, a new term came into vogue for characterizing[3] this combination of detachment and close attentiveness—the word "objective." *The Times* wrote in the summer of 1851, on the occasion of the Great Exhibition: "we want to place everything we can lay our hands on under glass cases, and stare our fill" (qtd. Mitchell 1988: 20). The word denoted the modern sense of detachment, detaching the self from the object. In accordance with that "objective gaze," the visitor's role was circumscribed as "passively curious." The display of the exhibited objects gave the notion of "imaginary structure" that exists before and apart from the "external reality" or the real world it represents. The traveller who desired the same accuracy of representation was to separate himself from the world and thus constitute it as a panorama.

To create for himself a 'point of view,' Edward Lane lived, while he was in Cairo, near one of the city gates, outside which there was a large hill with a tower and military telegraph on top. "This elevated position commanded a most magnificent view of the city and suburbs and the Citadel," Lane wrote. "Soon after my arrival I made a very elaborate drawing of the scene, with the camera Lucida. From no other spot can so good a view of the metropolis [. . .] be obtained" (Ahmed 1978: 26). Similarly, Gayer-Anderson enjoyed his privileged position in the Bait al-Kretliya on the elevated Yashkur hill, which overlooked the whole of the city of Cairo, and he could even see the Citadel. He was in perfect rhythm with the rest of the Western visitors who, while setting themselves apart in viewing the whole Eastern scene from a world-as-picture position, also wanted to experience it as though it were the real thing. Travellers wanted to immerse themselves in the Orient and "touch with their fingers a strange civilization" (Lane 1863–1893: vii). The desire for this immediacy of the real became a desire for direct and physical contact with the exotic, the bizarre, and the erotic. There was a contradiction, therefore, between the need to separate oneself from the world and render it up as an object of representation, and the desire to lose oneself within this object-world and experience it directly; a contradiction which world exhibitions, with their profusion of exotic detail and yet their clear distinction between visitor and exhibit, were built to accommodate and overcome.

Gayer-Anderson's museum was to fulfil this double desire. In the array of the objects and the creation of the showrooms Gayer-Anderson assumed the curious double position of the European as participant-observer that makes it possible to experience the Orient as though one were the visitor to an exhibition. The world is grasped, inevitably, as though it were 'a representation.' The exhibition (in our case the house/museum) persuades people that the world is divided into two fundamental realms—the representation and the original, the exhibit and the external reality, the text and the world. The so-called real world 'outside' is something experienced and grasped only as a series of further representations, an extended exhibition. The reality sought out by the European visitors was that which could be photographed, or else accurately represented that which presented itself as a picture of something before an observer. In the end the European tried to grasp the Orient as though it were an exhibition of itself. The European mind was continually searching for the certainty of representation—for an effect called 'reality.' The Orient is put together as this 're-presentation.' Such repetition and reworking is what Said has referred to as the citationary nature of Orientalism, its writings added to one another: "as a restorer of old sketches might put a series of them together for the cumulative picture they implicitly represent" (Said 1978: 176–177). As mentioned earlier when discussing the concept of exhibiting the Orient, the separation of an observed from an object-world was something a European experienced in terms of a code or plan. He expected something that was somehow set apart from 'things themselves' as a guide, a sign, a map, a text, or a set of instructions about how to proceed. However, the Orient refused to offer itself as a representation of something; it had not been arranged, that is, to effect the presence of some separate plan or meaning. The colonial process would try to re-order the Orient to appear as a world enframed. It was to be ordered as something object-like. It was to be made picture-like and legible—in the form of a museum.

In harmony with this concept Gayer-Anderson set out to put his select *objets d'art* in a certain order, to circumscribe, and to exclude. His framework set up the impression of something beyond the picture-world it enframed and displayed. Enframing is a method of dividing up and containing which operates by conjuring up a neutral surface or volume called 'space.' Within these containers, items can then be isolated, enumerated, and kept. Even the positioning of paintings, relics, statuettes, carpets, furniture, etc., can be specified to serve a function, a purpose, or a re-construction of an image. Articles in museums were arranged as 'signs of something further' and they conveyed the presence of history and culture. The absolute discernibility which was the principle of exhibitions was to be the principle of the world beyond as well. The careful ordering of the 'things' sought to make everything into a mere representation of something more real beyond itself, something original outside. However, the real outside was never quite reached. It was never represented. The cultural object was to be the primary signifier of a cultural, national, and ethnic identity which proclaimed and celebrated its integrity and 'difference' from the West. To accomplish this, the curators (as well as

Gayer-Anderson) deliberately selected cultural productions which straddled a number of different taxonomies, objects designated at various moments as the domains of ethnography, science, popular culture, and fine art. The cultural object was looked upon as a repository replete with meanings that were never immanent but always contingent. They had in their capacity aesthetic pleasure, exotic delectation, and spectacle. Racial purity, which characterized much of the aesthetic discourse around material culture from the colonies in the early part of the twentieth century, has been challenged to some degree by the current celebration of hybridity. As a means of validating the expansion of ethnographic collections, the argument was the necessity of conserving and preserving the material culture in the museum's custody, in the face of what was taken to be the inevitable extinction of the producers themselves. In this attempt to encapsulate the Orient, Gayer-Anderson's infatuation with the house, making it into a museum, and finally treating it like his muse and re-creating its legendary history, is all within the discipline of 'orientalism' and 'orientalising the orient.'

The Bait al-Kretliya. House and Legend

The house was built by Hajj Muhammad Salem Galmam el-Gazzar, as may be seen inscribed on the frieze surrounding the old ceilings in the loggia (*maq'ad*) and drinking fountain (*sebil*). At a later date (about 1800), the place came into the possession of a Muslim family from the Island of Crete, from which it derives its present name Bait al-Kretliya. 'The house of the Cretan Lady' is a beautiful example of a sixteenth–seventeenth-century Marnluk Bey's dwelling.[4] In detail the Bait al-Kretliya is typical of its period but in form it is unique, being in fact a double house. Like most houses of its kind, this ancient three-storeyed building is of local limestone and is somewhat austere and fortress-like in outward appearance. Its walls are relieved, however, by ample overhanging *mashrabiyyas* (latticed windows of intricate design) and graceful arched entrances.

The building stands by itself on the same rising ground called Jabal Yashkur or "Hill of Thanksgiving," as does the adjacent ninth-century mosque of Ibn Tulun. This is considered holy ground, for according to local tradition Noah's ark settled here after the deluge, the last waters of which subsided into the well which is now included within the courtyard of the house.

Here, too, it is said the Almighty revealed Himself to Moses in the Burning Bush, while close at hand at the Mastabet Faraoun this prophet confounded the pharaoh's magicians, whereas to the east of the mosque is the Fort of the Ram (Qal'at al-Kabsh), where Abraham made ready to sacrifice Isma'il, according to the Qur'an, and not Isaac as the Old Testament has it. Any house built on such a site and surrounded by such sacred traditions as these must surely be hallowed, all the more so by the presence of a saint on the premises, Shaykh Haroun al-Husayni.

The magic well (also referred to as the bats' well, or, "Bi'r el-Watawit") by reason of its sacred derivation from the flood waters, is said to possess magical properties. A lover looking in at full moon may behold the face of his true love reflected there, and at times one may hear sweet music and singing borne up from its depth, where dwells the beneficent King of the Jinn with his seven sleeping daughters who preside over a fabulous treasure.[5]

Gayer-Anderson's Position vis-à-vis the Local Inhabitants

After having lived in the Bait al-Kretliya for about a year, Gayer-Anderson learned that at first there had been considerable feeling aroused amongst the local inhabitants by the fact that a house with such sacred and legendary Islamic associations should be in the occupation of a Christian European. Gayer-Anderson appeased the anger of the mob, which he describes as "very tough and rough characters," by making various repairs to the tomb of the saint and restoring the *moulid* (a three-day festival). He commented that "it was not long before I felt that I had the confidence and even the affection of my neighbours and this, I think, was proved by their numerous visits to me in quest of advice, help and medical first-aid" (al-Kretli 1951: 15). Once again Gayer-Anderson was echoing the colonist attitude of the benevolent, superior, educated, knowledgeable, 'civilized' European.

In due time Gayer-Anderson befriended Shaykh Sulayrnan al-Kretli (head of the family from which the house took its name, and "the onlie begetter" of the tales). Shaykh Sulayrnan was the hereditary custodian of the tomb of Sidi Haroun al-Husayni (a direct descendant of the Prophet), whose remains he buried under the small white dome at the corner of the tiny front garden.

In perfect harmony with the Oriental stereotypical figure of the old wise man as storyteller, Gayer-Anderson is cleverly constructing the frame of the forthcoming legends. He goes on to say that the Shaykh's "voice was refined and well modulated from much recitation of the Koran" and adds that "his eyes had been 'burnt out' [. . .] when as a youth he had been trapped in a burning house from which saint Haroun, miraculously rescued him" and so the Shaykh perfectly fits the paradigm of the old, blind, wise, pious man who is full of stories from the past.[6] After establishing the narrator Gayer-Anderson moves on to identify the rest of the basic elements that feature in oral narratives of the East. He announces:

> It was not long before I sensed that, surrounding and enmeshing Sidi Haroun and his tomb, the House and its magic well, the Mosque and the neighbourhood in general, there was a network of legends which the Sheikh had acquired during his long life though he had never recorded them, and soon I began to question him concerning that complicated web. (al-Kretli 1951: 5)

Gayer-Anderson's role, like the rest of his fellow travellers to the Orient, was to discover, unravel, explain, and then ultimately record and document. He asserts: "It was only to be expected that this historic House of the Kretlis would have its own array of tales and legends waiting for me to set down from the lips of the Sheikh, its head." [7] Gayer-Anderson draws parallels between himself and translators of the *Arabian Nights*, and by doing that he is once more re-writing the Orient. He cleverly poses as the true tale-collector and echoes his contemporary travellers and orientalists in commending the East on its wealthy oral tradition, singling Egypt out as being still "richer in folk-yarns" (al-Kretli 1951: 5) than most of its neighbouring countries. In his introduction to the *Legends* he explains the exact process, methodology and technique that he followed in his collection and recording of the tales. He initially describes the daily sessions between him and the Shaykh, his narrator.

Needless to say, Gayer-Anderson's personal choice was the determining factor influencing and dictating his preference in relation to the stories. This in itself invites yet another query: were there any legends at the start? There are no documents or records of any sort that show any evidence of any Arabic legends related to the Bait al-Kretliya.[8] Gayer-Anderson, like many writers of his time, seemed to focus and crystallize current impressions and ideas. The general outline of what they conveyed, if not their detail, becomes part of the living body of knowledge and ideas of 'English' culture, and they play their part in shaping and influencing ideas, although it is a part that cannot easily be traced.

Method of Recording the Tales

Every representation exacts some cost, in the form of lost immediacy, presence, or truth, in the form of a gap between intention and realization, original and realization, original and copy. But representation does give us something in return for the tax it demands: the gap it opens. One of the things it gives us is literature.

Each cultural work is a vision of a moment, and we must juxtapose that vision with the various revisions it later provokes. The legends, like any other narrative, are a vision of a moment and as they were transmitted orally from one generation to the next they underwent various revisions, distillations, simplifications, additions, and were invariably changed by a set of choices made by the storytellers.

In that process of continuously telling and re-telling, the appropriation of history, the historization of the past, and the narrativization of society all gave these legends their force. "Such domestic cultural enterprises as narrative fiction and history are premised on the recording, ordering, observing powers of the central authorizing subject or ego" (Said 1994: 95).

In continuation of the museum-house discourse Gayer-Anderson went yet another step forward and registered the verbal discourse of the stories behind the house—the stories related to its first dwellers—and thus fulfilled the role of all the intellectuals who were infatuated by the East. After the re-discovering and re-collecting of the treasured cultural objects came the role of creating the aura that belonged to the imaginative realm of storytelling. What would be more fitting than folktales immersed in the cultural matrix of the house and its area? So Gayer-Anderson re-wrote the "Legends of Bait-al-Kretliya." A considerable proportion of the tales proved to be too trivial, crude, or repetitive to be worth recording, so they were discarded.

Finally, Gayer-Anderson states that the few tales he selected constituted an integral part of the history of the old house and its immediate neighbour-hood. There are fourteen tales altogether. "Seen from this [. . . .] perspec-tive the narrative may be regarded as a process of ordering or reordering, recounting, telling again what has already happened, or is taken to have already happened" (Miller qtd in Lentricchia 1995: 71).

Classification and Order

Four tales derived from Qur'anic sources come first as affording a back-ground to the rest. Gayer-Anderson compares these 'religious' legends to the bulk of Eastern legends that are a mixture of very doubtful ancient 'his-tory' embroidered with superstition and fancy. There is no indication that the order of the *arrangement* of the legends is meaningful. They persuade through their weight and cumulative effect and not through their develop-ment. This in itself gives the impression of their vulnerability and lends itself to manipulation. Gayer-Anderson admitted that he cut and pasted to suit his taste and since the text he worked from is nonexistent we are unable to judge his re-arrangement.[9]

Themes

The legends, whether of the mosque, the house or the well, centre around the tomb of the Saint Haroun al-Husayni. Legends, we are told, were originally miracle stories of saints—lives designed for instruction and read at religious services or meals—but the term now includes stories, presumably based on fact, in which traditional elements about people, places, or incidents have become inextricably mixed. A legend is told as if it is the truth. Like myths, legendary material is an indispensable part of man's literary culture.[10]

Most tales express a set of sentiments that are central to members of the community. As Stanley Fish explains, the text proceeds from the interpre-tive community of which the individual is a member and repeatedly empha-sizes that readers live and work within sets of institutions. The experience of reading, in turn, is therefore not open or free but constrained by a conven-tional way of thinking that is dictated by the community.[11] The emotional or affective component of a tale determines a group's attitude toward the tale.

Feelings about kinship relations; ethnic and religious groups; and significant objects, ideas, and values are major forces around which a tale coheres.

Classifications of Traditions

> Folk groups in Egypt recognize four broad categories of prose narratives: serious, non-serious, and humorous narratives, and un-delineated narrative talk. These categories are a product of the cognitive process of grouping; themes perceived to be similar are grouped together. (El-Shamy 1980: xliv)

The legends of Bait al-Kretliya belong to the first category. Moralistic, historical, and religious stories are known as *qissah,* and serious narrative is always described thus: "a true occurrence," "really took place," "did not really happen, but it could have," or "a story of wisdom." Occasionally, the term *qissah* is also used to refer to a traditional story which comes from a printed source.

Formulas in the Tale

Apart from the creative vocabulary which may distinguish the style of a narrator of an established oral tradition, Egyptian narrators employ numerous verbal formulas in the course of their communication with the audience. All this was preserved by Gayer-Anderson in his English translation of the legends. An example is the opening statement at the beginning of each story which praises God through the use of the formula "In the name of God the most merciful." Numerous verbal formulas current in oral tradition appear in tales as a matter of course: these include truisms, maxims, proverbs, proverbial phrases, proverbial similes, and recurrent quotations form religious literature. Most folk narratives do not have fixed titles. Tales are usually referred to in a descriptive manner, and a salient theme or episode serves as an identifying mark, as in "Ahmed Ibn Tulun builds his Mosque."

This particular legend serves as a typical example of how Gayer-Anderson represented the Orient. The main theme of this legend, as is clear from its title, is a narration of the history of the building of the Ibn Tulun Mosque. It explains why the Sultan chose the particular location of Jabal Yashkur to set his mosque upon. One of the main reasons is that "the holy Ark of Noah was still stranded here on the hill of Yashkur" (al-Kretli 1951: 48). The Sultan collected all the remaining planks and had the entire Qur'an carved on them. Gayer-Anderson then includes as many as six extensive footnotes explaining and commenting on the story.[12] Needless to say, these notes allow Gayer-Anderson to show off his knowledge of Egyptian history and folklore. In note number one, he gives a detailed explanation about the Sultan Ahmad Ibn Tulun and mentions names of Western and Arab historians like al-Jabarti, Creswell and Edward Lane to emphasize further the authenticity of his information. He also speaks as an authority on Islam and appends a note on the Imam al-Shafu "as the founder of the orthodox sect of Islam that bears his name and to which the majority of Egyptian Muslims belong" (al-Kretli 1951: 49). It is indeed noteworthy that Gayer-Anderson's comments and documentation are longer than the legend itself.

In terms of style, Gayer-Anderson closely adheres to all the conventions of the oral tradition. The story starts with the usual opening sentences praising God and the Prophet Muhammad, and the entire narrative is full of expressions that bless the main characters figuring in the events. In addition to that, Gayer-Anderson punctuates the entire discourse with phrases conjuring up God's name and asking for His mercy, compassion, and forgiveness. All these studied devices led to the creation of an assembly of tales that are firmly grounded in the Eastern folkloric tradition of storytelling. This 'semblance' of telling the truth, of recording the house's history, was further enhanced by the Arabic inscriptions engraved on the copper plates. Gayer-Anderson always made sure that a date was included (as in "here in the year 263 Hegira the generous Sultan Ahmed Ibn Tulun came and worked with his own hands and built his Mosque"), to serve as historical evidence proving that the legends hold some truth. Similarly, the recurrent motifs of folk literature like supernatural beings, evil spirits, magic, enchantment, and unusual happenings are all present in the various legends. In this particular legend Gayer-Anderson mentions the belief that a "fabulous treasure was revealed to Sultan Ibn Tulun by a beneficent jinn and this gold he set aside for no other purpose than his building" of the mosque (al-Kretli 1951: 48). In note number five Gayer-Anderson states that many searches for the residual treasure have been made without success, and that the approach was "from the large cistern in the salamlik of the Bait al-Kretliya almost directly under the main doorway of the Mosque." This conscious attempt on Gayer-Anderson's part to weave a common history between the Mosque and the House is in harmony with the general consensus, by most Orientalists, to add this extra dimension in their re-writing of the East.

Visual Discourse

In further connection with the idea of a museum house, Gayer-Anderson had the fourteen legends illustrated by 'Abd al- 'Aziz 'Abduh. This Egyptian craftsman/artist produced fourteen copper plates, each with one engraving corresponding to one of the legends. The collection of these dinner plates is kept in a cabinet in the museum.[13] The original drawings are printed at the beginning of each legend. Gayer-Anderson commends the illustrator on his excellent work by saying:

> I feel that the form of illustration which Abd-al-Aziz has employed could not have been improved upon justly to convey the sense, feeling

and atmosphere of the following folk and Koranic legends. (al-Kretli 1951: 12)

It is difficult to mistake the patronizing and condescending tone of Gayer-Anderson in the previous quotes. Once again he echoes the Western travellers' assumption that they were engaged in a holy mission to save the East and preserve its otherwise lost history.

As in much medieval work, the illustrator has shown several of the main incidents of a tale or scenes from other tales in the same illustration. There is a certain sameness about most of the backgrounds. This is by design and not due to lack of imagination or creative ability on the part of the artist. He has deliberately introduced into nearly every background four important motifs. Three of them are architectural and are labelled:

'the tomb of Haroon'	- (domed top)
'the Mosque of Ibn Tulun'	- (spiral minaret)
'the Bait al-Kretliya'	- (windows + arched doorway)

The fourth is not labelled and consists of a large pointed tree which will be seen to take a prominent place in all but four of the sixteen designs. The artist has introduced this device because 'a tree' is the author's 'Anderson' crest and therefore represents him historically throughout the legends just as Haroon, Ibn Tulun and the Kretlis are represented by their buildings. Gayer-Anderson is consciously establishing his equal stature as a key figure in the making of both the House's and the Mosque's history. On each design will be seen a main inscription in Arabic and usually some labelling as well; all are in the colloquial, not the classical language. The main inscription gives the general purport of the legend and as a rule includes the artist's name.

With the completion of the recording of the legends which "constitute an integral part of the history of the old House and its immediate neighbourhood" (al-Kretli 1951: 6), it is clear that Gayer-Anderson's contribution to the writing of the Orient is now terminated and is in its turn added to the repertoire of the Western imagination. The museum house, the collection of the oral tradition, the drawings that qualified the legends, have all fallen within the discipline by which the Orient has been approached systematically, as a topic of learning, discovery, and practice.

Gayer-Anderson's initial project was to exhibit the East in his precious collections which ranged from India and China to the Levant and Egypt that he so carefully displayed in the various rooms of the house with the metaphysical ambition that this *museum* would give an adequate ordered rational representation of reality. This project was doomed from the start. He came to realize that representation within the concept of the museum was intrinsically impossible. The museum can only display objects metonymically at least twice removed from that which they are originally supposed to represent or signify. The objects displayed as a series are of necessity only part of the totality to which they originally belonged. Spatially and temporally detached from their origin and function, they signify only by arbitrary and derived associations. Therefore, Gayer-Anderson chose another more forceful and possibly more permanent means of representing and hence preserving the Orient: the writing of the legends. As other sources of information on the Oriental world besides *The Arabian Nights* began to be available, new images began to be fed into the Oriental world that already existed for the English imagination.

Thus, in addition to making use of the usual paraphernalia of the Oriental tale, Gayer-Anderson added to the legends researched notes on Islam, particularly on its mythologies relating to supernatural beings and its personification of evil. Since the legends were set in a world as remote and unreal as that of dreams, they were insulated from the world of ordinary daily experience by their setting as well as their nature. Because of the richness of vivid concrete detail that forms part of their texture, they presented a world that possessed, as Conant has said, "a strange sense of reality in the midst of unreality" (Conant 1908: 5), and which, at the same time, was experienced above all on an imaginative plane. Irrational events and sequences that flout the laws of the everyday world, characteristic of most folk-tales, are apt and natural in the world of dreams. So aptly indeed did the world of the *Arabian Nights* represent that of dream that native literature (specifically oral tradition) adopted the 'Oriental world' as a means of signifying a reality other than that of ordinary daily experience. Soon, the Oriental world became established as the metaphor for the realities of dream, of imagination, and eventually, of poetry. Gayer-Anderson's *Legends of the Bait al-Kretliya* evoked an 'Oriental' world in their own right. Hence, they transcended the limitations of the traditional museum world and soared into the realm of the imagination. This effect was even further reinforced by the illustrations to the work: Translating the verbal description into the line, they continually gave the force and finish of permanent art. The engravings on the copper plates offer authentic glimpses of the Ibn Tulun Mosque, the sacred well, the Saint's tomb, the Bait al-Kretliya, and even Gayer-Anderson himself.

Finally, this cultural appropriation by the West, in its attempt to preserve 'the disappearing world,' produced visual narratives in ethnographic museums, art galleries, and private collections that all served the concept of yet another discourse. I would like to add here that in continuation of that tradition Gayer-Anderson's nephew produced a set of children's illustrations of one of the legends, "Lotfiya," which has been re-written, to be suitable for children, by yet another Englishman, Andy Smart, who resides in Cairo . . . So the discourse continues.

Notes

1. Bachelard explains further the significance of the house as an entity by saying: "[T]he sheltered being [. . .] experiences the house in its reality and in its virtuality, by means of thought and dreams. It is no longer in its positive aspects that the house is really 'lived,' nor is it only in the passing hour that we recognize its benefits. An entire past comes to dwell in a new house. [. . .] And the daydream deepens to the point where an immemorial domain opens up for the dreamer of a home beyond man's earliest memory. The house [. . .] permits us [. . .] to recall flashes of daydreams that illuminate the synthesis of immemorial and recollected. In this remote region, memory and imagination remain associated, each one working for their mutual deepening. In the order of values, they both constitute a community of memory and image. Thus the house is not experienced from day to day only, on the thread of a narrative, or in the telling of our own story. Through dreams, the various dwelling-places in our lives co-penetrate and retain the treasures of former days" (Bachelard 1969: 5).

2. See Timothy Mitchell's *Colonising Egypt* (Cairo: AUC Press, 1988: 13–14): "If Europe was becoming the world-as-exhibition, I am going to ask, what happened to Europeans who left and went abroad? How did they experience a life not yet lived, so to speak, as though the world were a picture of something set up before an observer's gaze? [. . .] Reality was that which presents itself as exhibit, so nothing else would have been thinkable."

3. McClintock also states: "At the Exhibition, the progress narrative began to be consumed as mass spectacle. The Exhibition gathered under one vaulting glass roof a monumental display of 'the Industry of All Nations'. Covering fourteen acres of park, it featured exhibitions and artifacts from thirty-two invited members of the 'family of Nations'. Crammed with industrial commodities, decorative merchandise, ornamental gardens, machinery, musical instruments and industrial ore and thronged by thousands of marveling spectators, the Great Exhibition became a monument not only to a new form of mass consumption but also to a new form of commodity spectacle" (McClintock 1995: 56–57).

4. It dates from the period AH 1040/AD 1631.

5. This is dealt with in legends eight and ten in *Legends of the Bait al-Krediya*.

6. Besides being a counsellor and composer of charms, philters and talismans, Shaykh Sulayman was also a sorcerer versed in magic and mysteries of all sorts but especially in *mandal* (divination).

7. The tales first appeared in "The Sphinx" of Cairo in 1940, and were published in the UK in 1951 by Gayer-Anderson's twin brother.

8. In all the folkloric collections and references in Arabic there is no mention of any stories, legends, or folktales related to this particular house.

9. See Jan Vansina, *Oral Tradition: A Study in Historical Methodology* (Vansina 1965).

10. For further definitions of the terms legend and folktale see V. Propp, *The Morphology of the Folk Tale* (Propp 1975a) and *Theory and History of Folklore* (Propp 1975b); Stith Thompson, *The Folktale* (Thompson 1946).

11. Stanley Fish states: "It is the reader who 'makes' literature" (*Is There a Text in this Class?*).

12. An example of these notes is the following: "All timbers are carved in Kufic characters, a script that may be compared to our early Gothic. A considerable proportion of them is still *in situ* and are certainly contemporary with the building of the mosque (ninth century). Though very extensive, the inscriptions carved on them can only have recorded a few chapters of the Koran."

13. The first to underscore the epistemological importance of archaeology and of museums is Raymond Swab in *La Renaissance orientale* (Paris: Payot, 1950). In particular, he writes: "The museum is no longer so much a conservatory of models as a storehouse of information; the masterpiece, formerly a source not only of pleasure and a standard of taste, now must share the same room with household artifacts; it is placed side by side with the commercial object on an exhibit table." (410)

Works Cited

Al-Kretli, S.S. (1951) *Legends of the Bait al-Kretliya*, trans. R.G.J. Gayer-Anderson. Illust. Abd al-Aziz Abdu, Ipswich: East Anglian Daily Times.

Ahmed, L. (1978) *Edward W. Lane*, London and New York: Longman.

Bachelard, G. (1969 [1994]) *The Poetics of Space*, Boston: Beacon Press.

Conant, M.P. (1908) *The Oriental Tale in England in the Eighteenth Century*, New York: The Columbia University Press.

El–Shamy, H.M. (1980) *Folktales of Egypt*, Chicago and London: University of Chicago Press.

Fish, S. (1980) *Is There a Text in this Class? The Authority of Interpretive Communities*, Cambridge, MA: Harvard University Press.

Hillis Miller, J. (1995) 'Narrative', in F. Lentricchia and T. McLaughlin (eds) *Critical Terms for Literary Study*, Chicago and London: University of Chicago Press.

Lane, E.W. (1863–1893) *Arabic-English Lexicon*, S. Lane-Poole (ed.), London: Williams and Norgate.

McClintock, A. (1995) *Imperial Leather*, New York and London: Routledge.

Mitchell, T. (1988) *Colonising Egypt*, Cambridge: Cambridge University Press.

Propp, V. (1975a) *The Morphology of the Folk Tale*, Austin and London: University of Texas Press.

——. (1975b) *Theory and History of Folklore*, Austin: University of Texas Press.

Said, E. (1978) *Orientalism*, London and Henley: Routledge and Kegan Paul.

——. (1994) *Culture and Imperialism*, London: Vintage.

Swab, R. (1950) *La Renaissance orientale*, Paris: Payot.

Thompson, S. (1946) *The Folktale*, New York: Holt, Rinehart and Winston.

Vansina, J. (1965) *Oral Tradition: A Study in Historical Methodology*, London: Routledge and Kegan Paul.

10 . . . What Will Count as the World

Indian Short Story Cycles and the Question of Genre

Dirk Wiemann

For a Reflexive Theory of Genre

"To look at literature through genres is to grasp the former historically," claims Stephen Heath (2004: 168), therewith summarily formularizing a consensus that appears to prevail amongst critical theorists in the West who attempt to map literature in the social at large. For Heath, the category of genre is indispensable in such a task inasmuch as genres

> are precisely not 'natural' forms or abstract categories, but specific socio-historical operations of language by speakers and listeners, writers and readers: orders of discourse that change, shift, travel, lose force, come and go over time and cultures. (Heath 2004: 168)

In the same vein, Fredric Jameson's programme of a historicizing reconstructive hermeneutics puts a premium on a contractual model of genre conceived as historically embedded "literary institutions that specify the proper use of a particular cultural artifact" (Jameson 1981: 106). Conceived as institutions, genres are thus not immanent to the text but "more appropriately regarded as themselves directly sets of social relations which, in structuring the sphere of reading practices, serve also to condition writing practices" (Bennett 1990: 103–104). These "sets of social relations" include, among others, the manifold paratextual signals deployed by publishing companies (mostly in order to slot texts for specific target groups) but also the ongoing proliferation of secondary discourses produced by professional critics. It could indeed be argued that genre is partly the result of its theorization: that it, in other words, presents itself as a reality only inasmuch as it is represented as that reality. Genre is not simply an explicatory 'tool' that helps to tame the singularity of the concrete text; more than that, the genres produced and consolidated by theory operate as devices with defining and discriminatory, inclusive and exclusive power effects. At stake is not only the acknowledgement of the mutability, and hence historicity, of genres but the historicization of the *production* of genre, that is, the concrete analysis of those processes and agencies through which genres are made to 'come and go over time and cultures.' In this line of enquiry, critical engagement with the category of genre has to become reflexive and hence an engagement with the production of genre-as-power in and by theory itself. It is at this stage that the question of genre begins to attain certain relevance for postcolonial projects inasmuch as a reflexive, self-historicizing genre theory may enable the critic to address not only how genres 'work' as literary institutions, but also how criticism itself is implicated in the consolidation—or unsettling—of the prevalent "monologism of literature's institutions" (Hitchcock 2003: 314). For it cannot go unnoticed that, even after some thirty years of academic postcolonialism, the various historicizations of genres as institutions have by and large remained stubbornly reluctant to engage in "reflections on the genre systems of different literary cultures [that] form an indispensable part of the intellectual preparation of more globally oriented perspectives on literary history" (Lindberg-Wada 2006: 1). In other words, reflexive genre theory is marked by the responsibility of the critic who contributes to the discourse of genre and thereby necessarily and ineluctably helps to (re)constitute the very genre s/he writes (about). In whatever miniscule way, then, every reflection on genre partakes of what Judith Butler asserts as the general effect of "the production of texts [that] can be one way of reconfiguring what will count as the world" (Butler 1993: 19).

Obviously, most Western genre theories have by and large contributed to the configuration and continuation of Eurocentric discourses by systematically neglecting non-Western modes of literary representation, by ascribing exclusively occidental origins to canonical literary forms, and by applying Western generic categories to types of text from widely discrepant traditions around the world. Twentieth-century theories of the novel are a pertinent case in point. Theorists as irreconcilable as F.R. Leavis, Ian Watt, Franco Moretti, and Margaret Anne Doody,[1] to name a few, seem to be in agreement on at least one issue: namely, that the dominant modern narrative genre—the novel—has emerged and been consolidated in Europe, and from European cultural resources alone, as a modular form that, in subsequent stages, got exported and differentially appropriated worldwide. As recently as 2003, Margaret Cohen, in an article that makes much of the novel's "cross-cultural and supranational" (Cohen 2003: 481) genesis, strictly omits any transcontinental or global history of the novel by reducing the generic cosmopolitanism of the novel to its mobility among the national literatures of the European heartlands: "What [she asks] is the first modern novel? *Don Quijote*? *La princesse de Clèves*? *Simplicissimus*? *The Pilgrim's Progress, La Télémaque, Orinooko* [sic]? *Robinson Crusoe*?" (Cohen 2003: 481). By what it includes and what it excludes, Cohen's catalogue tacitly produces comparative literature as the closed circularity of "cross-currents between European languages and within the western canon" (Helgesson 2006: 311).

From this position, the global history of the novel can only be conceived as the dissemination of an originally European form, as if cultural flows were always and invariably a 'voyage out' from the West. Franco Moretti's stimulating discussion of the literary world-system is a case in point: If, as Moretti has it, "the literature around us is now a planetary system," then this system operates in the mode of a "unified and uneven market" (Moretti 1998: 158), of centre and peripheries. With due precaution, Moretti proposes a cluster of laws of literary evolution resulting from the itineraries of genres from the centre to the margins:

> in cultures that belong to the periphery of the literary system (which means: almost all cultures, inside and outside Europe), the modern novel first arises not as an autonomous development, but as a compromise between a Western formal influence (usually French or English) and local materials. (Moretti 2004: 152)

On this account, then, the novel, having first 'risen' autonomously in some parts of Europe, gets exported to the intra- and extra-European peripheries where it is 'locally' modified in the process of its appropriation. A reflexive account of genre migration would have to acknowledge and address the politics involved in discussing the itineraries of genre. While postcolonial studies have traditionally focused on the transformative effects of creative genre appropriation or abrogation by writers from (formerly) colonized countries, the basic assumption of a primacy of European forms has largely remained intact inasmuch as these latter figure as "a basis on which the indigenous literature in English could develop" (Ashcroft et al. 1989: 182). Tracing the multiple postcolonial modes of writing back to the centre, however, this approach has to confirm the precedence of the centre in the first place and lose sight of the transcontinental interdependencies thanks to which that centre has historically evolved. As a result, there remains the residual risk to subscribe to the very "myth of the West" (Shohat and Stam 1994: 13) that has persistently underpinned the various discourses of Eurocentrism. Would it be possible to question the givenness of the centre's autonomy and thus effectively rule out the all-too-often prevalent notions of the dissemination of already established Western forms? Could the genesis of the novel as a genre be revised as a product of *planetary* cooperation?

Despite the scarcity of historical revisions of the 'global rise of the novel,' some suggestive work has been done in this direction. Nancy Armstrong and Leonard Tennenhouse, e.g., claim that "English fiction comes from captivity narratives" (Armstrong and Tennenhouse 1992: 216). In this perspective, the rise of the novel in eighteenth-century England cannot be grasped without taking into account the constitutive experience of captivity of British subjects at the hands of Native Americans. Hence it would be misleading to see the novel as "first and foremost a European genre, but rather one that simultaneously recorded and recoded the colonial experience" (Armstrong and Tennenhouse 1992: 197). In a similar vein, Firdauz Azim tries to show that the experience of colonialism—now not of captivity but of colonial mastery—is at the bottom of the unified narrative voice of the modern novel: According to Azim's revision, "the notion of the centrality of this subject and of the homogeneity of its narration had come into being within the colonising enterprise" (Azim 1993: 31). If these are revisions of Eurocentric notions of narrative voice, subjectivity and authorship, other scholars have tried to show how non-Western structural elements have been 'borrowed into' the western novel in the process of its consolidation. I mention only the work of Ros Ballaster, whose study on *Fabulous Orients* traces the modes through which, in the early eighteenth century, the genre of the 'Oriental Tale' was introduced in Europe via translation and simultaneously incorporated into the emergent novel form: "The 'form' of the eastern tale constantly resurfaces in the eighteenth-century European novel [. . .]. The realist occidental novel, like the western Enlightenment of which it was a part, was always already 'oriental'" (Ballaster 2005: 58). Certainly the works of Armstrong and Tennenhouse, Azim and Ballaster do not coagulate into one unified counter-narrative to the dominant story of the novel as a genre. Rather, they offer glimpses of the global genesis of a representational form whose full transmodern genealogy is still waiting to be written in a thoroughly reflexive perspective on genre: a genealogy, then, "that has to simultaneously produce the very position from which it can be elaborated" (Wiemann 2008: 308).

Beyond Novelism

If "we have become incapable of thinking beyond the nation-state, as if any other form of community is inconceivable" (Lal 2003: 206), then this impoverishment of the political imaginary finds its equivalent, in terms of economics, in the suspicion that "it seems easier for us today to imagine the deterioration of the earth and of nature than the breakdown of late capitalism" (Jameson 1998: 50). Could it be that this monoculture of the mind has extended its reach into the field of cultural production itself? After all, as far as literary narrative is concerned, "the habitual subordination of [all] writing to the novel" has given rise to a generic monologism that Clifford Siskin has aptly labelled "novelism" (Siskin 1996: 423). While Siskin is primarily interested in the historical impacts of this one-sided privileging of one genre over all others to the effect of "'domesticating' myriad practices and genres of modern writing that by the nineteenth century had come to be considered a social threat" (Rastegar 2007: 13), novelism in the contemporary postcolonial arena continues to "occlude the massive contribution made by oral narratives in decolonizing states" (Hitchcock 2003: 314). I would wish to add that the persistence and dynamic development of non-novelistic narrative forms in the postcolonial world is not necessarily restricted to *oral* genres.

For the rest of this article, I will focus on the genre of the story cycle which I propose to be read as conducive to a political imaginary that may possibly foster a 'thinking beyond the nation-state.' Therefore, the underlying assumption of my argument will be implicitly parasitical on the far more elaborate theorization of the novel, and indeed crucially indebted to Benedict Anderson's suggestions concerning the nexus between the literary genre of the novel and the political genre of the nation. For Anderson, the novel is *the* representational form that due to "its spectacular possibilities for the representation of simultaneous actions in homogeneous empty time" (Anderson 1991: 194) allows for the imagining of the nation. Both novel and nation, Anderson argues, are premised on secularism, on the vernacular, on print capitalism and on the experiential medium of homogeneous empty time. Postcolonial theorists, especially Partha Chatterjee, have taken Anderson to task for his elevation of the various nation-forms that evolved in the European context to a 'set of modular forms' with global validity and applicability: "If nationalisms in the rest of the world have to choose their imagined community from certain 'modular' forms already made available to them by Europe and the Americas, what do they have left to imagine?" (Chatterjee 1993: 5). Chatterjee argues in the name of a plurality of modes of political affiliation that he subsumes under the name of 'community' conceived as the umbrella term for all subjugated forms of polity that have historically been left "untheorized, relegated to the primordial zone of the natural, denied any subjectivity that is not domesticated to the requirements of the modern state" (Chatterjee 1993: 239). Still I would hold that Anderson's nation-novel nexus could be usefully applied as soon as one allowed for the coexistence of *other genres*. If Chatterjee's is a call to overcome nationism, then why not combine this with an analogous call to overcome novelism? Why not turn to alternative modes of narrative and their alternative modes of addressing and figuring collectivity? It is for this that I turn to the short-story cycle as a genre that, as I will suggest, provides a representational apparatus for imagining community without restricting this latter to the nation-form.

In spite of its proliferation and popularity, the short-story cycle has as yet received little critical attention and thus forms a kind of generic grey area. As a genre, the short-story cycle combines self-sufficient stories to create a linked series, evoking interrelations and coherence of apparently discrepant narrative units. This coherence may be achieved "according to one or more organizing principles" such as a setting, a single or collective protagonist, or a narrative pattern that all individual narrative units have in common (Dunn and Morris 1995: 14–16); most effectively, of course, coherence is ensured through the establishment of a frame narrative as fictional locus of enunciation of the individual narrative units. Such grouping of autonomous narrative pieces that together achieve the effect of whole-text coherence appears "at once ancient and avant-garde" (Kennedy 1995a: vii). Western readers will easily associate a book of interrelated narrative units with the architecture of the *Decameron* or the *Canterbury Tales* as much as with episodic films like Jim Jarmush's *Night on Earth* or such collective short film collages as *Ten Minutes Older* or *9/11*. In between these poles of the medieval and the (post)modernist, however, there lie "[l]acunae of centuries [that] call into question the very notion of a sustained tradition" of the genre in Western literary history (Kennedy 1995a: vii).

As a contrast, the composite narrative in India not only predates the discontinuous European tradition;[2] but seems to have enjoyed an unbroken continuity in Indian writing. Meenakshi Mukherjee asserts the persistent "influence of the puranic tradition, of interrelated oral narratives," the vitality in Indian writing of "pre-novel narratives" made up of "a larger story which contains a smaller one which in turn contains a smaller and so on" (Mukherjee 1985: 5). While Mukherjee relates this observation primarily to the nineteenth century, it goes without saying that short-story cycles have a veritable status in contemporary Indian writing as well, as such collections as Rohinton Mistry's *Tales from Firozsha Baag* (1987), Gita Mehta's *A River Sutra* (1993), Vikram Chandra's *Love and Longing in Bombay* (1997), or Rana Dasgupta's *Tokyo Cancelled* (2005) indicate. What becomes immediately apparent is that all these collections evoke a coherence of the independent narrative units by virtue of the unity of the chronotope. In fact, one could say that, in the story cycles from Mistry to Dasgupta, it is the function of each individual narrative to contribute to the construction and fleshing out of that overarching chronotope. In that sense, these volumes are all updated versions of the village sketch, a genre that Dunn and Morris identify as a nineteenth-century precursor of the contemporary short-story cycle. According to Dunn and Morris, the village sketch loosely combines a set of narratives that are linked primarily through setting: "In such works, one could capture a 'sense of place' in many minute particulars, including among these particulars an ethos of community that reflects a complex network of human lives" (Dunn and Morris 1995: 23). Thus, the eleven stories that make up Rohinton Mistry's cycle elucidate various facets of social life in the Bombay resident complex of Firozsha Baag. With clear resonances of Chaucer, Gita Mehta's *A River Sutra* comprises the tales of visitors (most of them pilgrims) at a remote rest-house on the Narmada river; these stories are interwoven with the framing narrative presented by the resident hostel overseer—a blend, then, of the figures of 'Chaucer-the-pilgrim' and 'the Host' in *The Canterbury Tales*—whose voice ensures that the individual tales fall into one coherent pattern and collaboratively evoke a multi-religious India held together by the common denominator of convivial spirituality. In a different but still compatible way, Vikram Chandra's five narratives in *Love and Longing in Bombay*—all presented by an evasive narrator figure named Subramaniam— can be read in their interplay as aspects of the metropolitan city, fleshing out particular modes of negotiating the urban experience that one inhabits. Arguably these story cycles are contemporary versions of the village sketch:

fictions of *localization*, however complex and complicated. In the broadest sense of the term, they focus on the basic categories of dwelling and belonging, even if they dramatize the loss of an intact 'organic' mooring. The place that such short-story cycles figure is therefore always social space which, as Henri Lefebvre insists, "implies, contains and dissimulates social relationships" (Lefebvre 1974 [1991: 83]). In that vein, the classical village sketch collection, Mary Mitford's *Our Village* (serially published between 1820 and 1830), celebrates and idealizes rural life in a social space "where we know every one, are known by every one, interested in every one, and authorized to hope that every one feels an interest in us" (Mitford 1986: 7). In line with this extrapolation of a chronotope as social space, the short-story cycle may moreover be conceived in a formal homology to the sociological category of community as a mode of affiliation under siege (see, for the Indian context, Chatterjee 1993). In that sense, J. Gerald Kennedy observes that "the genre [of the short-story cycle] embodies an insistently paradoxical semblance of community in its structural dynamic of connection and disconnection" (Kennedy 1995b: 195): Both independent and interdependent, the individual narrative units form an affiliation that link them "to a larger scheme of order and meaning" (Kennedy 1995b: 194), without, however, fully subsuming them as mere components of a larger whole. In this light, then, short-story cycles from Mistry to Dasgupta are, as updated village sketches, about a sense of *communal place*, about particular places that may be called Malgudi, Firozsha Baag, Bombay, or even India.

Tokyo Cancelled

In Rana Dasgupta's *Tokyo Cancelled* the village sketch has been blown up to the dimensions of a sketch of the global village. The global, "counterintuitive" (Spivak 1998: 329) and hence particularly resistant to representation, does of course not lend itself easily as a chronotope, that is, as the artistically processed, modelled or configured temporal space of a representable world. As Peter Hulme has pointed out, however, "allegories of the globe might possibly offer some improvement" of what he calls the "Eurocentric flat-earth imagery" that, with its "language of 'ends' and 'margins'" reiterates a geopolitical scenario of centres and peripheries (Hulme 2006: 51). In that vein, Dasgupta's global village sketch becomes ultimately readable as an attempt to figure a postcolonial planetarity articulated through the conjuncture of narratives from all over the world. Dasgupta appears to be keenly sensitive to the representational dilemma of the globe as chronotope. He chooses to locate his frame narrative in a setting marked by the full absence of all the criteria of Lefebvre's social space, namely in the paradigmatic 'non-place' of an airport lounge.

In a heavy snowstorm, a plane headed for Tokyo is grounded at nightfall at an unidentified provincial airport, somewhere in some unspecified country.

Of the 323 passengers, thirteen cannot be accommodated in the hotels and guesthouses of the adjacent nondescript town—they have to spend the night in the empty terminal building closed for the night. Stranded beside the baggage carousels in an echoing arrivals hall, they huddle up, passing around packets of peanuts and final cigarettes until one of them suggests that "when you are together like this then stories are what is required" (Dasgupta 2005: 7). And so the night is passed with each of the thirteen stranded passengers telling one story.

Some time ago, James Clifford has proposed that "the 'chronotope' of culture (a setting or scene organizing time and space in representable whole form) comes to resemble as much a site of travel encounters as of residence" (Clifford 1997: 25). While Clifford illustrates his thesis with the chronotope of the hotel as an apex of such travelling cultures of ephemeral encounters, French anthropologist Marc Augé goes further by elevating the airport (the setting of the frame narrative in *Tokyo Cancelled*) to the status of *the* emblematic chronotope of supermodernity—with the caveat that this type of chronotope is not a place at all but a 'non-place' devoid of all those residues of 'residence' that Clifford still allows for the hotel. Augé's airport is no longer a site of what Paul Virilio called "habitable circulation" (Virilio 2006: 31), but a space designed for the sole purpose of being passed through. Diagnoses or prognostications of this kind appear to usher in a brand new cultural condition of nomadic mobility, roots-to-routes fluctuation, and pervasive delocalization; and yet it cannot go unnoticed that—at least as far as narrative is concerned—there is *also* a note of 'return' implied in the deployment of the chronotope of the 'travel encounter': Bakhtin, one will remember, had identified 'the road as locale of chance encounters' as the historically earliest, emphatically premodern chronotope of epic narrative, for it is

> on the road (the "country road") that the spatial and temporal itineraries of the most discrepant characters, of the representatives of all strata and ranks, of all creeds, nationalities and age groups, may be made to converge in one single spatio-temporal point. (Bakhtin 1989: 192, my tr.)

Sites of transit, then, may figure as paradigms of some supermodern condition of cutting-edge global mobility while simultaneously harking back to some well-nigh archetypal locus of enunciation of narrative itself. In short, Dasgupta's airport lounge is as much an embodiment of Augé's non-place as it is a return to the *Panchatantra*'s ashram, to the caravanserai of the *Arabian Nights*, Bocaccio's Tuscan villa, or Chaucer's inn.

Marc Augé defines supermodern non-places (shopping malls, motorways, chain hotels, and most prominently, airports) in opposition to (older) 'anthropological place' that answers to the well-worn ideal of socially constructed and dynamically coproduced space (in the sense of Lefebvre) and hence in turn "creates the organically social" (Augé 1995: 94). As a contrast, non-places "cannot be defined as relational, or historical, or concerned with identity" (Augé 1995: 77–78): Even when they comprise cafés, restaurants, and retail spaces, they are by definition transit locations. In the words of Pico Iyer, the airport offers "all these amenities to people who don't really want to be there, whose only attention is on when they can get out" (Iyer 2000: 57). Apparently self-enclosed places, self-sufficient capsules in space, airports defy all vernacularization: Whatever 'local touch' the individual airport precinct may display, it will invariably be transformed into a simulation, a hyperreal theme park. Obviously, then, airports refuse to be 'localized.' Even if not all airports around the world may be identical, there still is "a sameness to them throughout the world" (Fuller and Harley 2004: 38). According to Fuller and Harley,

> a refrain of aviation aesthetics has emerged in the contemporary architecture of airports—the beep of metal detection, the expanses of glass overlooking the apron, the international pictograms, the slick retail space. This refrain seems to soothe the disorientation produced by the constancy of transit in modern lives. (Fuller and Harley 2004: 42)

In perceptual terms, then, airports (as well as other non-places) are not so much integrated into their immediate geographical environment as they are yoked into *global* networks. They connect with other airports rather than with the cities or countries beyond their confines. This, one will remember, is one of the key features that Fredric Jameson construes from his 'experience' of the L.A. Bonaventure Hotel as "a total space, a complete world, a kind of miniature city [which] does not want to be part of the city but rather its equivalent and replacement or substitute" (Jameson 1991: 40).

Next to this process of de-localization, Augé makes out a feature that could be called contractualization. The individual visitor is continuously interpellated into 'contractual relations' with the non-place (Augé 1995: 101) as passenger, client, or customer—in any case, a transitory figure passing through. Already Paul Virilio had, in his typically lyricist manner, described airports as "sites of accelerated ejection, rendered uninhabitable, where the particular individual becomes a particle" (Virilio 2005: 98). Furthermore, non-places "are defined partly by the words and texts they offer us"—the abundance of instructive, prohibitive, or prescriptive messages conveyed via loudspeakers, message boards, or pictograms—and through such heavy overcodings they implement "spaces in which individuals are supposed to communicate only with texts" (Augé 1995: 96). In this sense, the non-place interpellates the individual exactly in its own image: as claustrophobically self-enclosed in his or her "solitary contractuality" (Augé 1995: 94), that he or she, of course, shares with all the other individuals that happen to occupy the same non-place at the same time. In this supermodern system of permanent flows, however, this sharing of time/space with others is nothing more than

one of the many conjunctures in the global manifold that are constantly subject to disjuncture and reassembly. "Alone, but one of many," the denizen of
the non-place partakes of a spatio-temporal regime that "creates neither singular identity nor relations; only solitude, and similitude" (Augé 1995: 103).
For the anthropologist, therefore, the increasing importance of non-places
poses the serious problem of refocusing the very object of the discipline: to
replace an anthropology of localized cultures with an "ethnology of solitude"
(Augé 1995: 120).

Tokyo Cancelled endows its dominant chronotope—the empty airport lobby—with all the attributes and effects that Augé defines for the non-place:
delocalization, textualization, contractuality, and solitude. And yet Dasgupta's text does not subscribe, at least not fully, to the gloomy paranoid claus-
trophobia that marks the analyses by Virilio, Augé, or Fuller and Harley.
Narrative itself, it seems, works as a redeeming force that revokes the steril-
ity and hostility of the non-place: Delocalization becomes the condition of
possibility for the conjuncture of all these stories from all around the world;
textualization is transformed into the poiesis of narrative; contractuality gets
redefined as the thirteen stranded passengers make up their own mutual
pact of 'one story each,' with each story reaffirming the age-old narrative
contract of the willing suspension of disbelief; and yet as we will see, in the
end solitude remains.

Re-Placing the Non-Place

The airport of *Tokyo Cancelled* is introduced as "the Middle of Nowhere," "a
back corridor between two worlds, two somewheres," but also "devoid of any
obvious egress" (*TC* 1). The non-place of the airport lobby—a site of transit
and 'accelerated ejection' under normal conditions—is thus transmogrified
into one vast trap, a claustrophobically static limbo "full of lonely feelings
and terrible thoughts" (*TC* 3). With the onset of night, the almost completely
evacuated lounge turns to deep-sleep mode as

> lights went off in the Duty Free stores and the snack bar closed. Some-
> one summarily extinguished CNN's airport news service, and grandiose
> light boxes advertising American Express and *The Economist* flickered
> and became dull. (*TC* 4–5)

With its textual overcodings defunct, the dimly lit lobby, now fully disjunct
from the global networks in which it is designed to function as one modest
node, appears all the more "depressing and dead" (*TC* 5). It turns into a self-
enclosed capsule of space whose "great windows [. . .] revealed nothing but
blackened copies of the hall where they stood, with a huddle of thirteen in
each one" (*TC* 5). It is hence in a glass darkly, as it were, that the thirteen
remaining travellers first perceive themselves as a group of individuals no

longer protected by the contractual solitude of the supermodern non-place; or, positively put, no longer overdetermined by the atomizing dictates of jet-age travel. Conspicuously, Dasgupta's narrator resorts to the registers of both anthropology and chemistry in order to render this crucial moment of articulation: The thirteen passengers

> felt an inexplicable need to stay close, as if during the reconstitution of themselves around this new Situation a sort of kinship had emerged. They moved towards the chairs like atoms in a molecule, no closer but also no further away than their relationship dictated. (*TC* 5–6)

As the comparisons to kinship and molecular processes underscore, there is nothing voluntary, let alone decisionist, about this new loose affiliation that, interestingly enough, proceeds from a reformatting of each individual ("the reconstitution of themselves"). Virilio, as we have seen, determines the (functional) airport as a site at which the individual is reduced to the state of a particle; Augé as well as Fuller and Harley go further inasmuch as they observe an analysis of the individual into textual particles. For this is precisely what the non-place of the airport has been becoming ever since 9/11: "a space where a series of contractual declarations accumulate into a kind of password" as passengers–biometrically checked and scanned–are being "transformed into a series of pattern matches in the expanding databases of everyday life" (Fuller and Harley 2004: 79). Becoming a passenger, then, implies becoming a readable text. Dasgupta's book takes this process to the extreme, but by literalizing it, he turns it against the logic of the non-place. Where Augé asserts that the individual in the non-place is made to interact "only with texts" instead of other people, Dasgupta takes the textualization of the transitory denizen of the non-place seriously: If everybody has already been 'transformed into a text,' and if furthermore everybody is made to communicate only with texts, then why not communicate with other textualized passengers? Instead of the contractual solitude that Augé proposes as the ineluctable dictate of the non-place, Dasgupta's 'huddled' passengers begin tentatively to form a cosmopolitan community, however ephemeral: a completely anonymous community whose every member appears only as a story. As readers, we hardly learn anything about the storytellers as the narrator's strategic question, "who *were* those people?" (*TC* 5), remains largely unanswered. Neither do the passengers introduce themselves to each other, nor does the narrator shed any light on whose respective story the other twelve travellers are listening to in the course of the night. "Someone spoke" (*TC* 7); "Who will be next?" (*TC* 23); "Another story began" (*TC* 293); "There was only one person left to speak" (*TC* 349): Such are the brief connective interventions provided by the frame narrative that leaves the identities of the individual travellers as conspicuously underdetermined as the travellers themselves perceive "the Situation" they find themselves in. Their relation—the basis of their temporary community—is purely contractual and in that sense compliant to the airport setting; and yet, precisely because that airport has for the time being ceased to operate, it provides a largely unencoded, unconfigured site, a regulatory vacuum that leaves its occupants unexpectedly underdetermined and hence allows for a certain degree of self-determination. As one unidentified passenger muses in-between stories: "Was it not at times like this, when life malfunctioned, when time found a leak in its pipeline and dripped out into some hidden little pool, that new thoughts happened, new things began?" (*TC* 255). Programmatically, then, *Tokyo Cancelled* is in the last resort about the creation of newness: not only in the sense of opening a space for newness to "enter the world" (Rushdie 1991: 394), but even more emphatically about the creation of a theretofore inexistent world. The story cycle is itself about the prolific production of narrative texts that re-inscribe and re-place the non-place and thus contribute, cooperatively, to the reconfiguration of 'what counts as the world.'

As metonymies of globality, the thirteen individual stories seem to stand in for a world that is mainly brutal, exploitative, unjust, and murderous. The fate of many of the characters in this collection, bespeaks an acute sensitivity to the destructive dynamics of global neoliberalism as it persistently imposes its "standard of modernity" as a "global design" on discrepant "local histories" (Mignolo 2000: 297; 278). On the whole, though, *Tokyo Cancelled* cautiously advocates a strategy of undoing the hegemonic script of global designs, even if many of the short stories' protagonists—nearly all of them endowed with weak 'magicorealist' features—fail bitterly in that endeavour. It is the very fact that the stories of their failures can be told at all which is celebrated: that a space of enunciation can be cleared for the basic act of storytelling in which, as we learn from Walter Benjamin, "[e]xperience is passed on from mouth to mouth" (Benjamin 1968: 84). What is important is that that place of enunciation is socially and cooperatively coproduced by speakers and listeners alike, all of them anonymous 'texts' that seem to come from all over the globe. In the folds of the underdetermined genre of the short-story cycle, then, the dysfunctional airport—itself a semiotic vacuum—becomes the chronotope of a fully transmodern collaborative effort at world-making. The dysfunctional non-place, then, corresponds to the generic status of the text itself within which it functions as setting: both are sites of conjunctures of local histories that they do not subsume under global designs. As the anonymous travellers retrieve social place from the non-place, the story cycle gives room to a process of figuring a 'world of our making.' Subtly but emphatically, this creative claim forms the most exterior frame of the collection which starts with the sentence: "There was chaos" (*TC* 1), and ends with "Good morning" (*TC* 383). In between these two poles, allusive to the Genesis as well as other creation myths, lies the figurative labour of telling stories that (may), however modestly, help to reconfigure what will, temporarily, count as the world.

Notes

1. See F.R. Leavis, *The Great Tradition* (1948), Ian Watt, *The Rise of the Novel* (1957), Franco Moretti, *Modern Epic*, Margaret Anne Doody, *The True Story of the Novel* (1996).
2. The Sanskrit collections of the *Panchatantra* and the *Baital-pachisi* are antecedent to all Greek narrative cycles, while the *Kadambari* anticipates both Boccaccio and Chaucer by some 500 years.

Works Cited

Anderson, B. (1991) *Imagined Communities: Reflections on the Origins and Spread of Nationalism*, 2nd edn, London: Verso.

Armstrong, N. and Tennenhouse, L. (1992) *The Imaginary Puritan: Literature, Intellectual Labour, and the Origins of Personal Life*, Berkeley: University of California Press.

Ashcroft, B., Griffiths, G., and Tiffin, H. (1989) *The Empire Writes Back: Theory and Practice in Post-Colonial Literatures*, London and New York: Routledge.

Augé, M. (1995) *Non-Lieux: Introduction à une Anthropologie de la Surmodernité*, trans. J. Howe (1995) *Non-Places: Introduction to an Anthropology of Supermodernity*, London and New York: Verso.

Azim, F. (1993) *The Colonial Rise of the Novel*, London and New York: Routledge.

Bakhtin, M.M. (1975) Вопросы литературы и эстетики: Исследования разных лет; trans. M. Dewey (1989) *Formen der Zeit im Roman: Untersuchungen zur historischen Poetik*, Frankfurt/Main: Fischer.

Ballaster, R. (2005) *Fabulous Orients: Fictions of the East in England 1662–1785*, Oxford: Oxford University Press.

Benjamin, W. (1968) 'Der Erzähler', trans. H. Zohn (1968) 'The Storyteller', in H. Arendt (ed.) *Illuminations: Essays and Reflections*, New York: Schocken, 83–109.

Bennett, T. (1990) *Outside Literature*, London and New York: Routledge.

Butler, J. (1993) *Bodies That Matter: On the Discursive Limits of 'Sex'*, London and New York: Routledge.

Chandra, V. (1997) *Love and Longing in Bombay*, London: Penguin Books.

Chatterjee, P. (1993) *The Nation and Its Fragments: Colonial and Postcolonial Histories*, Delhi: Oxford University Press.

Clifford, J. (1997) *Routes: Travel and Translation in the Late Twentieth Century*, Cambridge, MA and London: Harvard University Press.

Cohen, M. (2003) 'Travelling Genres', *New Literary History*, 34/3: 481–499.

Dasgupta, R. (2005) *Tokyo Cancelled*, New Delhi: Harper Collins.

Dunn, M. and Morris, A. (1995) *The Composite Novel: The Short Story Cycle in Transition*, New York: Twayne.

Fuller, G. and Harley, R. (2004) *Aviopolis: A Book About Airports*, London: Black Dog Publishing.

Heath, S. (2004) 'The Politics of Genre', in C. Prendergast (ed.) *Debating World Literature*, London and New York: Verso, 163–174.

Helgesson, S. (2006) 'Going Global: An Afterword', in S. Helgesson (ed.) *Literary Interactions in the Modern World 2*, Berlin and New York: De Gruyter, 301–321.

Hitchcock, P. (2003) 'The Genre of Postcoloniality', *New Literary History*, 34/2: 299–330.

Hulme, P. (2006) 'Beyond the Straits: Postcolonial Allegories of the Globe', in A. Loomba et al. (eds) *Postcolonial Studies and Beyond*, Durham and London: Duke University Press, 41–61.

Iyer, P. (2000) *The Global Soul: Jet Lag, Shopping Malls, and the Search for Home*, New York: Vintage.

Jameson, F. (1981) *The Political Unconscious: Narrative as a Socially Symbolic Act*, London: Methuen.

———. (1991) *Postmodernism, or, The Cultural Logic of Late Capitalism*, London and New York: Verso.

———. (1998) *The Cultural Turn: Selected Writings on the Postmodern, 1983–1998*, London and New York: Verso.

Kennedy, J.G. (1995a) 'Introduction: The American Short Story Sequence—Definitions and Implications', in J.G. Kennedy (ed.) *Modern American Short Story Sequences: Composite Fictions and Fictive Communities*, Cambridge: Cambridge University Press, vii–xv.

———. (1995b) 'From Anderson's *Winesburg* to Carver's *Cathedral*: The Short Story Sequence and the Semblance of Community', in J.G. Kennedy (ed.) *Modern American Short Story Sequences: Composite Fictions and Fictive Communities*, Cambridge: Cambridge University Press, 194–215.

Lal, V. (2003) *Of Cricket, Guiness and Gandhi: Essays on Indian Culture and History*, Calcutta: Seagull.

Lefebvre, H. (1974; 2nd edn, 1984) *La Production de l'Espace*, trans. D. Nicholson-Smith (1991) *The Production of Space*, Oxford: Blackwell.

Lindberg-Wada, G. (2006) 'Introduction: *Genji Monogatari* and the Intercultural Understanding of Literary Genres', in G. Lindberg-Wada (ed.) *Literary Genres: An Intercultural Approach*, Berlin and New York: De Gruyter, 1–16.

Mehta, G. (1993) *A River Sutra*, London: Heinemann.

Mignolo, W. (2000) *Local Histories/Global Designs: Coloniality, Subaltern Knowledges, and Border Thinking*, Princeton, NJ: Princeton University Press.

Mistry, R. (1987) *Tales from Firozsha Baag*, London: Penguin Books.

Mitford, M.R. (1824–1832, illustr. edn, 1986) *Our Village*, New York: Prentice Hall Press.

Moretti, F. (1998) *Atlas of the European Novel, 1800–1900*, London and New York: Verso.

———. (2004) 'Conjectures on World Literature', in C. Prendergast (ed.) *Debating World Literature*, London and New York: Verso, 148–162.

Mukherjee, M. (1985) *Realism and Reality: The Novel and Society in India*, Delhi: Oxford University Press.

Rastegar, K. (2007) *Literary Modernity between the Middle East and Europe: Textual Transactions in Nineteenth-Century Arabic, English and Persian Literatures*, London and New York: Routledge.

Rushdie, S. (1991) 'In Good Faith', in *Imaginary Homelands: Essays and Criticism 1981–1991*, London: Granta, 393–414.

Shohat, E. and Stam, R. (1994) *Unthinking Eurocentrism: Multiculturalism and the Media*, London and New York: Routledge.

Siskin, C. (1996) 'Epilogue: The Rise of Novelism?', in D. Lynch and W. Beatty Warner (eds) *Cultural Institutions of the Novel*, Durham, NC: Duke University Press, 423–440.

Spivak, G.C. (1998) 'Cultural Talks in the Hot Peace: Revisiting the "Global Village"', in P. Cheah and B. Robbins (eds) *Cosmopolitics: Thinking and Feeling beyond the Nation*, Minneapolis: University of Minnesota Press, 329–348.

Virilio, P. (1984) *L'Horizon Negatif*, trans. M. Degener (2005) *Negative Horizon*, London: Continuum.

———. (1977) *Vitesse et Politique*, trans. M. Polizzotti (2006) *Speed and Politics*, Los Angeles: Semiotext(e).

Wiemann, D. (2008) *Genres of Modernity: Contemporary Indian Novels in English*, Amsterdam and New York: Rodopi.

Part IV
Emerging Narrative Genres

11 Saying Sorry

The Politics of Apology and Reconciliation in Recent Australian Fiction

Sue Kossew

The time has now come for the nation to turn a new page in Australia's history by righting the wrongs of the past and so moving forward with confidence to the future.

> (Prime Minister Kevin Rudd's apology made in the
> Australian Parliament, February 13, 2008)

The question is, what are we going to do, now that we are sorry?

> (Mr Isaacs in J.M. Coetzee's *Disgrace*, 1999: 172)

These two quotations provide a useful framework for the ongoing discussion of the problematics of apology for past wrongs, expressions of which have become an integral part of a number of contemporary national discourses (in Canada, Ireland, and Australia, for example). For Kevin Rudd, the need for a symbolic act of apology to Australia's Indigenous people, given in Parliament in February 2008 near the beginning of his term as Prime Minister, is justified by the necessity for "human decency" and the righting of an "historical wrong" in the form of statutes enacted by successive Australian parliaments that "inflicted profound grief, suffering and loss." However, he is also concerned, as he makes clear in this speech, that the apology is not merely symbolic (which would make it little more than, in his words, "a clanging gong") but also substantive, involving closing the gap between Indigenous and non-Indigenous Australians in the implementation of policies for material change.[1] The overwhelmingly positive response to his speech by Indigenous and non-Indigenous Australians alike marked a turning-point in the process of reconciliation. This was in dramatic contrast to the negative response to the opening speech by Prime Minister John Howard at the first Convention on Reconciliation held in May 1997 where, despite uttering the words "I am sorry," his refusal to accept responsibility on behalf of Australians of "this generation" for "past actions and policies over which they had no control" deeply offended many in the audience, who turned their backs to him in a gesture of contempt.[2] As Gooder and Jacobs point out, it was his decision not to apologize officially on behalf of the Australian government that led to other expressions of apology from state governments, police forces, church groups, and indeed from 'ordinary Australians' in the form of the collective symbolic apology of a National Sorry Day in 1998 (significantly held on the very date that marked the release of the *Bringing Them Home* report on the Stolen Generations) and in the form of 'Sorry Books' where people could leave their own messages of reconciliation. A clear link between 'saying sorry' and a process of reconciliation was made evident in the changing of the name Sorry Day to the 'Journey of Healing' in 1999.

What I want to posit here is the idea that there has arisen, out of the conservative political years prior to the Rudd apology, a peculiarly post-colonial fictional genre that I am calling the Sorry Novel, whose main feature is to rework, rewrite, or reimagine history in order to make a political point about the present. The hijacking of the 'meaning' of history by conservative politicians as well as historians in the now-infamous History Wars in Australia (where different versions of the past have been hotly contested, particularly with regard to black/white relations) has highlighted the importance of narratives of nationhood. Discussions at a national level about what should or should not be included in the Australian school history syllabus reflected attitudes at a time in Australian history when the Coalition Government under John Howard was speaking a language that many Australians disagreed with and that clearly excluded Indigenous perspectives on this 'whiteout history' or 'comfort history' which was being posited so forcefully in opposition to so-called 'black armband' history.[3] Howard's version of Australian history focused on stories of heroic sacrifice by white men (like that of Simpson and his donkey, a great Australian story of mateship and bravery[4]); for Howard, there was no moral ambivalence or room for disagreement in the narration of Australia's past and certainly no acknowledgement of what has been termed 'colonial guilt.'

Perhaps it was this very narrow version of history—one that denied any sense of 'shame'—that impelled a number of writers of literature to take the opposing view. Aboriginal writers have, of course, been concerned with rewriting history to correct what Anita Heiss has called the 'history books that have conveniently left out the facts around invasion, colonization [and] attempted genocide' (Heiss 1998: npn), much of which has been in the genre of life writing.[5] Both Kate Grenville and Gail Jones, (and these are the two authors I will concentrate on in this chapter), as non-Indigenous Australians, have used their novels to resist the *comfortable* narrative of the past. For Grenville, her novel, *The Secret River* (2005), was a way of engaging with her own family history as it dovetailed with a national remembering that coincided with post-Bicentennial Australia. She has said in a *BBC World Book Club* interview with Harriet Jones:

> For 200 years we white Australians have pretended that massacres didn't happen; we have brushed under the carpet the whole ugly history of our

relationship with the Indigenous people. I wanted to bring it out into the open. (Grenville 2009b: transcribed from podcast: npn)

Similarly, Gail Jones, in discussing her own novel, *Sorry* (2007a), has empha-sized the centrality of remembering, forgetting, and recovering history, sug-gesting that "the first responsibility [of the novelist] is to *remember* what it serves the state to *repress*" (Jones 2007b: npn, my emphases). She describes her novel, too, as a "kind of testing of ideas of responsibility and history" (Jones 2007b: transcribed from podcast: npn) and this is clearly in line with Grenville's sense of bringing "the whole ugly history [. . .] out into the open."

In particular, it seems more than coincidence that a number of recent Australian novels by non-Indigenous writers have specifically engaged with the idea of an apology to the stolen generations and/or with the concept of reconciliation, either in the text itself or in comments by the writers. Also more than coincidental is the engagement of such texts with history, or, as Kate Grenville prefers to call it (to avoid further tussles with historians[6]), "the past." It seems that by revisiting the past in fictional form—whether by reimagining actual people and events from the distant colonial past as in Grenville's *The Lieutenant* (set at the time of the First Fleet in 1788) and *The Secret River* (set in the early nineteenth century), and Richard Flanagan's *Wanting* (2008), or the more recent past of the Second World War as in Gail Jones's *Sorry*, all of these writers wish to *refigure* the past (as well as revisiting it) in order to understand or comment *on the present*. As Grenville has sug-gested, her books are

> essentially not about the past [. . .] What I'm really writing about is the present and the only way you can really understand the present obvi-ously is to go back and look at where the problems began and unknot those tight knots that have been there for 200 years. (Grenville 2009b)

Similarly, Gail Jones has said in an interview with Rob Cawston that she is "very interested in what is forgotten, the way that certain voices in history are forgotten, [and] the rights and values of Indigenous people in particular are lost or locked away" (Jones 2007b: npn). In the same interview, she char-acterizes the replaying four times in four different versions of a particular traumatic moment in her book, *Sorry*, as a way of suggesting that "history is a complicated process of repressions and revelations" in which it is sometimes "in certain people's interests not to have the real story told" (Jones 2007b: npn). Grenville uses remarkably similar language in another interview, given *after* Kevin Rudd's historic apology:

> There is a blankness at our hearts, a great Australian forgetting and silence [. . .] a repressed history that we haven't wanted to look at

[. . .] Until recently, we haven't been able to voice it to ourselves. We are now starting to look at it in Australia now, it has come to consciousness. We've done the talking cure [. . .] To tell stories truthfully is the essential starting point. Next, a conversation should begin [. . .] listening as well as talking, learning as well as patronizing. (Grenville 2009a: transcribed from podcast)

All three novels, of course, were written before Kevin Rudd's formal apology to the Indigenous people of Australia in Parliament. But for both Grenville and Jones, even Rudd's Sorry speech signals only "a new initiative for reconciliation and dialogue between Aboriginal and other Australians" (Jones 2007b: npn) that does not "necessarily atone or repair the hurt" (Jones 2008) and as a starting point for the next conversation (as Grenville suggests in the quotation above). So the questions remain: Can literary works, particularly those written by non-Indigenous writers, play a productive part in the process of reconciliation between Indigenous and non-Indigenous Australians? How do such literary works help contemporary post-colonial nations to come to terms with the 'shame' of their pasts? Can telling stories 'truthfully' help to heal the wounds of past silences? And what are the potential pitfalls of saying sorry? These are some of the questions I hope this chapter will raise, if not answer.

It is striking that both Grenville and Jones mark the moment of their own personal participation in the March for Reconciliation in May 2000 across Sydney Harbour Bridge as turning-points, not only for the nation but also for the process of writing books that were subsequently informed by this experience. Grenville's chapter entitled "Walking for Reconciliation" in her writing memoir *Searching for the Secret River* pinpoints the moment when her own thinking shifted. She was walking across the Bridge to support the "idea of reconciliation" but it wasn't, she suggests, until she made eye contact with an unnamed Aboriginal woman in the crowd with whom she shared "one of those moments of intensity" that she felt the need to "cross [the bridge] the hard way, through the deep water of our history" (Grenville 2006: 13). And it was later in conversation with Aboriginal writer Melissa Lukashenko that she fully realized the implications of her ancestor's "taking up" land on the Hawkesbury River as equating to "taking" land from its Aboriginal owners. Clearly, the Bridge walk marked an important moment in the birth of *The Secret River* where a search for her own family history and the narrative of her ancestor Solomon Wiseman coincided with her sense of the need to rethink the whole settler-Indigenous relationship as it had been presented to her generation in Australian history and in a contemporary Australia seeking reconciliation. As she writes in *Searching for the Secret River*, where she outlines the process of researching her novel: "My mother's story was full of gaps [. . .] I realised that, like Lord Nelson, the family story had been holding the telescope up to its blind eye" (Grenville 2006: 19). Linked with the idea of saying sorry is the idea of personal guilt:

Because my ancestor was there in 1806, it was inescapable for me, so I had to live with a huge weight of grief. Which is actually what 'sorry' means in Aboriginal English [. . .] it means grieving, mourning, acknowledging loss. (Rustin 2007: npn)

Gail Jones also describes her participation on the Bridge walk that day in 2000 as significant for her personally, and for her novel, *Sorry*:

. . . I was one of the demonstrators who went on Sorry Day marches across bridges and saw written in the sky in sign-writing the words 'sorry' and 'hope' 10 years ago and really thought that this was a new moment in Australian history, an interventionist moment that would just change things and it hasn't happened. So although this seems very late [10 years later] to bring out a book called *Sorry*, it's my form of activism, I suppose, to say this is still an issue. (Jones 2007b: npn)

She also includes a postscript to her novel entitled "A note on 'sorry'" in which she describes the refusal of John Howard to "say 'sorry' to Aboriginal Australians for past government policies of mistreatment" (Jones 2007a: 215), most specifically those referring to the Stolen Generations. In addition to an explanation of the Sorry Day marches, she, like Grenville, notes the meaning of "sorry business" for Aboriginal people as referring to "matters of death and mourning." In another essay entitled "Sorry-in-the-Sky," she movingly describes a photograph on her desk taken at the time of the walk for reconciliation of the word "sorry" as it was written in the sky by a skywriting plane. By referring to its "exquisite ephemerality" (it is "clearly dissolving even as it appears") and by linking it to traditional Aboriginal ceremonious "sorry business" which is a way in which grief is shared and the spirits of the dead are quieted and honoured, she suggests that the "sorry-in-the-sky is emblematic of the speech act which it betokens," in which "apology and mourning are [. . .] interlaced" (Jones 2004: 168–169). This is, she suggests, indicative of an "incipient communal ethics" (Jones 2004: 168), a sharing of the apology, however frail and transitory that shared responsibility may have been in real time, by all those people who saw it, whether they admitted liability or not. Like those sharing in "sorry business," it had a healing quality; it became performative of both an apology and a mourning, a marking of loss and trauma, despite its brief and shaky appearance in the sky. This idea of a shared space of what John Frow has called "ethical listening" gives us, I think, a useful way of thinking about these Sorry Novels.

However, this notion of what we might call the ethics of apology opens up another minefield, one that is captured in the title of a chapter in John Hirst's book, *Sense and Nonsense in Australian History*, entitled "How sorry can we be?" Accusing Kate Grenville of applying a twenty-first century mentality regarding guilt and responsibility to Australian history, Hirst differentiates between shame and guilt, following Raimond Gaita:

> I accept what Ray [sic] Gaita has argued that if a nation can feel pride at its past achievements it can properly feel shame (though not guilt) for its past misdeeds. Forcibly removing Aboriginal children was undoubtedly a misdeed. What finally makes the case for apology compelling in this instance is that some of the victims are still alive. (Hirst 2005: 91)

It is perhaps useful at this point to turn to J.M. Coetzee, whose experience (like my own) encompasses both South African and Australian "colonial guilt." In his most recent novel, *Diary of a Bad Year*, which incorporates a number of "strong opinions" written by an ageing writer, JC, the writer considers the issue of national shame and the burden of responsibility for the actions of the state. In the context of the "war on terror," he refers to the shame of Australia's complicity with America as "the most abject" member of the Coalition of the Willing. The writer figure here compares the contemporary British attitude towards "collective guilt"—which involves simply declaring "their independence from their imperial forebears" (Coetzee 2007: 44)—that is, not taking on any responsibility—with the "heavy burden" of the "shame of crimes committed in their name" borne by generations of white South Africans. It is, he implies, a shame from which there is no escaping, even if some individuals refuse to "bow before the judgement of the world" (Coetzee 2007: 44). In another 'opinion' entitled "On Apology," the writer figure refers to an advertisement by an American lawyer who will coach Australian companies "in how to word apologies without admitting liability" (Coetzee 2007: 108). What is important is to be seen to perform a convincing "act of apology" (Coetzee 2007: 108). It is of course such a performative "act"—one that is essentially without substance—that David Lurie refuses to participate in when requested to by the University's Committee of Inquiry into the charge of sexual harassment in Coetzee's novel, *Disgrace*, an act that would have enabled him to retain his professorial position.

Coetzee suggests that the ambivalence that surrounds any act of contrition, apology or confession concerns the issue of its sincerity. The "double thought[s]" that Coetzee refers to in his essay on "Confession"[7] is its performative nature: It is possible to 'say' sorry without meaning it. An act of apology, in other words, can make the perpetrator feel better without having any material effect on the victim (and it is in the context of South Africa's Truth and Reconciliation Commission that Coetzee's nuanced and complex analyses of apology and confession took on a national significance). Sara Ahmed makes a similar point in her discussion of national shame and identity in Australia. She starts by quoting the words of Australia's Governor-General, Sir William Deane, cited in the preface of the 1997 *Bringing them Home Report*:

It should, I think, be apparent to all well-meaning people that true reconciliation between the Australian nation and its indigenous peoples is
not achievable in the absence of acknowledgement by the nation of the
wrongfulness of the past dispossession, oppression and degradation of
the Aboriginal peoples. That is not to say that individual Australians
who had no part in what was done in the past should feel or acknowledge personal guilt. It is simply to assert our identity as a nation and the
basic fact that national shame, as well as national pride, can and should
exist in relation to past acts and omissions, at least when done or made
in the name of the community or with the authority of government.
(Governor-General of Australia, Sir William Deane 1996: 19–20; quoted
in *Bringing them Home Report*, Preface 1997)[8]

In response to this, Ahmed points out the problematic nature of separating
the individual from the nation, personal guilt from national shame and of
linking national shame with national pride. She comments:

Recognition works to restore the nation or reconcile the nation to itself
by 'coming to terms with' its own past in the expression of 'bad feeling'.
But in allowing us to feel bad, shame also allows the nation *to feel better
or even to feel good* [. . .] Such expressions of national shame are problematic as they seek within an utterance to finish an action, by claiming the
expression of shame as sufficient for the return to national pride. In other
words, such public expressions of shame try to 'finish' the speech act by
converting shame to pride: *it allows what is shameful to be passed over in the
very enactment of shame.* (Ahmed 2004: npn, emphases in original)

The paradox of this movement from shame to pride is exactly the ambivalence at the heart of confession that Coetzee identifies in his essay, where
the performance of an act stands in for 'genuine' contrition. In similar vein,
Gooder and Jacobs point out that "apology is as much an act of narcissistic
will and desire as of humility and humanity" (Gooder and Jacobs 2000:
244). In the context of Australian apologies, they suggest that "in apologiz-
ing, settler Australians ask indigenous Australians to see them more as they
would like to see themselves: as settlers who properly belong, who have a
kind of indigeneity" (Gooder and Jacobs 2000: 245). The suggestion that
there is a self-interested aspect to national apologies complicates the way we
offer and receive them.

   This is of particular relevance to these Sorry Novels as both authors
have identified, more or less overtly, the implication of their texts in a
national politics of apology. Grenville, for example, while distancing herself from claiming *The Secret River* as her own personal apology on behalf
of her ancestor, has preferred to position the book as written in a spirit of
'acknowledgement' of past injustices as evidenced in her own dedication of

the book to the Aboriginal people of Australia, past, present, and future.[9] The novel makes clear Thornhill's desperate need to establish himself in this new place where punishment can be converted to success; and at the same time expresses the writer's moral repugnance at his joining in a massacre of local Aborigines through the text's violent representation of this event. It is in the voicing of this suppressed history of violence that this novel inserts itself into the contemporary politics of apology and reconciliation. In Grenville's more recent novel, *The Lieutenant*, a kind of prequel to *The Secret River*, language becomes the vehicle for a close relationship between the character Daniel Rooke (closely modelled on the historical figure, William Dawes) and a young Aboriginal girl, Tagaran. It is in trying to understand and communicate across cultures that Rooke finds common humanity (including a sense of humour) with Indigenous culture. His recording of his interactions with Tagaran (based virtually verbatim on Dawes's notebooks) provides a model of cross-cultural communication that shows the potential that existed for peaceful coexistence between colonizers and colonized. However, it is the more violent encounters that dominate, arising from the spearing of a convict gamekeeper intruding on Aboriginal land. Thus, the Governor's injunction to the settlers to treat the natives with "amity and kindness" (Grenville 2008: 61) and his reminder that "their feelings are no different from ours" (Grenville 2008: 111) are undermined and contradicted by the action of revenge against the Indigenous people to teach them a lesson as, in his justificatory terms, "an act of mercy to all the others" (Grenville 2008: 274). Grenville's novel, though, is offered as a reminder that a more positive form of intersubjective recognition was (and is) possible between Indigenous and non-Indigenous Australians.

Reviewer Kerryn Goldsworthy makes a case for a more overt reading of Gail Jones's novel as "a lament for the country's failure to offer a formal apology to the Aboriginal people for the sins and crimes of the past" and suggests it may also be read as

> Jones' own personal, formal and explicit statement of apology: [. . .] as a kind of enactment in fiction of her ideas about Australian race relations and reconciliation, and as a suggestion that if the country's government cannot bring itself to offer an apology then perhaps its artists, at least, might step up to fill the gap. (Goldsworthy 2007: 2)

In Jones's novel, the personal functions as an allegory of the nation, as in the following statement by its central character, Perdita, who develops a disabling stutter following the traumatic witnessing of the murder of her father (although it later emerges she is more directly implicated than this):

> This is a story that can only be told in a whisper [. . .] There is a hush to difficult forms of knowing, an abashment, a sorrow, an inclination

towards silence. My throat is misshapen with all it now carries. (Jones 2007a: 3)

Here, Perdita's stuttering, which amounts to silencing, could be seen to represent the historical "gulf of silence" to which Grenville referred (Grenville 2009b; cf endnote 9). The uncertainty of the truth of what happened to her father, despite the confession of guilt by Mary, Perdita's childhood Aboriginal friend, and Mary's subsequent arrest for murder, continues to haunt Perdita at a bodily level:

> It was possible to believe that what had happened was a terrible dream [. . .] Yet Perdita found that some trace of the violence remained like congestion in her mouth [. . .] something mangled her speech, syllables jammed in her mouth. (Jones 2007a: 96)

It is both a personal trauma and also a national one. For in addition to being present at her father's murder, the child Perdita has also previously witnessed him "hurting" Mary, in an act of sexual abuse. Perdita, whose name translates as "the lost one," is silent about this witnessing of an act whose meaning "she did not want to know" (Jones 2007a: 60). Perdita's witnessing and suppression of this betrayal by her colonizing father of her Aboriginal 'sister' symbolizes both her own loss of innocence and that of the settler nation which has chosen to "forget" its own violent treatment of Indigenous people. Jones thus shows an acute awareness both of the ambivalence of such silence and of voicing it.

In this novel, she focuses this ambiguity around language. In an interview, she put it this way:

> . . . there is a kind of hinge mechanism in the book that talks about the problems with a governing culture taking over linguistically but also uses that as a redemptive space and comes down on the side of saying that language is not just one thing: there are spaces of both authority and dissent within every language act in the same way that *saying sorry might also be quite ambivalent*. It might actually be a way to make white people feel very self-righteous and good about a history that cannot be repaired. (Jones 2007b: npn, my emphases)

Jones's awareness of the ambivalence at the heart of "saying sorry" enables her to explore in her novel the links between forgetting and speaking and what she has called the "rupturing of language" that "ironically speaks what is being suppressed in the past" (Jones 2007c: npn). Her novel, she suggests, can best be read as an "allegory about cultural forgetting." This focus on language enables her to characterize Perdita's father, Nicholas, as a colonial anthropologist whose "imperial and arrogant" ideas about other cultures are echoed in his language and his desire to "crack open the code of primitive humanity" (Jones 2007a: 30) and discover "the why and wherefore of primitive man" (Jones 2007a: 13). On the other hand, the text also emphasizes the potential of language for cross-cultural communication. So Perdita learns from the Aboriginal women who raised her both the warmth of the language of the body as well as the "full-mouthed sounds of indigenous nouns, the clever and precise onomatopoeia of the bird names, the cyclical songs, full of sonorous droning" (Jones 2007a: 32). From Mary, she and Billy Trevor, the deaf-mute boy, also learn the hidden language of the bush so that "even the glass-clear sky was a fabric of signs" (Jones 2007a: 55).

Like language itself, silence is employed as a post-colonial trope in the novel with both redemptive and negative potential. Mary's self-imposed silence protects her 'sister' Perdita from punishment while Stella, Perdita's Shakespeare-obsessed mother, refuses to corroborate Perdita's eventual remembering of the circumstances of her father's murder even though "a few words [from Stella] might release Mary from prison" (Jones 2007a: 202). The only other witness to the story, Billy, is mute. Mary's explanation for her silent self-sacrifice is heart-rending, given the context of her having been taken from her own mother as part of the Stolen Generations: "mothers and daughters, they need each other" (Jones 2007a: 203). Literature, too, can both connect and dissociate. For Stella, a volume of Shakespeare contains "everything one needed to know about life" (Jones 2007a: 37) but Perdita soon understands that "the dazzling light of Australia" represented "more on heaven and earth than was dreamt of by Mister Shakespeare" (Jones 2007a: 38). While Stella's excessive quoting from Shakespeare is used to distance herself from her sense of displacement in Australia and to find a way of communicating her otherwise-suppressed "declaimed desires" (Jones 2007a: 7), encouraging Perdita to recite Shakespeare also enables Dr Oblov, the speech therapist, to help her to speak without stuttering. For Mary, books provide a form of community so that "when people read the same words they were imperceptibly knitted" (Jones 2007a: 73). The two key canonical books in the text, *The Lives of Saints* and *The Plays of Shakespeare*, then, could be seen to operate both as potentially colonizing but also as providing spaces of redemption.

It is, I suggest, in what Gail Jones has called this space of "both authority and dissent" that these Sorry Novels operate. While all acts of "saying sorry" are potentially open to the claim that apology is just "a way to make white people feel very self-righteous and good about a history that cannot be repaired," as Gail Jones has acknowledged (Jones 2007b: npn), such acts can also contribute to a shared space of ethical understanding. Indigenous writer Larissa Behrendt indeed praises Kate Grenville for the image she uses in *The Secret River* of the carved stone fish that lies beneath the foundations of the colonist Thornhill's house as a symbol of the ways history has sometimes "been deliberately suppressed to give the impression of more noble beginnings" (Behrendt 2006: 2) and of the "deeper foundations of our past" (Behrendt 2006: 12). It is only, Behrendt suggests, by uncovering such layers that what she calls the "psychological *terra nullius*" will be overcome and may lead to a more equal reciprocity and, in her words, "a future for all Australians" (Behrendt 2006: 12). This positive response by an Indigenous Australian to Grenville's text—despite the misgivings and ambiguities that remain unresolved around the process of saying sorry in literature—could be seen to perhaps signal the beginnings of the cross-cultural conversation called for by Grenville and possibly also to mark a step in the right direction of the walk towards reconciliation. While, as in Gail Jones's description of the 'sorry-in-the-sky' sign, the writing may well be somewhat shaky and ephemeral, it does, at the very least, perform a communal act of ethical engagement.

Notes

1. A full transcript of Kevin Rudd's Apology to Australia's Indigenous Peoples can be found online at: http://australia.gov.au/about-australia/our-country/our-people/apology-to-australias-indigenous-peoples. Accessed: Feb. 26, 2009.
2. For a full discussion of the implications of this 'improper' apology, and on the link between apology and reconciliation, see Gooder and Jacobs (2000: 229–247). This article provides a useful historical–political background to the issues discussed in this chapter.
3. Stuart Macintyre and Anna Clark's book of that name drew much debate at the time of its publication.
4. For more information on Jack Simpson Kirkpatrick and his ANZAC story, see http://www.anzacs.net/Simpson.htm. Accessed: March 5, 2009.
5. For a useful account of Indigenous women's writing about the Stolen Generations, see Barrett (2005).
6. Grenville was criticized by historian Inga Clendinnen for purportedly overstepping the boundary between history and fiction. See Inga Clendinnen, "The History Question: Who Owns the Past?", *Quarterly Essay* 24 (October 2006): 227–244 and subsequent responses in that journal.
7. "Confession and Double Thoughts: Dostoevsky and Tolstoy", see Coetzee (1992).
8. The full text of the *Bringing Them Home Report* can be found online at: http://www.hreoc.gov.au/Social_Justice/bth_report/report/content_page_full.html, Accessed: March 10, 2009.
9. The full transcription is: "The book was written, not so much in a spirit of apology, but a spirit of perhaps acknowledgement is a better word. What had been done to the Aboriginal people had been so thoroughly glossed over and prettified for all of my learning about Australian history. It was very important to say let's forget about all these pretty stories we're telling each other about how things were in early Australia, let us be absolutely frank about what happened because, until we non-Indigenous Australians are prepared to look that in the face, no conversation is possible, no progress is possible, nothing will happen and there will continue to be a gulf of silence and denial between black and

white in Australia. So certainly acknowledgement and that is why the book is dedicated to the Aboriginal people of Australia past, present and future" (transcription of Grenville 2009b; in response to a question about whether the book could be seen as an apology on behalf of her ancestor).

Works Cited

Ahmed, S. (2004) 'Declarations of Whiteness: The Non-Performativity of Anti-Racism', *Borderlands e-journal*, 3/2.

Barrett, S. (2005) 'Reconstructing Australia's Shameful Past: The Stolen Generations in Life-Writing, Fiction and Film', *lignes* 2: 1–13, http://www.lignes.fr/lines2/01barrett.pdf. Accessed: April 13, 2009.

Behrendt, L. (2006) 'What Lies Beneath', *Meanjin, New Writing in Australia*, 65/1: 4–12.

Clendinnen, I. (2006) 'The History Question: Who Owns the Past?', *Quarterly Essay*, 24: 227–244.

Coetzee, J.M. (1992) 'Confession and Double Thoughts: Dostoevsky and Tolstoy', in D. Attwell (ed) *Doubling the Point: Essays and Interviews*, Cambridge, MA: Harvard University Press.

———. (1999) *Disgrace*, London: Secker & Warburg.

———. (2007) *Diary of a Bad Year*, Melbourne: Text Publishing.

Flanagan, R. (2008) *Wanting*, New York: Knopf.

Goldsworthy, K. (2007) '*Sorry*: A Literary Reconciliation' (Review), *The Age* (5th October 2007), http://www.theage.com.au/news/books/sorry-a-literary-reconciliation/2007/05/10/1178390472932.html. Accessed: April 13, 2009.

Gooder, H. and Jacobs, J.M. (2000) '"On the Border of the Unsayable": The Apology in Postcolonizing Australia', *Interventions*, 2/2: 229–247.

Grenville, K. (2005) *The Secret River*, Melbourne: Text.

———. (2006) *Searching for the Secret River*, Melbourne: Text.

———. (2008) *The Lieutenant*, Melbourne: Text.

———. (2009a) 'Interview with John Mullan', *Guardian Book Club* 13.2.09. Available as podcast at: http://www.guardian.co.uk/books/audio/2009/feb/13/kate-grenville-bookclub. Accessed: Feb. 21, 2009.

———. (2009b) 'Interview with Harriet Jones', *BBC World Book Club* (April 2009). Available as podcast at: http://www.bbc.co.uk/programmes/p002mbrl. Accessed: April 13, 2009.

Heiss, A. (1998) '*Sister Girl*, the Writings of Aboriginal Activist and Historian Jackie Huggins' (Review), *Australian Humanities Journal*, http://www.australianhumanitiesreview.org/archive/Issue-December-1998/heiss.html. Accessed: Jan. 29, 2009.

Hirst, J. (2005) *Sense and Nonsense in Australian History*, Melbourne: Black Inc. Agenda.

Jones, G. (2004) 'Sorry-in-the-Sky: Empathetic Unsettlement, Mourning and the Stolen Generations', in J. Ryan and C. Wallace-Crabbe (eds) *Imagining Australia: Literature and Culture in the New New World*, Cambridge, MA: Harvard University Press, 159–171.

———. (2007a) *Sorry*, North Sydney: Vintage.

———. (2007b) 'Interview with Rob Cawston', in *OpenDemocracy*, 11 June 2007, http://www.opendemocracy.net/podcast/gailjones.mp3. Accessed: Jan. 29, 2009.

———. (2007c) 'Interview with Sarah L'Estrange', Australian Broadcasting Corporation's *Bookshow*. Available as podcast at: http://www.abc.net.au/rn/bookshow/stories/2007/1962061.htm. Accessed: April 13, 2009.

———. (2008) 'Interview with Summer Block', *January Magazine*, May 7, 2008. Available as podcast at: http://www.januarymagazine.com/profiles/gailjones. html. Accessed: April 13, 2009.

Macintyre, S. and Clark, A. (2003) *The History Wars*, Melbourne: Melbourne University Press.

Rudd, K. (2008) 'Apology to Australia's Indigenous Peoples', Australian Government, Feb. 13, 2008. Available at: http://australia.gov.au/about-australia/our-country/our-people/apology-to-australias-indigenous-peoples. Accessed: Feb. 26, 2009.

Rustin, S. (2007) '"Past imperfect", Review of *The Secret River*', *The Guardian*, Saturday, Aug. 18, 2007. http://www.guardian.co.uk/books/2007/aug/18/featuresreviews.guardianreview12. Accessed: Aug. 31, 2007.

12 Remapping Territories of Fiction in Ahdaf Soueif's *The Map of Love*

Noha Hamdy

Some people can make themselves cry. I can make myself sick with terror.

When I was a child-before I had children of my own—I did it by thinking about death. Now I think about the stars and imagine the universe. Then I draw back to our galaxy, then to our planet—spinning away in all that immensity. Spinning for dear life. And for a moment the utter-precariousness, the sheer improbability overwhelms me. What do we have to hold on to? (Soueif 10:1999a)

Spinning is a kinesis which not only informs the manifold geographical trajectories of travelogue—in Soueif's *The Map of Love*, it becomes part and parcel of a 'narrative' cartography which problematizes the concept of realism. With this "sheer improbability" which sweeps through the novel, I would like to begin my investigation of a concept of motion in Soueif's *The Map of Love*, a spinning motion which is created through the travelogue both as a narrative genre and as a metaphor for cultural translation, negotiation and transformation. What makes travel literature generically interesting is precisely this flexibility and mobility with which images from a visual cultural depository, discourses, and referential systems traverse borders and create hybrid forms: The multiple trajectories in Soueif's travelogue engage both travellers and travellees, narrators and narratees in a negotiation, and translation of various representational narrative paradigms, among which is the rather problematic notion of realism, which figures here not as an objective, ontological reality, but rather as an ordering and organization of a world constituted by our experience. James Clifford aptly describes travel writing as a metaphor for the contemporary postcolonial condition; "a figure for different modes of dwelling and displacement, for trajectories and identities, for storytelling and theorizing in a postcolonial world of global contacts" (Clifford 1989: 17).

Soueif's text is therefore a paradigmatic example of a 'translational novel' not just because it involves a code-switching aesthetics of interlinguistic cross-cultural communication, but also because it enacts more broadly a poetics of cultural and cognitive translation through the act of traveling. The novel offers a map of translational practices which occur in the space between translators and translated, painters and viewers, travellers and travellees, narrators and narratees. And it is precisely this in-between space that I would like to look into: On the one hand, kinetic convergences between travel literature and the typically Victorian ekphrastic tradition in terms of common narrative and cognitive paradigms. For example, one of the intriguing questions is the possibility of locating a latent kinesis in Victorian ekphrasis that informs much of the narrative dynamics of the colonial travelogue. On the other hand, I would also like to examine how at the same time these convergences between ekphrasis and travel literature are possibly dismantled as part of an anticolonial agenda in a postcolonial narrative, in a way similar to what Graham Huggan describes as counter-travel writing, "possibilities inherent in travel writing as cultural [subversion or] critique" (Holland and Huggan 2000: 48).

Departing from Pratt's notion of a "contact perspective" (Pratt 1992: 43), this chapter will explore the ontological boundary(ies) at which chafe two synchronous yet opposing narrative paradigms: the orientalist tale and its postcolonial counterpart. In mapping the narrative transformations/relocations in this generic postmodern hybrid, this chapter aims at investigating these problematic politico-aesthetic junctures at which the novel seems to pull in opposite directions.

The novel is a postmodern hybrid interweaving Anna Winterbourne's diary and letters dating back to the turn of the last century with a contemporary reconstruction (1990s) of those British orientalist tales through the eyes of Amal, an Egyptian woman. While the love story pulls the reader into the seductive orientalist tale, the revisionist historical information requires a politicized and committed reading. The novel pulls its readers into two periods in the turbulent history of modern Egypt, with the narrative spanning approximately 100 years of Egyptian history, thus juxtaposing several generations of an Egyptian-British family against the backdrop of a colonial and a postcolonial Egypt. The story, which is mediated primarily in a first-person point of view through the eyes and reflections of an Egyptian translator of novels named Amal El Ghamrawi, travels back and forth between present-day Egypt/New York and Egypt in the early 1900s, unwinding across the contents of a 100-year old family trunk containing diaries, letters, journals, and thus creating parallels between past and present, East and West. Isabel, an American journalist, finds a trunk full of documents in the form of journal entries and personal letters in her dying mother's apartment in New York. This family archive, partly documented in Arabic, partly in English, it turns out, belongs to her English great grandmother Anna Winterbourne. Plunging in Egypt out of orientalist desire fanned by Frederick Lewis's oil canvasses hanging in the South Kensington Museum, Anna Winterbourne ends up marrying the Egyptian nationalist Omar El Ghamrawi. Almost a century later, and in a geographically parallel trajectory to Anna's journey to Egypt, Isabel travels to Egypt to seek the help of Amal, who unpacks and translates the contents of the family trunk for her. A family tree drawn at the beginning of the novel reveals interesting familial entanglements as Amal and Isabel turn out to be distant cousins. The narrative then vacillates between Anna's letters and Amal's growing obsession with the reconstruction of Anna's life.

A cursory glance at the critical reception of the novel in the West notably reveals a marked discrepancy between the critical reception of the novel in the postcolonial world and its marketing by mainstream newspapers and book reviewing publishers. In the academic world, reception was not always very favourable, detecting in Soueif's novel an example of Native Informant Literature which does not speak for the large oppressed minorities in the postcolonial world.

Engaging an orientalist and an apologist vision at once, the novel was proclaimed "a harlequin romance for the anti-Western intelligentsia" (King 2000: 453), "employing a postcolonial counterdiscourse which [recasts] the nature of colonialism" (Burt 2001: 153), and thus imperilling Ahdaf Soueif's position as a postcolonial writer and relegating her rather to that of the Native Informant.

In 1999, *The Map of Love* was shortlisted for the Booker Prize, yet for politico-aesthetic reasons, it failed to go beyond a nomination; for one thing, it was deemed anti-Semitic in its endorsing of the Palestinian cause, but more significantly, critics found it hard to accept the mongrel version of an orientalist romance forcibly yoked to a postcolonial narrative. In her "Fictionalising Post-Colonial Theory: The Creative Native Informant" Anastasia Valassopoulos poses the vital question: "How can a novel be a harlequin romance, an oriental version of a British Mills and Boon book, and an embodiment of postcolonial discourse at once?" (Valassopoulos 2004: 28).

It is interesting to note here that the book reviews, on the other hand, and obviously due to marketing purposes, are mostly engaged in an act of domesticating the mongrel novel, and assimilating it into the canon of Western narrative. In what we could presumably call a trend of neo-orientalist book marketing, (and I believe this is relevant insofar as it relates to the question of genre marketing in the capitalist book reviewing industry), the Guardian proclaims *The Map of Love* as a "romance of the desert" (Soueif 1999a, cover page), in an exoticizing grain that serves only to highlight the orientalist romance at the expense of its political/postcolonial commitment. Similarly, Big Issue's review is no less romanticizing and impartial: "Filled with subtlety, grace and beauty [. . .] *The Map of Love* is honest and intellectual. It takes on a range of topics in the way Dickens did, fusing life, art, history, class, and culture into a huge, vibrant novel," an observation which once again overshadows Soueif's rather hybridized narrative style and confines it to a Victorian heritage of novel writing. It is evident that underlying this critical reception of the novel, which seeks to appropriate *The Map of*

Love into an extended heritage of Western narrative writing, are politico-aesthetic tensions inherent in the novel which problematize the question of genre and narrative typology.[1]

The novel displays a curious interdisciplinarity, raising questions of whether Soueif is writing in her capacity as postcolonial theorist-critic, novelist, or both at once. Weaving elements of postcolonial theory into the fictional tapestry and offering what Graham Huggan describes as a heavy "blend of sociology, history and political science" (Huggan 2001: 239), the novel vacillates here between various practices and disciplines, fictional and non-fictional. Bruce King contends that the book is "at times modeled after and a critique of the Oriental tale. It can be read as literary criticism, a criticism of Western readings of the Arab world" (King 2000: 453). There is even a passage defending diaspora intellectuals [like Said and Soueif] from claims that they are unrepresentative cosmopolitans who tell an alienated Western intelligentsia what it wants. What complicates the game even more is Soueif's deployment of a code-switching aesthetics in terms of language, discourse, and genre in a process of continuous cultural translation.

In terms of language, the novel is charged with discourse strategies which employ a wide range of cross-linguistic phenomena such as lexical borrowing, culture-bound references and translational transfer. In the tradition of postcolonial writers producing contact literatures, Soueif seems to be pushing the frontiers of the English language to simulate the multicultural experience of her characters. These linguistic phenomena may not be interesting per se, but their functional motivation casts a shadow over their effectiveness and readability in a postcolonial context. The process of translational transfer from English into Arabic and vice versa is emblematic of an ethnopoetics of representation which often functions as politically subversive, an instance of anticolonial resistance. Soueif's use of Arabisms/colloquialisms with minimal glossing and hardly any translational mediation is described by her as an attempt to "render a dynamic of the Arabic language into English" (Soueif 1999b: 85) without any syntactic, lexical, or other mediating compromises. However, this cross-linguistic strategy is questionable in its efficacy to provide an alternative model of narrativity. The story is mediated mainly through the eyes of Egyptian Amal, a translator of novels, and is thus predicated on an act of translation, mediation, and decoding. The power differential, which lies predominately in the use of English, serves to recuperate and contain alien Egyptian cultural forms and concepts or indigenous practices via a process of familiarization and domestication. According to Anuradha Dingwaney, this process often "entails varying degrees of violence, especially when the culture being translated is constituted as that of the other" (Dingwaney 1995: 3). In the process, many indigenous narrative practices, especially epistemic narrative cognates, are either completely lost or denuded of their radical inaccessibility through an act of approximation to typically English narrative paradigms. In this opening passage of the novel, Amal, the Egyptian translator of novels, appears as a modern-day Scheherazade-narrator trying to conjure a story out of her imagination or as a Western Alice in Wonderland who has stumbled over some interesting doorway leading her into the forays of another quasi-mythical world.

> Last night I dreamt I walked once more in the house of my father's childhood: under my feet the cool marble of the entrance hall, above my head its high ceiling of wooden rafters: a thousand painted flowers gleaming with distance. And there was the latticed terrace of the haramlek, and behind the ornate woodwork I saw the shadow of a woman. Then the heavy door behind me swung open and I turned: [. . .] I saw the tall broad-shouldered figure of my great uncle. As I opened my eyes and pulled the starched white sheet up close against my chin, I watched him pause and take off his tarbush and hand it [. . .] to the Nubian sufragi who leaned towards him with words of greeting. (Soueif 1999a: 10–11)

The passage also reverberates with echoes from classical frame stories which are employed in cinematographic narration, with Amal making the typical dream flashback to her ancestral home and unravelling the story piecemeal as she begins to unpack the contents of the trunk. In the process, however, we notice that Soueif's intention to employ Amal as a differential Arab narratorial agency and to juxtapose her with a typically Victorian colonialist discourse found in Anna Winterbourne's letter diaries falls short of transcending those very colonial paradigms it has set out to challenge. Instead, Amal's discourse is marked by a subtle form of self-orientalizing where elements of surprise, romantic enchantment and mysticism are employed in order to lure the reader into the orientalized tale. Besides its self-orientalizing, the 'Sheherezadization' of Amal points to a rather stereotyped construction of Arab or oriental narrators. Even worse, her focalization is paradigmatic of an orientalist voyeurism which seeks to look through the latticed window, in Arabic 'the mashrabiya' to visualize, fixate, and expose the usually opaque roaming shadows of the otherwise black-clad harem women. Even though Soueif may have been using the *mashrabiya* to evoke an interesting historical detail of female segregation around the turn of the century, the voyeur/ viewed dynamic is unrealistically turned upside down, with a pseudo-empowerment of a focalizer, who is seen rather than seeing. Therein lies also further proof that Amal, though representing the Egyptian lens, is employed unconsciously as an agent of the Western ethnographic gaze in her attempt to screen a world that is usually censored out of sight, and to objectify Arab womanhood in an eluding focalizing gesture. This is just one example of how Soueif's deployment of Amal as a postcolonial narrator does not transcend Western logocentric narratorial cognates which are predicated on a visibility/invisibility opposition.

While, on the one hand, Soueif's deployment of Arabisms, (in this passage, we have *sufragi*[2], *tarbush*[3], and *haramlek*[4]) serves admittedly to interweave the novel with rich historical information by simply evoking details of an extinct historical setting—hence describing a social stratification/class consciousness which is typical of the period around the turn of the century—her choice of culture-specific references pulls the story into the exotic, rather than the realistic. The violence of colonialism is completely levelled out here while the story panders to a cosmopolitan audience hungry for the exotic. Clarissa Burt remarks here that

> such true-to-life and touristy elements confirm the clear slant of the novel to an English-reading audience, even as they embody Soueif's personal reckoning with her Egyptian background and her current relationship with Egyptian intellectual culture [. . .]. (Burt 2001: 155–156)

This model of transculturation, which is based on a code-switching aesthetics, is a function of the ambivalence and dispersal of colonial power and is dubiously complicit with neo-colonialist/neo-orientalist paradigms of narrative representation which emanate from metropolitan centres. I wish to argue therefore that this trend of self-orientalizing falls short of providing an alternative postcolonial narrative agenda and that such borderline narrators like Amal, who inhabit several worlds at once, display a degree of culturally schizoid self-reflexivity. Valassopoulos argues that

> works such as *The Map of Love* make it difficult, if not impossible, to discover a new interpretation or understanding of the effects and aftershocks of colonialism in the Orient. Instead it offers us a revisionist history married to an exotic remake of the oriental tale. The result is a mixture of high post-colonial criticism and a fantasy harem rolled into one; a critique and a copy of the ongoing postcolonial paradigm between colonizer and colonized; an interdisciplinary exercise? (Valassopoulos 2004: 43)

As a twentieth-century postmodern hybrid, *The Map of Love* foregrounds more explicitly and self-consciously conceptual schemes and representational paradigms governing colonial as well as postcolonial discourse. This self-reflexivity is clearly reflected in the internalizing and juxtaposing of multiple paradigmatic realisms which are questioned and whose discourse is clearly problematized throughout.

I am particularly interested in and tempted to look into the nexus between rhetorical operations, which determine narrative-epistemic cognates in Victorian travel writing, and ekphrasis as a form of narrativity which is based on a remediating, translational act. Anna Winterbourne's cognitive experience of colonial Egypt does not begin in Egypt; it is in fact virtually initiated by her visit to the Kensington museum in the heart of the English empire, London. The journey already begins with Anna's repeated visits to the museum which represents what Donald Rosenthal identifies as "a mode of thought for defining, classifying, expressing the [. . .] vast control mechanism of colonialism, designed to justify and perpetuate European dominance" (Rosenthal 1982: 9). Anna's fascination does not only lie in an aesthetic appreciation of the paintings; her delight is raised by the ontological specificity of the museum as a space of Western epistemological and visual superiority over the Islamic Orient where physical mobility, colonial fantasy, and the Western ethnographic gaze converge towards the privilege of slipping into and maintaining a viewer-focalizer position, thereby freezing the paintings in the discursive stasis of ekphrasis and anchoring the Orient in a fixture of harem tropes. Together they constitute a system of control in the production of narrative discourse.

Describing those paintings as a "world of light and colour," Anna proceeds, in an ekphrastic fascination which places Egypt in an idealized timelessness and non-historicity: "the wondrous colours, the tranquility, the contentment with which they are infused."

> Later in Egypt I woke up from what must have been a deep and peaceful slumber and my first thought on waking was that I had slipped into one of those paintings [. . .] There above me was the intricate wooden latticework and beyond it a most benevolent blue sky. Sherif Pasha asks: "What brought you to Egypt, Lady Anna?" "The paintings", I said. (Soueif 1999a: 102)

In what Anna Winterbourne describes as a slippage into one of those paintings lies a clear convergence between Victorian ekphrasis and discursive/ narrative formations which have become prosaic and commonplace in nineteenth-century colonial travelogues.

This loop-effect or cross-feeding across genres and modes of representation is achieved through the introduction of narrative devices that "create an impression of fidelity to the real world by stressing prior representations through dependence on conventions of genre and style" (Brinker 1983: 254). While normally the act of slipping into the painting would signal a borrowing from a lexical depository of travel adventure, in this case, it interestingly reflects the reverse, namely how narrative-epistemic cognates of the travelogue derive from a kinesis that is originally localizable in ekphrastic descriptions. Notably, this ekphrasis-inspired travel narrative depends on an absence/presence paradox where the Western voyeur is narratologically present only through the gaze, the perspective through which the painting is rearranged. The visual image of the Orient therefore represents an absence, insofar as it exists only inside paintings or a visualization that is predetermined by the act of framing.

According to Rifaterre, these shared conventions of a narrative paradigm are rationalizations which reduce strangeness in the text to something known and familiar. In the same vein, Sabina D'Alessandro contends in *Oriental Painting as a Place of Absence*:

> the perceptual process on which the formation of the image of the Orient depends doesn't reveal itself only at the moment when individuals and a specific reality meet, but often there is an overlap of the same pre-existing images, filtered through the deformed and kaleidoscopic lens of their values and their culturally determined preconceptions. (D'Alessandro 2005: 401)

Similarly, Richard Brown's notion of realism seems to fit in here as he contends realistic representation appears as such only when a given genre or paradigm has become common (Brown 1986: 223). Though originally based on a model of metaphoric or figurative exchange, ekphrasis as a translational act where the visual is remediated but not replaced through the verbal, is flattened out here in an exchangeability of words and images, travel and ekphrasis, which constitutes a valorization of a colonialist realism. Even Anna's description of Layla, the sister of her future Egyptian husband, is governed by an ekphrastic impulse to frame people and settings in a way that is no less fixating than the Lewis paintings:

> She was Egyptian, and a Lady—the first I had seen without the black cloak and the veil. She had pulled a cover of black silk up to her waist, her chemise above that was the purest white, and then again, her hair vied with the silken cover for the depth and luster of its black. Her skin was the colour of gently toasted chestnut, and she lay on cushions of deep emerald and blue, and the whole tableau was framed, yet again, by the lattice of a mashrabiyya. (Soueif 1999a: 134)

Alongside these narrative paradigms in the novel, there exists a mimetic or what Mack Smith in his *Ekphrasis and Literary Realism* terms an ekphrastic discontinuity, where the multiple narrations of art present a variety of aesthetic models and construct a cacophony of epistemic worlds. Soueif uses the double-gaze as a narrative device by means of which multiple focalizations are simultaneously embedded in the novel.

The transformation is effected through an inversion of the critical gaze where Anna's diaries are re-focalized and reconstructed through Amal's point of view. This interpolation of an oppositional representational paradigm, which collides with Victorian narrating and viewing mechanisms, constitutes an instance of anticolonial resistance. In what seems to be a multidirectional translational narrative act, Soueif appropriates and subverts the typically Victorian genre of the travelogue through an inversion of gazes:

I forgive her the mannered approach as she feels her way into my home. Does she know yet? [. . .] I find myself curious: wondering what she will make of Egypt, how much she will see really see. (Soueif 1999a: 58–59)

In an example of cross-cultural interpolation, Soueif employs metaliterary criticism to subvert travelogue conventions: Amal finds Anna's early letters and diary entries contrived, "a little self-conscious perhaps, a little aware of the genre—Letters from Egypt, a Nile Voyage, More Letters from Egypt [. . .] Perhaps she was thinking of future publication. In any case I forgive her [. . .] What else does she know yet?" (Soueif 1999a: 60).

In a further kaleidoscopic twist, Soueif's narrative strategy is to depict Anna as a principal first-person narrator whose diary evidences a shift from a Eurocentric to an idealized Western observer of, and participant in, Egypt's struggle for independence. As the narrative proceeds, the travelogue spins away from the conventional rhetorical operations found in ekphrastic references, and orientalist representations are brushed off in favour of a more nuanced exploration of a systematically gendered typography of a female/feminist counter-travel writing. In a complicated game of cross-dressing, Anna's wearing of the Islamic veil results in a reversal of the gaze and turns the classic scene of travel literature inside out. Though often regarded as a sign of Muslim women's invisibility and oppression, the veil becomes here an empowering narrative device, a focalizing lens, an authorizing presence for Anna. In Western epistemology of narrative, there appears to be an intuitive association of visibility with presence, voice, and subjectivity which is subverted here through the veil. This last instance amazingly opens up a spectrum of focalizing possibilities for Anna and functions as a horizon for cultural translatability. Joseph Massad contends in this regard:

When Anna dresses as an Egyptian Muslim woman in public, not only are her looks transformed but so are her perceptions as well as those of others towards her. (Massad 1999: 82)

It is a most liberating thing, this veil. While I was wearing it, I could look wherever I wanted and nobody could look back at me. Nobody could find out who I was. (Soueif 1999a: 205)

The ability of the owners of the gaze and interpreters of the Orient to see, record, and describe in a narrative context is radically questioned.

It is pretty obvious that Soueif is exploiting the potential for alternative narratorial paradigms that women travel writing provides where, as Blunt observes, "the intersection of colonial and gender discourses involves a shifting, contradictory subject positioning," where Western women represent centre, periphery, identity and alterity at once. This becomes obvious in a spinning motion towards a counter-travel narrative epistemology which less and less relies on deterministic visual and verbal operations of ekphrasis and rather preserves a space for the non-writerly, the non-painterly, the non-readerly, in short, the untranslatable:

> I sit in my room at Shepheard's Hotel possessed by the strangest feeling that still I am not in Egypt [. . .] there is something at the heart of it which eludes me [. . .] and which [. . .] seems far from my grasp. (Soueif 1999a: 102)

I go back to the very beginning to close on Amal's contemplation of the precariousness of life and our existence in her question "What do we have to hold on to?", to conclude that Soueif's novel *The Map of Love* is structurally inspired by a concept of motion, which sees in realism a narratological construct yielding to the discursive conventions of particular ideologically motivated genres, like travel literature. This last appears, as Clifford aptly describes it, a "figure for different modes of dwelling and displacement, for trajectories and identities, storytelling and theorizing in a postcolonial world of global contacts" (Clifford 1989: 177), with a translational potential which can subvert genre, viewing and narrating conventions. The question remains, however, whether Amal's and Anna's subversion of the ethnographic gaze really succeeds in reinforcing a postmodern/postcolonial narrative paradigm that opposes the aesthetics and epistemology of the Victorian travelogue. While the novel is politically bent on obliterating the Victorian tale and countering its imperial epistemological dominance, there remains an overpowering Victorian narrative sensibility about the novel which refashions itself as a 'neo-self-orientalizing' tale deflecting its political motivations and narratorial agendas.

Notes

1. For these references see http://www.middlemiss.org/lit/prizes/booker/booker 1999.html (Middlemiss 2005) Accessed: Nov. 20, 2011.
2. The Nubian *sufragi* was the typical Egyptian butler-cook who served in Egyptian aristocratic households and usually came from Upper Egypt and spoke in a typical Nubian accent. The *sufragi* reflected a code of conduct that was marked by utter politeness, submission, and devotedness to the family.
3. The red *Tarbush* is the close-fitting, brimless, flat-topped, red cap, in shape similar to a truncated cone, which was worn by Egyptians enjoying a privileged social status (Pasha, Beik) under the Ottomans and right up to the Revolution in 1952, and so functioned as a social class marker in a socially stratified society.
4. The *haramlek* was the woman's quarter in an Egyptian household, with latticed windows which allowed women to look out without being seen. The *haramlek* was often associated with confinement or imprisonment of women or conjured orientalist visions of opulent surroundings, ornate woodwork, and sensuous

women-concubines who were supposed to entertain men. Contrarily, and as this vision is later subverted in the novel, the harem is shown to be a place where women can have fun, be socially and even politically active and, most significantly, where they can be independent from men.

Works Cited

Brinker, M. (1983) 'Verisimilitude, Conventions, and Beliefs', *New Literary History*, 14: 253–272.

Brown, R.H. (1986) 'Toward a Sociology of Aesthetic Forms: A Commentary', *New Literary History*, 17: 223–228.

Burt, C. (2001) 'The Map of Love', *Feminist Review*, 69: 153–156.

Clifford, J. and Dhareshwar, V. (1989) 'Notes on Travel and Theory', in J. Clifford and V. Dhareshwar (eds) *Traveling Theories, Traveling Theorists, Inscriptions 5*, Santa Cruz: Centre for Cultural Studies, USCC.

D'Alessandro, S. (2005) 'Oriental Painting as a Place of Absence and *The Map of Love* by Ahdaf Soueif', Textus XVIII: 397–408.

Dingwaney, A. and Maier, C. (eds) (1995) *Between Languages and Cultures: Translation and Cross-Cultural Texts*, Pittsburgh: University of Pittsburgh Press.

Holland, P. and Huggan, G. (2000) *Tourists with Typewriters: Critical Reflections on Contemporary Travel Writing*, Ann Arbor: University of Michigan Press.

Huggan, G. (2001) *The Postcolonial Exotic: Marketing the Margins*, New York: Routledge.

King, B. (2000) 'The Map of Love', *World Literature Today*, 74/2: 453.

Luo, S.-P. (2003) 'Rewriting Travel: Ahdaf Soueif's *The Map of Love* and Bharati Mukherjee's *The Holder of the World*', *Journal of Commonwealth Literature*, 38/2: 77–104.

Malak, A. (2000) 'Arab-Muslim Feminism and the Narrative of Hybridity: The Fiction of Ahdaf Soueif', *Alif: Journal of Comparative Poetics*, 20: 140–183.

Middlemiss, P. (2005) *1999 Booker Prize*. http://www.middlemiss.org/lit/prizes/booker/booker1999.html. Accessed: Oct. 15, 2009.

Massad, J. (1999) 'The Politics of Desire in the Writings of Ahdaf Soueif', *Journal of Palestine Studies*, 28/4:75–80.

Pratt, M.L. (1992) *Imperial Eyes: Studies in Travel Writing and Transculturation*, London and New York: Routledge.

Rosenthal, D. (1982) *Orientalism: The Near East in French Painting, 1800–1880*, Rochester, NY: University of Rochester Memorial Art Gallery.

Soueif, A. (1999a) *The Map of Love*, London: Bloomsbury.

———. (1999b) 'Interview with Jospeh Massad', *Journal of Palestinian Studies*, 28/4: 85.

Valassopoulos, A. (2004) 'Fictionalising Post-Colonial Theory: The Creative Native Informant', *Critical Survey*, 16/2: 28–44.

13 Reading Short Stories as a Postcolonialist

Jhumpa Lahiri's "This Blessed House"

Renate Brosch

What sorts of narratives lend themselves particularly to postcolonialism? I would like to make a case for short stories, firstly because they are disproportionally canonical in the literatures of colonial and postcolonial cultures, so that some critics have argued that they are particularly suited to the representation of liminal or problematized identities (A. Hunter 2007: 138). In spite of the prominent role short stories play in cultures that have experienced colonial disruption, they are marginalized in literary history and criticism as the genre has been bypassed by most of the theoretical developments in the past decades. Postcolonial criticism also—astonishingly—has tended to privilege the novel to the exclusion of other genres. The short story's figural and formal density certainly makes it a less convenient medium to annex as textual synecdoche for historical or social circumstances. A reason for its neglect may be that "postcolonial criticism is largely grounded in mimetic suppositions about literature" (Edwards 2004: 2), a tendency which too often leads to stale and "ossified" criticism (Huggan 2007: x).

Postcolonial criticism has not often given much attention to the aesthetics or poetics of genre. When there is a professed interest in genre, as in an essay on the postcolonial short story by Catherine Ramsdell, its consideration remains vague, leading to a general admonishment to move beyond binary categories, opposing victims, and oppressors, and to "eliminate the stereotypes and create something new, something that is in Bhabha's words, neither the one nor the other" (Ramsdell 2003: 99). Such celebratory adoption of Homi Bhabha's idea of cultural hybridity as an "in-between space" which provides the terrain for "elaborating strategies of selfhood that initiate new signs of identity" (Bhabha 2000: 1), has become typical of the vague exhortations and pious platitudes echoed in a lot of postcolonial readings. It is easy to see how convenient this rhetoric is, since it provides the language for a conflation of interpretation with a widely accepted and politically correct theory, but the problem remains how to develop critical readings that go beyond a mere metaphorical conclusion (like "in-between-space"). The topic of this collection is therefore a welcome opportunity to combine an aesthetic and generic interest with a postcolonial one. Of course, it would be silly and presumptuous to want to prescribe any form of expression for authors with a postcolonial agenda; what the following chapter will attempt to do is address the problem of genre from another angle.

My argument in the following is motivated by the conviction that the postcolonial is not something that can be found in textuality at all, whether of the individual or the generic type, but a mode of reading. As such, it is encouraged by certain textual features, but it emerges only in the interaction between reader and text. This means that the achievements of postcolonial criticism in relating literature to social and political power structures past and present need to be supplemented with a consideration of the context of reception, as the cultural history of literary texts is the history of their varying uses in and through the act of reception. Only by including reading practices can we adequately judge the cultural work literature performs. I am convinced that we need to combine discourse analysis with a phenomenology of reading as an analytical tool. Such an inclusion of reading processes into the analysis of texts is not meant as an erasure of the need for an ethical position in postcolonial studies, it will rather lead to an identification of the political effect of texts in a very concrete and material sense, I hope, by interpreting certain textual demands on reception as impulses towards forming interested temporary reading communities (L. Hunter 2001), and thus add another dimension to the analysis of the social function of literature.[1]

In processing texts, readers allow themselves a certain amount of "wish-fulfillment" which reshapes and re-describes the collective cultural imaginary. The presentational nature of literature allows wide-ranging uses, the principle one of which is "identificatory transfer;" hence, when fictions are said to construct identity, they do so primarily through their making available figures for the reader's identification and judgement. Though most of this relation to the fictive text is temporary and elusive, it is such cultural work that little by little creates what we think of as ourselves and our world. Thus the utopian potential in acts of reading lies not only in the fact that the fictional text restructures reality, but that the reception is similarly creative.

There are, of course, textual markers designed to elicit certain reactions on the reader's part, and the success of literary communication depends on both the writer and the reader of the text agreeing to play their assigned parts in connection with those markers; "once upon a time," for example, signals that readers are not supposed to worry about the referential nature of the text in question (Lefevere 1999: 76). Similarly, the generic marker 'short story' impacts on readers in distinct ways, reminding them of whatever definitorial knowledge they possess.

Coming back to the question of genre, I would like to make a crucial distinction: The difference between novels and short stories is one of kind, not of quantity. This difference, however, lies primarily in the kind of aesthetic experience the short story promotes. The short story "invites a degree of reader participation not frequently found in other narrative texts" (Korte

2003: 5), because when a text is compressed to such a degree that it leaves many things unexplained, readers tend to charge it with meaning. This is the reason why short stories can be most profitably approached from the vantage point of the experience involved, rather than as texts with a set of determinate generic characteristics. The approach allows us to look at the participatory organizational acts which depend on both the structure of the text as well as on the disposition of the reader.

Experiencing short stories unfolds in a tension between verbal economy and imaginative projection. Whereas the novel presents a large and largely interdependent intratextual system, understanding a short story must have greater recourse to contextual supplementary knowledge (Hanson 1989: 23). This is made evident by comparing interpretations of shorter and longer narratives. Interpretations diverge less in the latter case because a long reading process educates readers in the belief system of the implied author and enables them to compensate dissonance and ambivalence. Because stories do not have room to elaborate on the determining factors of the fictional world and its values, they demand a dual understanding in the reading process, one in which one's own perspective is constantly copresent with, projected onto and interactive with that of the fiction. Hence, short stories profit from a supplementary imaginative reaction to gaps of meaning which correlates different frames and world pictures. This dependence on extrinsic ways of constituting meaning is an advantage for short stories, because they depend on causing cognitive participation in the reader for making themselves memorable.[2]

Another strategy which short stories use to compensate for brevity is the creation of memorable images and metaphors, a feature that has often been remarked on by critics. Clare Hanson argues from the perspective of production that the compulsion for writers to compress results in a tendency to evoke iconically. She therefore regards the short story as a form of preference for the visual in place of the discursive (Hanson 1989: 5f). Supplementing her argument with regard to reception processes, one could point out that it is obviously easier to organize textual material mentally when there is less quantity for our memories to deal with. There are reasons to believe that brevity in narration inclines readers to foreground "visual configurations" (Brown 1989: 242f). In short story reading, the cognitive and emotional process involves forming units of visualization which retain a semantic essence of the text, balancing the dissonance with which short narratives necessarily challenge our imagination and, at the same time, projecting the unresolved ideas and contradictions proffered by the narrative into the larger framework of the reader's world-picture. Reader participation thus creates visual images as configurations which simultaneously function as units of containment and as enablers of their mental transgression.

Hence, the effect of narrative visuality leads back to the projective blending of story elements with an extrinsic contextual framework mentioned before. The cognitive process of reading is a constant and ongoing interaction between what is presented and an attempt on the part of the reader to maintain or impose his or her own order on the manifold story world. In these dynamic operations an imaginary is constructed at the same time as it is undermined. Thus stories make assaults and inroads on the expectations and assumptions brought to them and lead readers in turn to construct configurations which allow them to come to terms with them. Short stories, at least in their more recent modern version since the beginning of the twentieth century, are opposed to what Said called the "representational circularity" of the novella, where "the perfect closure of the whole thing is not only aesthetically but also mentally unassailable;" these aesthetics seemed imperialist to Said (cf. Lane 2006: 6). The disadvantage of stories that they command less space for the depiction of a fictional world hence becomes an advantage in the present postcolonial situation: Shorter narratives cannot create and sustain narrative authority to the same extent as longer ones; they must therefore speak to the need to make imaginative connections, to discover and yoke together similarity in difference in a "webworking creative act" (Stafford 1999: 8). This opportunity of spanning boundaries and weaving particulars into a partial concordance is part of the distinctiveness of the short story experience, in which we must negotiate the singular and the exemplary—or in postcolonial terms, the local and the global.

Some critics have attempted to argue that the short story is particularly suited to the representation of liminal or problematized identities (Frank O'Connor) and that "in the ruptured condition of colonial and postcolonial societies, the form speaks directly to and about those whose sense of self, region, state or nation is insecure" (A. Hunter 2007: 138). According to Adrian Hunter, narrative voices which speak from the affective experience of social marginality, from a disjunctive, displaced agency, and from the perspective of the disempowered, are congenial to short fictions. His argument goes some way to explain the prevalence of these positions taken in postcolonial fictions. The short story's preference for problematized identities becomes, in a Western context, a dramatization of cultural multiplicity, such as prevails in diaspora.[3]

But it is obviously not the short story that turns an author into a postcolonialist. She must have taken up certain conceptual positions before she began to write, and the decision to write a short story means to be willing to omit a lot of things that would be spelt out in a novel. She must have been prepared to be read by people making 'imaginative projections.' Instead of presenting a dialogic polyphony, she must have been concerned to engage readers cognitively by other means.

Jhumpa Lahiri's short stories occupy a place in between single story and short story cycle. This in-between-ness of her narratives ties in with her second generation diasporic project. Her story collections contain the unifying pattern characteristic of the cycle in that they thematize diasporic displacement and isolation, yet this common theme is too weak an argument for the categorization as a short story cycle. The volumes of stories are not quite linked consecutive narratives, yet more than independent tales. The author exhibits a specific interest in culture clashes, preferring to represent the peculiarities of diasporic identities of second generation American Indian immigrants. The immigrants portrayed in Lahiri's work are part of a 'new diaspora,' which is highly educated and successful in U.S. culture but which nevertheless maintains a connection to its home culture. These new diasporic characters reveal an identity construction different from both cultural sources. It is based on an imaginary construction of homelands, rather than a genuine memory of their country of origin. While the first generation immigrants in her fictions maintain a tenacious connection to the past, conserving in their memories an idealized version of their home as an entity frozen in time, the second generation is more flexible and productive in its construction of an imaginary homeland.

This conflict is dramatized in a story called "This Blessed House." The couple in the story, Sanjeev and Tamina, nicknamed Twinkle, are Americans of Indian origin, who have been introduced to each other by their parents, married soon after and have now moved into their new home. The difference in background between them is significant: Twinkle is a Californian by birth with no first-hand experience of India, while Sanjeev is a more recent migrant.

Among the textual markers designed to elicit certain reactions on the reader's part, titles and beginnings are the most successful for initial literary communication. As short story titles very often signal dissonance, the religious overtones in combination with the demonstrative pronoun in this example alert us to a sceptical reading of the phrase, creating pleasant expectations of upheaval, for instance. The story proper then opens with a portentous sentence: "They discovered the first one in a cupboard above the stove . . . " (Lahiri 1999: 136). The discovery motif is of course one that has been deployed in the discourses of imperial exploration and expansion to justify territorial claims. Hence the act of discovering and its description as being the first one suggest a chain of findings that has colonial resonances, especially as we soon find out that the story takes place around the time of "Columbus Day," the anniversary of the so-called discovery of America.

What is it that they discover? The objects they find are kitsch paraphernalia of Christian devotion left behind by the previous owners. The first, a white porcelain effigy of Christ, produces a disturbance as startling as Robinson's footprint. Subsequently, the further objects they light upon cause serious trouble since husband and wife react very differently to these objects: While Sanjeev wants to throw them away, Twinkle becomes more and more intrigued and determined not only to keep them but to exhibit them prominently on the mantelpiece of their drawing room. This is cause for increasing tension between them as Sanjeev dreads the impression they will make on his colleagues at the upcoming housewarming party.

'We're not Christians,' Sanjeev said. Lately he had begun noticing the
need to state the obvious to Twinkle [. . .] She shrugged. 'No, we're not
Christians. We are good little Hindus.' (Lahiri 1999: 137)

This irritable repartee is not only indicative of growing estrangement but
alludes to the wider context of postcolonial and diasporic circumstances.
Twinkle's ironic iteration of religious and cultural belonging resists a con-
fined, predetermined identity and emphasizes her unstable and hybrid
self-perception. The findings multiply, "each day is like a treasure hunt"
(Lahiri 1999: 141), bringing to light: a 3-D postcard of Saint Francis done
in four colours; a wooden cross key chain; a framed paint-by-number of the
three wise men against a velvet background; a tile trivet depicting a blond,
unbearded Jesus, delivering a sermon on a mountaintop; a plastic snow-dome
containing a miniature Nativity scene; salt and pepper shakers designed to
resemble Mary and Joseph; a larger-than-life watercolour poster of Christ
weeping translucent tears the size of peanut shells and sporting a crown of
thorns; switch plates in the bedroom decorated with scenes from the bible; a
dishtowel with the ten commandments printed on it; and a waist-high lawn
statue of the Virgin Mary. Sanjeev deeply resents this sizable collection of
what he calls "a biblical menagerie," commenting that if the former inhabitants had wanted to convert them, they obviously succeeded in her case. But
he is mistaken, Twinkle never treats the items in a pious or reverential way,
rather she appropriates them for an ironic play on cultural semantization.
The story culminates in a climactic scene when the drunken housewarming party ascends to the attic to join in the treasure hunt, while Sanjeev
stays behind. Eventually he sees Twinkle stagger down the stairs carrying a
"solid silver bust of Christ, the head easily three times the size of his own [
. . .] Unlike the other things they'd found, this contained dignity, solemnity,
beauty even" (Lahiri 1999: 156f).

Most critics celebrate Lahiri's stories as innovative rewritings of the concept of hybridity, taking their cue from an interview in which Lahiri used
the term "translating" for her repossession of her parental culture and an
adaptation of the past into her fictional creation (cf. Kuortti 2007: 217).[4]
In one such reading, Joel Kuortti argues that this particular story is "resistant to hegemonic formations" (Kuortti 2007: 212). He applauds the female
character's uninhibited mixing of cultural heritages, which he perceives as
rewarded with a "solid trophy" in the shape of the silver bust of Christ, the
undeniable value of which even her husband is forced to recognize. What
is being dramatized, Kuortti sums up, is the clash between assimilation and
resistance—in husband and wife respectively—finding its compromise and
happy end in hybridity (Kuortti 2007: 216).

Such a reading misses the multiple meanings of the story, as well as the
ambiguous references to the postcolonial or diasporic dilemma. By investigating the story in relation to the specifics of short narratives, we will be able
to reveal more possibilities for the construction of meaning.

Because of their textual constraints, short stories not only eschew character development, they often create ambiguous characters whose intrinsic value cannot be decided on and who hover somewhere between empathetic and non-empathetic agent.[5] "This Blessed House" employs this textual strategy: It is told by a third person narrator, but for the main part the focalizer is Sanjeev. Hence, we perceive Twinkle's superstitious obsession with her new possessions from a detached and disapproving point of view. One of the cognitive challenges common in short stories is that they force the reader to "counterfocalize," i.e., to push imaginatively against the privileging of one perspective (Edwards 2004: 8). Since Sanjeev is evidently a spoil-sport due to his conservative 'migrant's' convictions, his inferiority in terms of the ideological position of the text as a whole is easily taken for granted. In the final scene, moreover, Twinkle lives up to her nickname, becoming the star of her party glowing in the admiration of the male guests. But the public appreciation of what he privately disapproves, leads to Sanjeev's final epiphany when he realizes that he can reach out to her with love in spite of her thoughtless and superficial irresponsibility.

Short stories, their limited textual space notwithstanding, frequently use repetition as a strategy for pointing out significant terms. In this case the repetition of the word "menagerie" recalls the vulnerable crippled girl in Tennessee Williams's play. *The Glass Menagerie* suggests Sanjeev's sympathetic nature on the one hand and the crippling nature of the diasporic situation on the other. This alternative reading shows Lahiri's second generation immigrant characters to be

> emotional outsiders: having grown up translating the mysteries of the United States for their relatives, they are fluent navigators of both Bengali and American culture but completely at home in neither; they always experience themselves as standing slightly apart, given more to melancholy observation than wholehearted participation. (Kakutani 2008: 1)

This reading could be called an immersive one, intuitively relating to the emotional effects of a victim's narrative. In this reading, the surprise effect, which readers would have to accommodate, lies in the reversal of the power balance of perspective: Though Twinkle's attitude is valorized for most of the story, it is Sanjeev who finally experiences a spiritual development and whose moral deliberations become the end-note of the narrative, forming the ending which challenges the reader's imaginative projection to carry on.

However, such an interpretation (of melancholy hybridity triumphing over playful hybridity) privileges the effect of the ending over that of the narration leading up to it. It takes inadequate account of the emphasis on inequality in marital power relations, of Sanjeev's decidedly inferior position. Besides, it does not address style, a style manifested in the mocking attitude of Twinkle towards the devotional objects, which is condoned by the third person narrator, so that the visual immediacy of all the trumpery items becomes the story's best comic effect. And Twinkle who doubles over laughing at the statue of the Virgin Mary can be regarded as the reader's proxy. Visual configuration in ongoing reception thus conflicts with and undercuts interpretive judgement.

Moreover, an empathetic response to the emotional aspect of the narrative is forestalled by the allegorical level of the story. As mentioned before, in order to engage the reader in creative participation, short stories often deliberately provoke the mental activity of projecting beyond the textual boundary—be it structural or thematic. This projective blending beyond the frame of the text occurs typically immediately after a first reading experience; in a conscious act of interpretation, these projections are again compared and juxtaposed with the proposals of the text. In the process, the best short stories will aim to transcend the level of individual psychology. Rather than engaging us in psychological assessments, the "provocation into counterfocalization" can happen not just in terms of perspective or figuration but also on another level of the text, in terms of mode (Edwards 2004: 7). It is the allegorical mode which most often performs this cognitive function in postcolonial texts. According to Edwards, allegory, a discontinuity between modes, is mobilized to force readers to think against the current of the narrative (Edwards 2004: 8). Short stories with their artful ellipsis have long trained readers to do this; in postcolonial readings the force of allegory combines with an ethical interest or attention.

As events accelerate, another element that mystifies is the increasingly fantastic nature of the objects. While the first items found seem ordinary enough, the findings later become implausibly numerous and outrageously gross. This transformation from realism to fantasy is typical of the short story's affinity to folklore and myth. Merging allegory and fantasy is a short story strategy for projective reading. "This Blessed House" provides subtle hints that an exclusively referential reading is not sufficient. Indeed, it has perplexed readers looking for realistic explanations. No explanation is provided for why the objects were left behind in the first place and the identity of the former inhabitants is not revealed. The fictive situation can be said to mirror allegorically that of missionary first encounter when worthless trinkets are offered for barter and the continuing process of colonization produces growing pressure on the 'heathen' subject when oppression gradually shifts from coercion to a reward policy holding out the promise of increase in material or cultural capital.

In the allegorical reading, Sanjeev and Twinkle represent two types of colonists entering the supposedly empty space of a newly "discovered" land. But the couple's idea of entering an empty territory in their new home is as illusionary as the idea of *terra nullius* in the invasion of the Australian continent. Like the countries of colonial exploration, the "blessed house" into which the characters are trying to insert themselves is already inhabited by another culture.

The many references to material value support this idea, hinting at the true cause for colonization. Moreover, Twinkle's adoption of the devotional objects follows the stages of the colonizing process: first, there is appropriation when she claims the things are their rightful possession since they have bought the house; second, there is re-presentation when she exhibits them on the mantelpiece without bothering about their proper context; and third, there is re-interpretation when she interprets the discovery of the objects as a sign ("'Face it. This house is blessed,'" Lahiri 1999: 144), appropriating their sacred nature for her own agnostic purposes (Kuortti 2007: 212f).

What unsettles this neat reading is the story's potential for reversing familiar hierarchies and agency positions. In an allegorical reading of the discovery plot as colonial encounter, the house must figure as an image of a colonizing situation. This understanding contains a challenging reversal of expectations for the reader as the diasporic situation of the protagonists involves the discovery, appropriation, and suppression of a Western location and the spoliation of the recipient culture's most highly valued symbolic objects. In a complex figuration, the process of colonization is written onto the process of constructing a diasporic identity. According to Kuortti, the transfer of the colonizing process into a diasporic situation performs a denial of the very foundation of the colonial project (Kuortti 2007: 213). But since the spoils are responsible for unprecedented conflict between the fictional characters, the story expresses personal loss as well as playful reinterpretation. Rather than recommend a triumphalist diasporic hybridity, the text shows the colonial subject to work within the same parameters as the colonists. Gradually the fantastic agency and power of the iconic cult objects transform the house owners into different people, in the end even working a kind of magic reconciliation. And the dissonant (and comic) effect of the reversals of power positions advances an ambivalent postcolonial critique at most.

The genre's central strategy of effecting visual configuration is evident in the central trope of the house—of mixed blessings—as it turns out. It provides the enunciatory space for the focalizer, who wishes the house to be an empty space. As a metaphor, the emptiness is ambivalent, suggesting a colonizing attitude as well as a diasporic identity, an identity to be constituted out of contrasts. Sanjeev's desire for an empty space is thwarted by the presence of remnant belongings from earlier inhabitants. The anxiety resulting from an intrusion of traces which disrupts the couple's initial illusion of security and harmony is underscored in the increasingly fantastic descriptions of the objects. But if diasporic identity has to come to terms with an Other, it can negotiate the Other in different ways. A love-hate relationship to the recipient culture is expressed in the contrasting reactions of the two protagonists: While Twinkle stages intentional hybridity to "shock, change, challenge [. . .] or disrupt through deliberate, intended fusions" (Werbner 1997: 5), it is Sanjeev whose epiphanic realization promises a future of indefinitely repeated acts of conscious tolerance.

As in many of Lahiri's stories, the first generation Indian-Americans try to overcome their loneliness and homesickness by creating a "little India" abroad, while the second generation finds itself at odds with the community of traditional expatriates. Ultimately, all the concepts of home available to these diasporic characters are shown to be imaginary. While the first generation immigrants maintain a tenacious connection to an increasingly imaginary past, conserving in their memories an idealized version of their home, the second generation is engaged in a flexible construction of an imaginary homeland different from both cultural sources. Lahiri's representations of both the traditional and the new hyphenated identities deconstruct the notion of an authentic identity or home. The second generation attitude of fluid negotiable identities appeals to readerships who value mixed alliances. Moreover, since the stories themselves engage in the construction of imaginary homelands for diasporic identities, it can be said to be privileged on a metafictional level. But the short story text as a whole refuses to lend itself completely to an unequivocal celebration of hyphenated identity.

In conclusion, I want to come back to the cultural and political effect of the interaction of genre and reception. As these different readings exemplify, fictional literature offers a unique experience unavailable elsewhere: the dual experience of being participant and observer at the same time. The function of fiction is to allow us to take up various fictional positions for identification, identification based on difference and identification based on similarity.[6] Yet this multiplicity is not always appreciated. According to Winfried Fluck, fiction can affect its recipients through one textual element only. When readers make segmented use of a narrative, the effect on the reader may be the exact opposite of its ideological intention (cf. Fluck 2007). The effect of projection can potentially enlarge on any aspect of the text. As short stories depend much more than other fictional texts on exterior frameworks, textual markers that alert readers to a diasporic situation tend to produce a convergence of readers towards certain accepted opinions. Rather than preventing an emotional response on the part of the audience, this appellative structure often produces vehement partisanship which sometimes has little grounding in the text, a partisanship especially strong in postcolonial literature.

The genre of short story particularly invites the reader to participate in the process of signification by its necessarily elliptical form. The reader is placed in a strategic position, charged with determining meanings—ethnic, racial, or cultural—by imaginatively bridging textual insularity. This is where the particular affinity to the postcolonial is produced, according to Rocío Davis:

> The characteristic of contemporary writing of encouraging participation of the reader in the production of meaning [. . .] or using fragments or incompleteness to force the reader to make the connections [. . .] is not merely descriptive of how ethnicity is experienced, but more importantly is an ethical device attempting to activate in the reader a desire

for *communitas* with others, while preserving rather than effacing differences. (Davis 2001: 18)

Thus the fragmentary nature of the text encourages the confluence of temporary interested reading communities. Reading as a postcolonialist means bringing a set of firm expectations and attitudes to a text. Even though this is a conscious act of employing a set of ethics and political convictions in reading, it can also degenerate into a conventional response from which literature's famous defamiliarizing strategies are unable to remove the veil of familiarity. It may mean having to accept fervid communities of believers who sometimes produce predictable criticism because directed interest leads them to focus on one aspect of a fiction, and academic pressures often necessitate participation in common discourse.

A postcolonial critical approach obviously cannot content itself with increasing the multiplicity of textual meanings. Rather, postcolonialism can be acknowledged as a power which not only shapes our reading, but also our lives through the formation of interpretive communities where we exchange views and share opinions beyond regional and national boundaries. This web-working can be welcomed as a positive transnational side-effect. After all, it is not to be regretted if an aspect in a literary work is found that justifies the ethical or moral positions brought to the reading. Reading as postcolonialist then promotes acts of cultural transfer which turn the individual into a much more complex and interrelated subject, connecting with different fictional voices as well as with other readers in sharing second narratives of (selective) response. For this social and political function of literature the genre of short story provides ample opportunity.

Notes

1. In referring to the reading process, I want to expand the idea of the implied reader. This concept by Wolfgang Iser was a productive construction in his attempt to define the textual strategies which occasion valid readings. However, as it is ultimately hermeneutic, it does not tell us enough about the effect of the "act of reading" (Iser 1984). This mental organizational act involves transfer processes that are part of the reading experience and therefore largely invisible in textuality. In "processing online," in Mark Turner's phrase (Fauconnier/Turner 2003), the reader parasitically uses the fictional text as host to realize a plethora of repressed desires. This processing of text is not accessible except through introspective description. With this empirically broadened concept of reception, I do not mean to infer that the text is not open to each and every reading. Documents of the reader's experience (whether arrived at through hermeneutics or more emotional, intuitive responses) are necessarily "interpretations" and hence exist inevitably as "second narratives" (Fluck 2005: 34). However, they are not only the result of subjective predispositions, since the text contains references to preexisting discourses which constitute what Iser calls a "repertoire" of a narrative (Iser 1984: 115), a

repertoire which consists of familiar territory within the text, reflecting the culture from which the text has emerged, so that the reader relies not only on the text, but also on a context or "cultural imaginary" determining meaning in the production as well as in the reception.

2. The basic theoretical arguments made here are developed at greater length in my book *Short Story: Textsorte und Leseerfahrung* (2007); also cf. Brosch 2009.

3. But there are demurrals to this argument. It is extremely difficult to think what generally applicable relationship can be said to exist between the short story and the experience of postcolonialism per se (Hunter 2007: 139). As an onto-logical understanding of cultures has vanished, authenticity seems to be also receding from the horizon and processes of hybridization cannot be depicted as unique to postcolonial or diasporic experience.

4. Lahiri encourages these notions by saying: "Unlike my parents, I translate not so much to survive in the world around me as to create and illuminate a non-existent one. Fiction is the foreign land of my choosing, the place where I strive to convey and preserve the meaningful. And whether I write as an American or an Indian, about things American or Indian or otherwise, one thing remains constant, I translate, therefore I am" (cf. Kuortti 2007: 217). Harish Trivedi calls this an "abuse or, in theoretical euphemism, [a] catachrestic use, of the term translation" (Trivedi 2007: 285). Trivedi rejects the use of "translation" as an overarching metaphor "for the unequal power relationship" whether in the for-mer colonies or in diaspora, so that "[t]he colonial subject fixed to his native site as well as the unsited migrant post-colonial are thus equally translated persons" (Bassnett and Trivedi 1999: 12f).

5. For an elaboration on these terms cf. Hogan 2003: 212.

6. This imaginary transfer in reading fictional texts not only gratifies by extension of subjective interiority, it also performs the feat of taking up multiple identifica-tory positions; we can identify with different characters, simultaneously enact and observe different experiences and indulge in memory saturated mental images of elements of the text. In the process of reading, we become participant and observer at the same time, shifting our attitude (not always consciously) from abandonment to evaluation (Appleyard 1991: 53f; cf. also Gallagher and Greenblatt 2000: 17).

Works Cited

Appleyard, J.A. (1991) *Becoming a Reader: The Experience of Fiction from Childhood to Adulthood*, Cambridge: Cambridge University Press.

Bassnett, S. and Trivedi, H. (1999) 'Introduction: Of Colonies, Cannibals and Ver-naculars', in S. Bassnett and H. Trivedi (eds) *Postcolonial Translation: Theory and Practice*, London: Routledge, 1–18.

Bhabha, H.K. (2000 [1994]) *The Location of Culture*, London: Routledge.

Brosch, R. (2009) 'Migrating Images and Communal Experience', in S. Säckel, W. Göbel, and N. Hamdy (eds) (2009) *Semiotic Encounters: Text, Image and Trans-Nation*, Amsterdam: Rodopi, 51–65.

———. (2007) *Short Story: Textsorte und Leseerfahrung*, Trier: WVT.

Brown, S.H. (1989) 'Discourse Analysis and the Short Story', in S. Lohafer and J.E. Clarey (eds) *Short Story Theory at the Crossroads*, Baton Rouge, LA: Louisiana State University Press, 217–248.

Davis, R.G. (2001) *Transcultural Reinventions: Asian American and Asian Canadian Short Story Cycles*, Toronto: TSAR Publications.

Edwards, B.H. (2004) 'Introduction: The Genres of Postcolonialism', *Social Text*, 78, 22/1: 1–15.

Fauconnier, G. and Turner, M. (2003) *The Way We Think: Conceptual Blending and the Mind's Hidden Complexities*, New York: Basic Books.

Fluck, W. (2005) 'Imaginary Space; Or, Space as Aesthetic Object', in K. Benesch and K. Schmidt (eds) *Space in America: Theory, History, Culture*, Amsterdam: Rodopi, 25–40.

——. (2007) 'Playing Indian: Media Reception as Transfer', in G.S. Freyermuth (ed.) *Intermedialität / Transmedialität*, Köln: Böhlau, 67–86.

Gallagher, C. and Greenblatt, S. (2000) *Practicing New Historicism*, London: University of Chicago Press.

Hanson, C. (1989) *Re-Reading the Short Story*, Basingstoke: Macmillan.

Hogan, P.C. (2003) *The Mind and its Stories: Narrative Universals and Human Emotion*, New York: Cambridge University Press.

Huggan, G. (2007) *Australian Literature: Postcolonialism, Racism, Transnationalism*, Oxford: Oxford University Press.

Hunter, A. (2007) *The Cambridge Introduction to the Short Story in English*, Cambridge: Cambridge University Press.

Hunter, L. (2001) *Literary Value / Cultural Power: Verbal Arts in the 21ˢᵗ Century*, Manchester: Manchester University Press.

Iser, W. (1984) *Der Akt des Lesens: Theorie ästhetischer Wirkung*, München: Fink.

Kakutani, M. (2008) 'Wonder Bread and Curry: Mingling Cultures, Conflicted Hearts', *The New York Times*, 4 April 2008: 1–2. http://www.nytimes.com/2008/04/04/books/04Book.html. Accessed: 28 April, 2010.

Korte, B. (2003) *The Short Story in Britain: A Historical Sketch and Anthology*, Tübingen: Francke.

Kuortti, J. (2007) 'Problematic Hybrid Identity in the Diasporic Writings of Jhumpa Lahiri', in J. Kuortti and J. Nyman (eds) *Reconstructing Hybridity: Post-Colonial Studies in Transition*, Amsterdam: Rodopi, 205–219.

Lahiri, J. (1999) 'This Blessed House', *Interpreter of Maladies*, New York: Houghton Mifflin Harcourt, 136–157.

Lane, R.J. (2006) *The Postcolonial Novel*, Cambridge: Polity Press.

Lefevere, A. (1999) 'Composing the Other', in S. Bassnett and H. Trivedi (eds) *Post-colonial Translation: Theory and Practice*, London: Routledge, 75–94.

Ramsdell, C. (2003) 'Homi Bhabha and the Postcolonial Short Story', in F. Iftekharrudin et. al. (eds) *Postmodern Approaches to the Short Story*, Westport, CN: Praeger, 97–106.

Stafford, B.M. (1999) *Visual Analogy: Consciousness as the Art of Connecting*, Cambridge, MA: MIT Press.

Trivedi, H. (2007) 'Translating Culture vs. Cultural Translation', in P. St-Pierre and P.C. Kar (eds) *In Translation: Reflections, Refractions, Transformations*, Amsterdam: John Benjamins, 277–287.

Werbner, P. (1997) 'Introduction: The Dialectics of Cultural Hybridity', in P. Werbner and T. Modood (eds) *Debating Cultural Hybridity: Multi-Cultural Identities and the Politics of Anti-Racism*, London: Zed, 1–26.

14 Postcolonialism and Nostalgia in Michael Ondaatje's *Divisadero*

Georgiana Banita

The raw truth of an incident never ends.

(Michael Ondaatje)

The leave-it state. You got money you want to gamble, leave it here. You got a wife you want to get rid of? Get rid of her here. Extra atom bomb you don't need? Blow it up here. Nobody's gonna mind in the slightest. The slogan of Nevada is, 'Anything goes, but don't complain if it went.'

(Arthur Miller, *The Misfits*)

Narrative in Transit: Michael Ondaatje and the World Novel

The global community of Michael Ondaatje's readers was rocked in 2007 by the publication and critical success of *Divisadero*, a transnational yet also deeply regional novel for which Ondaatje's previous works had not quite prepared us. Briefly, the narrative is divided between a family (a father and his daughter, Anna, adopted daughter Claire, and the orphaned hired hand Coop) in the 1970s California countryside, and the story of the obscure writer Lucien Segura in pre-World War I southern France. The novel's cross-cultural, transhistorical narrative strands are linked by a violent act that splits the family apart. Upon discovering his daughter's sexual involvement with Coop, Anna's father explosively interrupts the teenagers' lovemaking and banishes them both from the farm. Years later, Anna resettles in France where she researches Segura's life, partly in an attempt to escape her own past. Claire relocates to San Francisco, but still visits her adoptive father on a weekly basis, while Coop is left to wander through the neon landscapes of Nevada's casinos, watching footage of the Gulf Wars on TV to break the dull pattern of gambling.

Despite the apparent dislocations and disjunctions this plot implies, *Divisadero* is filled with parallels and echoes across time and place, giving an impression of transnational literature as closely related to the cinematic art of editing[1] and suggesting the central observation of this chapter: The television images of America's post-Cold War involvement in the Middle

East, images that were "fought over rhetorically as evidence for this or that claim about the war" (Simons 2007: 184), resonate with the politically sensitive poetics of Ondaatje's novel. Of course, Canada participated in the 1991 military operations in the Persian Gulf and supported sanctions against Iraq throughout the 1990s, thus challenging the bedrock tradition of Canadian peacekeeping. More recently, Canada also participated in the 2001 U.S.-led war efforts in Afghanistan, again troubling Canada's image as peaceable nation. Of concern in *Divisadero* is not so much the issue of Canada's military interventions, but a kind of postcolonial nostalgia that revolves less around memory or repression than around distortion and desire.

Critical responses to *Divisadero* have overlooked the novel's postcolonial stakes and its nostalgia for a model of power and difference that a transnational paradigm (which is what most critics see in both *Anil's Ghost* and *Divisadero*) has successfully obscured. My primary concern is to rectify this perception by exploring the parallels between the post-traumatic nostalgia that traverses the novel's layered narratives, on the one hand, and the traumatophilic return of imperialist desire in the novel's sporadic treatment of America's past and current wars on the other hand. In other words, I seek to reveal the connections between the sphere of intimate relations and the geopolitical in a novel that condenses discourses of nostalgia and colonialism. Some critics have dismissed the presence of the Gulf Wars in the novel as a jarring political interlude in what is mainly a prose study of poetic language. I argue that far from being awkward or superfluous, the Gulf War episodes expose the colonial relations of power that obtain in the world—both in a larger geopolitical context and in the private realm.

The Domesticity of Empire

My own understanding of the interactions between transnationalism and domesticity is indebted to the insights of Amy Kaplan, who contends that "domestic and foreign spaces are closer than we think, and that the dynamics of imperial expansion cast them into jarring proximity" (Kaplan 2002: 1). *Divisadero* confirms Kaplan's sense that "cultural phenomena we think of as domestic or particularly national are forged in a crucible of foreign relations" (Kaplan 2002: 1). To cite the most obvious example, the novel depicts Nevada as a blurred borderland between one of America's most iconic visual symbols (Las Vegas) and the country's imperialist explorations in the Middle Eastern desert. As an ambiguous space that is both foreign and domestic, the desert suggests a deterritorialized arena riddled with instability that prompts a reconsideration of the terms and issues clustering around post-1989 U.S. expansionist exploits: (post)colonialism, Empire, imperialism, and globalization. Kaplan persuasively contests the distinction posited by Hardt and Negri between Empire as denoting the contemporary world of globalization, and imperialism as revolving around a territorial centre of power: "these two tendencies are not as distinct as Hardt and Negri contend," she writes (Kaplan 2002: 15). Similarly, to separate postcolonialism from globalization in *Divisadero* is to ignore post-Cold War American history and the veiled colonial frontiers inscribed by the two Gulf Wars in particular.

The critical eagerness to remove the postcolonial from the sphere of Ondaatje's geographically transgressive narratives was sparked by the politically uncommitted stance adopted by *Anil's Ghost*. As Brian May observes, Anil is a figure of alterity "but not subalternity, too westernized, too hybridized, too cosmopolitan" (May 2008: 909) to successfully play a subaltern role. This assessment is echoed by Heike Härting, who argues that *Anil's Ghost* favours "a nomadic configuration of identity," which keeps Anil "suspended in a state of perpetual foreignness and transition rather than allowing her to inhabit multiple cultural and historical spaces at once" (Härting 2003: 50–51). However, as Timothy Brennan compellingly cautions, "if one means by globalization the creation of new 'world subjects' who are not bound by the laws and territorial limitations of locality—or indeed, are necessarily happy in their uprootedness—one is indulging in a fiction" (Brennan 2001: 673–674). Both *Anil's Ghost* and many of its scholarly readers indulge in a similar fantasy. The much more territorial *Divisadero* chooses America as its central setting on account of its global localism (illustrated, among others, by casino iconography) and of its imperial inflections, particularly the two Gulf Wars. This choice makes sense to the extent that "the key to the link between classical imperialism and contemporary globalization in the twentieth century has been the role of the United States" (Ashcroft, Griffiths, and Tiffin 1998: 112–113).

My claim is that *Divisadero* contains both a sentimental desire for postcolonialism's straightforward dynamics of power, and the opposite of this affect (suggested by Coop's amnesiac rootlessness), thus enacting an ambivalent aesthetic that points beyond both postcolonialism and utopian global imaginaries. In fact, any clear-cut distinction between postcolonialism and so-called fictions of globalization would overlook the ways in which "the postcolonial often seems to be the name for the critical practice that precedes and provides the foundations for global or transnational cultural studies" (O'Brien and Szeman 2001: 605). The novel encodes both the private and the political, two levels connected by the idiom and imagery of nostalgia. Public matters, such as the endless war in Iraq, echo the violent childhood trauma still resonating in the characters' lives, just as personal habits (Coop's gambling for instance) and the very evasiveness of the novel's poetic style come to stand in for a kind of public policy as disjointed and fluctuating as Ondaatje's own fictional aesthetics, one that denies readers a clear grasp on the political events described. Margaret Scanlan's statement on the political import of *Anil's Ghost* aptly encapsulates the apparent political stakes of *Divisadero*: Anil, Scanlan writes, "reproduces no political rhetoric, adjudicates no political claims, projects no political solutions" (Scanlan 2004:

302). Ondaatje himself has kept activist interpretations of the novel at arm's length: "I didn't want to make assured judgements about what should be done—which is often incendiary and facile [. . .] I was very careful to try and avoid the easy solutions" (Jaggi 2004: 253). Like *Anil's Ghost, Divisadero* is a study of "unhistorical lives" (Ondaatje 2007: 55) within a historical moment, or moments, lives which give a temporary contour to the liminal spaces where a random series of events become history. About Segura, for instance, Ondaatje writes:

> For much of his life the man was unknown, save that he was a poet and later the author of a jeremiad about the Great War. And in the years since his death, knowledge of him has sunk into the fabric and soil of this region, so he is almost forgotten by his countrymen. Anna loves such strangers to history; for her they are essential as underground rivers. (Ondaatje 2007: 85)

In *Anil's Ghost*, Victoria Cook writes, "Ondaatje reveals Anil's transnational nature as being a continually changing mixture of a variety of cultures, which incorporates, encompasses and contains various fragments in one unified being" (Cook 2004: 3). *Divisadero* punctures this image of a unified being containing a variety of cultural elements, and does so by showing how individuals fall prey to traumatic histories that they attempt to escape by invading, as it were, the geographic and emotional territories of others, just as nations, in this case the U.S., cave in to historical obsessions they constantly re-enact in a bid to salvage their past. In both cases the psychological infrastructure needed to maintain this extraterritorial impetus relies on a form of nostalgia as the desire not to recuperate what has been lost, but to reach a utopian state of fulfilment that never previously existed. *Divisadero* thus approaches postcolonialism not from the conventional perspective of the colonized subject but that of a hybrid, destabilized, rudderless formerly colonial power. Yet, instead of portraying the former empire as irresponsibly postmodern, Ondaatje displays a profound awareness of the historical traumas that reduced the "empire" to merely the "world" (or worlds), and its ordered possession to a chaos of the dispossessed. Writing about *Anil's Ghost*, Victoria Burrows has argued that

> Ondaatje's famously fragmentary and ambivalent narrative exposes the way in which the developed world turns away from the experience of trauma that so often blights the existence of many postcolonial subjects in different parts of the developing world. (Burrows 2008: 162)

However, for colonial powers the loss of their former territorial outreach can be just as traumatizing and often leads to a frantic replay of precisely those colonial interventions that doomed them in the first place. Thus *Divisadero* may be interpreted as a literary obituary for the melancholy spectre of America's colonial power, especially as it relates to the First Gulf War and the 2003 invasion of Iraq—both events being invoked at key junctures in the novel.

Fragmentary Fiction and Transnational Aesthetics

Divisadero not only obliquely places its domestic plot "in the complicated broader context that repels a sense of satisfaction or even connection" (Keen 2007: 156), but reassembles the broken lives of its protagonists into a narrative that orbits around multiple centres of consciousness. Having abandoned his family, the French poet Lucien Segura—who forms the subject of a biography written by Anna—encounters a family of gypsies in southern France in the early decades of the twentieth century. Only the wife, Aria, is ethnically Roma, the husband having adopted her habits and lifestyle as a result of their union. When Lucien asks him about his name, which the husband is reluctant to reveal, the answer he receives is both ambivalent and very telling: "I am not Roma, the husband said. I have simply attached myself to her, I live in *her* world. I am not important" (Ondaatje 2007: 175). Segura comes to inhabit the world of these strangers and to covet the kind of anonymity that the husband cultivates, who "used names like passwords, all of them with a brief life span" (Ondaatje 2007: 182). In the manner of nomads, Ondaatje's protagonists in this novel float free of all fixed locations, abandoning points and coordinates while retaining, as the husband's statement intimates, a sense of entering each other's worlds and attaching themselves to their uniqueness, however far-flung and geographically disparate these worlds may be. The gypsy that Segura encounters in fact delineates features that are common to most of *Divisadero*'s characters. "His sentences were half-hearted, unpersuasive," Ondaatje writes. "He appeared uncertain of all things, and was content to reside in a state as humble as a sparrow" (Ondaatje 2007: 176). He is "not quite of this world, his remarks porous, his talents invisible, the paths he took almost erased" (Ondaatje 2007: 176). The opacity of his image and the fluidity of his trajectories encapsulate the fragmentary aesthetics of this book, where "everything is collage" (Ondaatje 2007: 16).

Many critics have noted *Divisadero*'s fragmented, discontinuous narrative, which deconstructs spatial and temporal boundaries. Indeed, *Divisadero* seems incoherent, or, as Brian May would put it, "philosophically incoherentist" (May 2008: 905). Claire's words are instructive in this regard: "In spite of her desire for a contained universe, her life felt scattered, full of many small moments, without great purpose" (Ondaatje 2007: 157). The novel's protagonists float on the viscous texture of their lives like what Canadian writer Daphne Marlatt would call "islands cut off from the main" (Marlatt 1996: 16).[2] If marriage and family life represent alliances that help cement national identities, *Divisadero* employs extramarital romances, short-lived affairs, and incest as metaphors of loose transnational bonds among the protagonists.[3] Both temporal and territorial, the past shared by Anna, Claire, and Coop survives in odd fragments that barely suggest what lies behind them, yet in their tempo and texture these fragments form independent if interrelated worlds. The tangled web of connections the three protagonists maintain toward their origins leaves them oddly positioned geographically, yet firmly at home in their private, deterritorialized worlds, in turn separated by what Ondaatje elsewhere calls "moats of privacy" (Ondaatje 2000: 278). It is inside these small gaps that *Divisadero*'s multiple stories huddle, creating an impression of static inactivity. Yet Ondaatje's particular brand of transitorial fiction in *Divisadero* also involves various means of transportation that help un-map the novel's landscapes. Countless vehicles are mentioned in the novel, yet far from invigorating the narrative, the transitoriness they facilitate is more often "experienced as the dizziness of hypertension" (Stewart 1988: 231). The historical lack of progression that the novel evinces is thus marked by its vehicular circularity: the narrative features, in this particular order, horses, cars, trailers, trains, planes, a skateboard, and finally a sinking boat as instrument of Segura's suicide at the end of the novel.[4]

In this sense, although both *Anil's Ghost* and *Divisadero* work with what Wolfgang Iser would call a poetics of the blank—"Not knowing something essential makes you more involved," Segura opines (Ondaatje 2007: 208)—while Anil seeks to solve a mystery contained partly in the narrative and partly in her own identity, *Divisadero*'s mysteries form a wide, permeable net of countless gaps through which identities and stories are permanently seeping. Far from encapsulating transnationalism in one character, *Divisadero* is more diffuse, its narrative subjectivities more provisional and shifting. "She too has lived a stranger's life," Ondaatje writes of Anna. "There are layers of compulsive secrecy in her. She knows there is a 'flock' of Annas" (Ondaatje 2007: 88). In other words, what separates *Anil's Ghost* from *Divisadero* is the difference they illustrate between an aesthetics of embeddedness and an aesthetics of adjacency. Taking her cue from Sigmund Freud's theory of the unconscious and Julia Kristeva's work on uncanny strangeness, Hilde Staels proposes that "poetic discourse in *Anil's Ghost* disrupts the rules of 'normal' communicative discourse and gives expression to the Other within the self" (Staels 2007: 978). The uncanny in *Divisadero*'s figures, I would argue, lies not within but in-between, as a repressed distance. As Carmen Concilio remarks, "*Divisadero* designs both a precise topography as well as the direction of a destiny: it is the name of a street in San Francisco, and it vaguely hints at distancing" (Concilio 2009: 13). Linking the spatial and temporal levels implied in Concilio's statement is a form of nostalgia that mediates between the novel's space and time as both magnet and repellent.

Nostalgia—Place—Time

The term 'nostalgia' is a vexed one. "What is nostalgia," Daphne Marlatt asks in her novel *Taken*—which is similarly haunted by the Gulf War—"but the longing for a place the body opens to" (Marlatt 1996: 7). The place in this case is faraway Baghdad, where Operation Desert Storm is underway, pointing out, in the dim light of night explosions, "this sense of an enemy again" (Marlatt 1996: 19). Although Ondaatje's previous works often traced the stories of real historical figures (such as Billy Bud or himself in *Running in the Family*) and *Divisadero* is clearly set against a post-Cold War background, the novel zeroes in on unhistorical characters and plots that merely adumbrate larger historical narratives, while floating loosely around the margins of history. "What the novelist is responsible for," Ondaatje observes, is the "unhistorical, unofficial— what goes on in private" (Jaggi 2004: 254). Ondaatje's interest in unhistorical lives is itself a form of nostalgia, belied by recurring references to historical events. The novel thus inhabits both past and present, deriving its strength from the tension-filled gap that separates them, thereby exposing nostalgic sentiment "to be a mere façade covering over an affect tending towards its opposite, which is an interest in what is really, materially, bodily there" (May 2008: 912). In contrast to what Homi Bhabha describes as the nostalgia that underwrites narratives of nationhood, *Divisadero* details not the integration of self and nation through the work of mourning but their dissolution.

As a result, despite the international ramifications of the plot, *Divisadero*'s characters remain locked in their discrete, solitary, silent entities, inhabiting multiple worlds in both space and time. *Divisadero* constructs memory by juxtaposing personal and collective geographies as a formal technique and organizing principle. The novel thus not only illustrates current theories of trauma narrative as adopting primarily modernist or non-linear forms, but also provides fresh insight into the transnationalism of trauma and its function at the intersection between colonialism and transnationalism. According to Ondaatje, his novels are "about searchers trying to find the mysterious central character" (Jaggi 2007: npn), yet the world depicted in *Divisadero* is flat, as it lacks a centre of gravity, raising the question, repeatedly invoked by Anna herself, whether anyone can really play the central part in their own stories. From this, the larger issue arises of what determines the centrality of a spatial position in a transnational continuum and how this centrality still mirrors colonial formations.

With its forensic interest in the fresh bodies of political killings, *Anil's Ghost* can already be said to inhabit a post-traumatic narrative space, displaying an aftermath aesthetics that critics of the novel have condemned as apolitical and ethically suspect. The blood of the Sri Lankan civil war is not on their hands but, as Anil's co-worker, Sarath, puts it, on their clothes (Ondaatje 2000: 48), sprayed from a distance and unable to penetrate the protective shield of their Westernized profession, which leads them to "expect clearly marked roads to the source of most mysteries" (Ondaatje 2000: 54). The sudden irruption of the First Gulf War and of the 2003 Iraq invasion in *Divisadero* (further complicated by conversations about Vietnam between Claire and her employer) suggest both the latency and the perpetual presence of trauma. Left unassimilated by the narrative, the footage of desert explosions carries unspeakable suffering over time zones and geographical locales and, like the eruption of violence that flung Anna, Claire, and Coop on separate trajectories, the desert war never ends. Under scrutiny, the war even appears to awaken echoes of old traumas to which the characters realize they have never been able to resign themselves. Once "the war machine gears up across all media," Marlatt writes of the first Gulf War, "once it begins, where does it end?" (Marlatt 1996: 15). This continuity is a cross-generational one, Marlatt suggests, inherited like weather and pervading both personal and public realms—"a set of atmospheric conditions another *we* will live within" (Marlatt 1996: 38, emphasis in original). Writing about *The English Patient*, Marlene Goldman interprets the novel as an allegory of what she calls the "non-progressive character of human history" (Goldman 2001: 903). *Divisadero* further accentuates this understanding of history as a repetitive, stalled continuum.

Specifically, the traumatic violence that sets fire to everyone's lives is perpetrated by the father figure, who violently disrupts Anna's short-lived affair with Coop. Drawing on the pain and confusion caused by this punctual yet deeply traumatic intervention ("something that might occur within just a square inch or two of a Brueghel," Ondaatje 2007: 140), *Divisadero* creates a narrative structure that replicates the experience of nostalgia, which decelerates both the evolution of the characters and the narrative that documents it. As Kathleen Stewart writes: "Nostalgia, like the economy it runs with, is everywhere. But it is a cultural practice, not a given content; its forms, meanings, and effects shift with the context—it depends on where the speaker stands in the landscape of the present" (Stewart 1988: 227). At times nostalgia conjures up a memory of the idyllic life on the Californian farm for Anna, now engaged in other affective liaisons, at other times it creates a caesura that enables her to distance herself from her own past and to inhabit the memories of the poet she is researching. More often, both directions are involved, as in this paragraph:

> There are times when she needs to hide in a stranger's landscape, so that she can look back at the tumult of her youth, to the still-undiminished violence of her bloodied naked self between her father and Coop, the moment of violence that deformed her, all of them. (Ondaatje 2007: 75)

By recreating a sense of time and place, and of a subjectivity in time and place, Anna's nostalgia for the lost Paradise of the childhood triangle helps her attach points and coordinates to her displaced existence. As Stewart observes, in those situations "where the self is a pastiche of styles glued to a surface, nostalgia becomes the very lighthouse waving us back to shore—the one point on the landscape that gives hope of direction" (Stewart 1988: 229).

Yet the characters' grief cannot simply be regarded as a private affair. Their post-traumatic rituals accrue wider cultural significance and should be interpreted as modes of collective melancholia—a repetitive and stunted labour replicated in the process of reading. The narrative often dissolves into a mode of waiting, hovering between interest and apathy. The text appears to be dispersing, flowing back and forth, curling and swivelling, forcing the reader to remember—where remembering involves a strong dose of refashioning and reinvention—in a gesture that might be called hermeneutic nostalgia. Ultimately, the reader longs for a coherent story instead of the jagged timeline Ondaatje offers with almost perverse relish:

> It's like a villanelle, this inclination of going back to events in our past, the way the villanelle's form refuses to move forward in linear development, circling instead at those familiar moments of emotion. Only the rereading counts, Nabokov said. [. . .] For we live with those retrievals from childhood that coalesce and echo throughout our lives, the way shattered pieces of glass in a kaleidoscope reappear in new forms and are songlike in their refrains and rhymes, making up a single monologue. We live permanently in the recurrence of our own stories, whatever story we tell. (Ondaatje 2007: 136)

Just as Anna, Claire, and most obviously Coop, who loses his memory as a result of a violent beating at the hand of fellow gamblers, constantly struggle to rearrange their lives according to an adequate sequence of tenses, narrative memory is revealed as an essentially incomplete process which has as its aim the ultimately impossible recovery of a narrative subject. This impossibility is reinforced by the inclusion of several photographic segments into the novel, which suggest the unstable subjectivities of those depicted, and function as a concretization of the nostalgic tendencies inherent in the narrative itself. Once he loses his memory, Coop comes to inhabit a world of images, and feels burdened by their lack of history. This also determines the uncanny materiality of Coop's spectre as it haunts the narrative, remaining obdurately unfamiliar, despite the novel's attention to his physical presence. Coop cannot be plotted or objectified. He remains a spectre, unhoused by the narrative in which he fleetingly appears:

> Why was Coop never in our father's photographs? There were a few pictures taken of him, but these seemed preoccupied with texture and light. And there were some abstract reflections of him in a window, or of his shadow on the grass or on the flank of an animal. How many things could you throw your image against? (Ondaatje 2007: 20)

The ideal décor for Coop's oblivion is the state of Nevada, recalling what Paul Virilio—relying on the idiom of neuropathology—calls "topographical amnesia" (Virilio 1994: 1). The images of the Iraq War punctuate images of the Nevada desert, underlining the novel's representation of space as disrupted yet continuous. This sense of continuity derives to some extent from the perception of the 2003 Iraq invasion as a repetition of the 1991 Gulf War, a recurrence that adds weight to the novel's "overall formal and thematic preoccupation with repetition, doubling, and splitting" (De Smyter 2009: 99). History repeats itself here neither as tragedy nor as farce but as sustained continuum, a temporal and spatial cadence dimly perceptible in the background of domestic events.

The Forever War[4]

In fact the whole novel serves to memorialize a single traumatic event without placing it in a chronology—suggesting even the breakdown of chronology—until the Iraq moment, which functions to indicate both a breach in time and its final suture. Ondaatje's narratives often gravitate towards war (Sri Lanka's civil war in *Anil's Ghost*, World War II in *The English Patient*); in the more oblique *Divisadero*, Ondaatje's allusions to the Gulf Wars are fleeting but significant. In fact, the novel's fragmentary style contributes to the sense of menace emanated by these sequences. After all, *Divisadero*'s chief concern lies with the representation of invisible trauma (as atemporal and unlocalized trace of psychological stress), as opposed to *Anil's Ghost*, whose protagonist examines the concrete traces of occupational trauma on human bones. In fact, I would go as far as to claim that the constitutive role of the Gulf Wars in *Divisadero* is highlighted precisely by the novel's general refusal to represent these events. Like the Nevada gamblers, the narrative fails to register the beginning of the war, let alone consider its methods and consequences:

> The Gulf War begins at 2:35 a.m. during the early hours of January 17, 1991. But it is just another late afternoon in the casinos of Nevada. The television sets hanging in mid-air that normally replay horse races or football games are running animated illustrations of the American attack. For the three thousand gamblers inhaling piped-in oxygen at the Horseshoe, the war is already a video game, taking place on a fictional planet. The TV screens are locked on mute. [. . .] Simultaneously, in the other desert's night, orange-white explosions and fireballs light up the horizon. [. . .] During the next four days, one of the great high-tech massacres of the modern era takes place. (Ondaatje 2007: 53)

The setting of the games which Coop and his friend engage in is aptly invoked to suggest not merely the gamble of yet another Gulf War but also the correspondence between the desert of Nevada and that of Iraq, and finally as a subtle reference to the desert that formed the backdrop to *The English Patient*. As an environment bereft of any props, the desert is an ideal background to history, a place of amnesia, suggestive of emotional dryness and catatonic passivity. Like the depressives described by Julia

Kristeva in *Black Sun,* Coop "wanders in pursuit of continuously disappointing adventures and loves; or else retreats, disconsolate and aphasic" (Kristeva 1989: 13), alone with his memories and then entirely alone, the slate wiped clean by his amnesia. Coop's depression is coupled with a certain eroticization of suffering, rooted in his short-lived sexual relationship with Anna, echoed in his affair with the jazz-singer Bridget, and finally exorcised by his encounter with Claire and the prospect, displaced beyond the end of the story time, of a cathartic reunion with the girls' father. Coop is riveted to the past, as is the spectrum of America that follows him everywhere, a country nailed to its imperialist illusions. Coop's convulsive desire for a past of which he has been orphaned can thus be read as an allegory of America's nostalgia for what Freud would call the psychic object of its imperial construct, located within the imaginary space of the desert as ground zero of colonization, for which Las Vegas provides an apt objective correlative.[5] "Las Vegas is a kind of testimonial to contemporary modes of power, and functions oddly like the symbols of bygone imperial dominance that Vegas so gleefully appropriates," Jeffrey Nealon writes, referring to the Egyptian, Roman, and Ottoman iconography cited by the city's simulacral architecture (Nealon 2002: 80). The object of nostalgia, both domestic and historical, is not a concrete memory event, but a blurred representation put together in the imaginary realm, a fata morgana.

The parallels between the American and the Iraqi deserts can even be said to stage what Ken Cooper has described as the larger political "conflation of Las Vegas and the [nuclear] bomb as the symbol and landscape of the cold war and its attendant reign of terror" (Cooper 1992: 528). Indeed, a conflict such as the 1991 Gulf War unfolding in a desert that Baudrillard dubbed "a place of collapse" (Baudrillard 1995: 70) is excellently paired with Nevada as the place where the F–117 Stealth Fighter, the most widely used bomber of choice in the 1991 Persian Gulf War, was developed and tested, but also as the home of Baudrillard's simulacra and the hyperreal. Places like Disneyland or Las Vegas, Baudrillard contends, are "presented as imaginary in order to make us believe that the rest [of America] is real" (Baudrillard 1983: 25). Conversely, the Baghdad bombings are presented on casino television as the only reality of the Gulf War to suggest that "the massacre in the 'troublesome desert'—with American planes pouring down ten thousand rounds a minute onto a crowded highway of escaping soldiers" (Ondaatje 2007: 56)—is not an indubitable fact but a fleeting impression. To use the terminology of Gilles Deleuze and Félix Guattari, Las Vegas is not a place or "extension" in form and substance, but a pure "intensity," a shorthand for phantasmatic reinvention and the longing for more.[6] Imperial Las Vegas, then, "functions *not* by conquering or assimilating new territory, but rather by intensifying new versions of familiar things" (Nealon 2002: 81, emphasis in original). The repetition of the Gulf War, both as military intervention and media event, mirrors this intensification of the past that manifests itself as chronic postcolonial nostalgia. For Coop, Las Vegas and Lake Tahoe, the other casino area he frequents, occasion introverted meditations rather than opportunities to confront some other. This isolation chimes with the ways in which "since the fall of the Berlin wall in 1989 and the millennial 'defeat' of Soviet power worldwide, it seems like there is no 'out there' for casino capitalism to vanquish, no dialectical 'other' against which to define or test itself" (Nealon 2002: 83). The return to the father, which the novel stops short of recounting, reinstates Coop's bond with the earth and a land that offers greater stability than the desert, after years of wondering without touching the land of reality in a way reminiscent of the coloured flags he and Anna used to attach to the house they briefly inhabited as a couple, flags that were not permitted to touch ground. It is the rootedness of this house that he built with his own hands, and implicitly also the disciplinary domination of Anna's father (which made the girl all the more enticing), that Coop longs for in the non-place of the Nevada desert.

Nor does the environment of the casinos facilitate clear-cut territorial distinctions, serving instead as an artificial oasis of slow-motion, remembered time. As Venturi, Brown and Izenour aptly observe:

> The combination of darkness and enclosure of the gambling room and its subspaces makes for privacy, protection, concentration, and control. The intricate maze under the low ceiling never connects with outside light or outside space. This disorients the occupant in space and time. He loses track of where he is and when it is. Time is limitless, because the light of noon and midnight are exactly the same. Space is limitless, because the artificial light obscures rather than defines its boundaries. (Venturi, Brown and Izenour 1972: 44)

Illustrative of this ambiguity is the parallelism between the medieval costume carnival in which Coop and Claire participate and a contemporary protest march. The juxtaposition collapses historical time, as medieval monks clad in fourteenth century European village costumes carry anti-American placards. The novel also connects one scene set during the build-up to the first Gulf War with another on the eve of the 2003 Iraq invasion. Both Coop and the invading colonial power are seen as amnesiac and as such unaware of the traumatic loop they are caught in. Although he cannot recall anything about his life, Coop is startled by the footage of the Iraq invasion, and almost feels remnants of memories slowly surfacing, yet his attempts to retrieve a historical consciousness of the events remain fruitless and repetitive. Significantly, the music that accompanies the anti-war *slash* medieval carnival marches is the 'endless' version of *Fire on the Mountain*, one of Grateful Dead's most repetitive songs (Ondaatje 2007: 162), featuring a very unique beat, the very same one for the entire length of the piece.

Conclusion

In its traumatophilic style, *Divisadero* proposes an answer by telling a story whose narrative texture mimes trauma, whose characters replay it, and whose purportedly transnational, unmarked spaces secretly repeat the trauma of their colonial histories. The novel disrupts transnational plots of identity that centre on the trope of disconnection (witnessed earlier in *Anil's Ghost*), reinstating those discourses of nostalgia that inscribe a desire for unity and origin—a desire that lacks temporal and spatial dimensions, is never fulfilled, and feeds on itself as a movement without target. Ondaatje's evasions of conventional narrative development make a telling political point: the longing that permeates Coop, Anna, and Claire's sense of their past resonates with America's obsessive sifting through its military past in search of colonial authority. By challenging the traditional vision of colonialism as connected to temporal succession and territorial conquest, *Divisadero* exposes nostalgia as constitutive of contemporary colonialism. In positing a past in relation to a present while at the same time blurring the boundaries between the two, this kind of nostalgia creates a frame of relational meaning that responds to an increasingly fluid post-Cold War political landscape. The seduction of nostalgia is to construct a code of distinction in a 'world' where distinctions no longer obtain, to dramatize the separation between the self and the other. As alienation effect in the Brechtian sense, *Divisadero*'s nostalgia ultimately lies in the search for the never-ending truth of an incident (be it sex, violence, or war) that left an enticing, recoverable trace yet did not, as Baudrillard would put it, take 'place.'

Notes

1. For evidence of Ondaatje's interest in the editing process and its fragmentary aesthetics, see his book *The Conversations: Walter Murch and the Art of Editing Film*.
2. In the following I will refer repeatedly to Daphne Marlatt's 1996 novel *Taken* because this text may be seen as a predecessor and possibly as a model for *Divisadero*'s transnational, transhistorical plot and for its interest in the 1991 Gulf War (see also Sprout).
3. On sexual and geographical transgression in Ondaatje's work, particularly *The English Patient*, see Hsu.
4. Corresponding to this eclectic mobility aesthetics is the novel's genre syncretism: *Divisadero* features the "adventure story" narrative of Segura's life in France; the hard-boiled-western-film noir around Coop, with its smoky rooms and back alleys of poker-playing and drug addiction; the harlequin novel lifestyles of Segura's daughters; the picaresque road narrative of Segura's search for a country house in southern France; and finally, the academic life writing style of Anna's biography of the French author.
5. For the source of this section title, see Filkins 2008.

6. *The English Patient* already connected the history of Western imperialism with "a desert dream of nationlessness" (Shin 2007: 213). As Ondaatje writes, "the desert could not be claimed or owned—it was a piece of cloth carried by winds, never held down by stones, and given a hundred shifting names" (Ondaatje 1992: 138–139).

7. On Deleuze and Guattari's terminology, see Massumi 1992: 66.

8. A better term than amnesiac would probably be "forgetful," in the sense proposed by Ali Behdad in his book *A Forgetful Nation*, which argues that forgetting and recollection are not mutually exclusive, but differential aspects of the same process of cultural remembering. Behdad constructs his argument around America's selective forgetting or "negation" of its own history of immigration so as to ensure a state of cultural innocence, but his thesis seems applicable to the similar practices employed in the preparation of the Iraq invasion and of the public discourse around the U.S.' liberatory role in the region.

Works Cited

Ashcroft, B., Griffiths, G., and Tiffin, H. (1998) *Key Concepts in Post-Colonial Studies*, London: Routledge.

Baudrillard, J. (1983) *Simulations*; trans. P. Foss, P. Patton, and P. Beitchman, New York: Semiotext(e).

———. (1995) *The Gulf War Did Not Take Place*; trans. P. Patton, Bloomington: Indiana University Press.

Brennan, T. (2001) 'Cosmo-Theory', *The South Atlantic Quarterly*, 100/3: 659–691.

Burrows, V. (2008) 'The Heterotopic Spaces of Postcolonial Trauma in Michael Ondaatje's *Anil's Ghost*', *Studies in the Novel*, 40/1–2: 161–177.

Concilio, C. (2009) 'Michael Ondaatje's *Divisadero* and Photography', in C. Concilio (ed.) *Image Technologies in Canadian Literature*, Brussels: Peter Lang, 13–29.

Cook, V. (2004) 'Exploring Transnational Identities in Ondaatje's *Anil's Ghost*', *Comparative Literature and Culture*, 6/3. http://docs.lib.purdue.edu/clcweb/vol6/iss3/2/. Accessed: Nov. 9, 2011.

Cooper, K. (1992) '"Zero Pays the House": The Las Vegas Novel and Atomic Roulette', *Contemporary Literature*, 33/3: 528–544.

De Smyter, S. (2009) '"We Live Permanently in the Recurrence of Our Own Stories": Michael Ondaatje's *Divisadero*', *Studies in Canadian Literature*, 34/1: 99–119.

Filkins, D. (2008) *The Forever War*, New York: Knopf.

Goldman, M. (2001) '"Powerful Joy": Michael Ondaatje's *The English Patient* and Walter Benjamin's Allegorical Way of Seeing', *University of Toronto Quarterly*, 70/4: 902–922.

Härting, H. (2003) 'Diasporic Cross-Currents in Michael Ondaatje's *Anil's Ghost* and Anita Rau Badami's *The Hero's Walk*', *Studies in Canadian Literature*, 28/1: 43–70.

Hsu, H. (2004) 'Post-Nationalism and the Cinematic Apparatus in Minghella's Adaptation of Ondaatje's *The English Patient*', *Comparative Literature and Culture*, 6/3. http://docs.lib.purdue.edu/clcweb/vol6/iss3/6. Accessed: Nov. 9, 2011.

Jaggi, M. (2004) 'Michael Ondaatje in Conversation with Maya Jaggi', in S. Nasta (ed.) *Writing across Worlds: Contemporary Writers Talk*, London: Routledge, 250–265.

———. (2007) 'Rhymes of the Ancient Narrator', *The Sunday Times*, Sept. 16, 2007.

Kaplan, A. (2002) *The Anarchy of Empire in the Making of U.S. Culture*, Cambridge, MA: Harvard University Press.

Keen, S. (2007) *Empathy and the Novel*, Oxford: Oxford University Press.

Kristeva, J. (1987) *Soleil Noir: Dépression et mélancholie*, trans. L.S. Roudiez (1989) *Black Sun: Depression and Melancholia*, New York: Columbia University Press.

Marlatt, D. (1996) *Taken*, Concord: Anansi.

Massumi, B. (1992) *A User's Guide to Capitalism and Schizophrenia: Deviations from Deleuze and Guattari*, Cambridge, MA and London: MIT.

May, B. (2008) 'Extravagant Postcolonialism: Ethics and Individualism in Anglophonic, Anglocentric Postcolonial Fiction; Or, "What Was (This) Postcolonialism?"', *English Literary History*, 75: 899–937.

Nealon, J.T. (2002) 'Empire of the Intensities: A Random Walk Down Las Vegas Boulevard', *Parallax*, 8/1: 78–91.

O'Brien, S. and Szeman, I. (2001) 'Introduction: The Globalization of Fiction / the Fiction of Globalization', *South Atlantic Quarterly*, 100/3: 603–626.

Ondaatje, M. (1992) *The English Patient*, New York: Knopf.

———. (2000) *Anil's Ghost*, London: Picador.

———. (2002) *Walter Murch and the Art of Editing Film*, New York: Knopf.

———. (2007) *Divisadero*, New York: Knopf.

Scanlan, M. (2004) '*Anil's Ghost* and Terrorism's Time', *Studies in the Novel*, 36/3: 302–317.

Shin, A. (2007) 'The English Patient's Desert Dream', *Literature Interpretation Theory*, 18: 123–136.

Simons, H.W. (2007) 'From Post-9/11 Melodrama to Quagmire in Iraq: A Rhetorical History', *Rhetoric & Public Affairs*, 10/2: 183–194.

Sprout, F. (2009) 'Ghosts, Leaves, Photographs, and Memory: Seeing and Remembering Photographically in Daphne Marlatt's *Taken*', in C. Concilio and R.J. Lane (eds) *Image Technologies in Canadian Literature*, Brussels: Peter Lang, 81–98.

Staels, H. (2007) 'A Poetic Encounter with Otherness: The Ethics of Affect in Michael Ondaatje's *Anil's Ghost*', *University of Toronto Quarterly*, 76/3: 977–989.

Stewart, K. (1988) 'Nostalgia—A Polemic', *Cultural Anthropology*, 3/3: 227–241.

Venturi, R., Brown, D.S., and Izemour, S. (1972) *Learning from Las Vegas*, Cambridge, MA: MIT.

Virilio, P. (1994) *The Vision Machine*, Bloomington: Indiana University Press.

Contributors

Bill Ashcroft is a renowned critic and theorist, founding exponent of postcolonial theory, coauthor of *The Empire Writes Back*, the first text to examine systematically the field of postcolonial studies. He is author and coauthor of sixteen books and over 150 articles and chapters, including *Post-Colonial Transformation* (2001), *On Post-Colonial Futures* (2001), and *Caliban's Voice* (2008).

Georgiana Banita is an Assistant Professor of Literature and Media Studies at the University of Bamberg and Honorary Research Fellow at the United States Studies Centre, University of Sydney. Her first book, *Plotting Justice: Narrative Ethics and Literary Culture after 9/11* (2012) proposes an ethical approach to post-9/11 literature, linking narrative ethics with literary portrayals of racial profiling, psychoanalysis, and globalization. Her research has appeared in *Textual Practice*, *LIT: Literature Interpretation Theory*, *Biography*, *Critique*, *Parallax*, and *Peace Review*, in addition to chapters for several edited volumes. She is currently at work on a transnational cultural history of the American oil industry since 1850.

Renate Brosch holds the chair of English Literature at Stuttgart University. Her main research interests are in visual culture, narratology, fiction of the 19th century and modernism, and Australian Literature. She has published on Henry James (*Krisen des Sehens: Henry James und die Veränderung der Wahrnehmung im 19. Jahrhundert*, 2000), on text-image-relations, on neglected women authors in the modern period, and on short story theory (*Short Story: Textsorte und Leseerfahrung*, 2007) as well as on Australian literature and culture.

Sharae Deckard is a Lecturer in World Literature at University College Dublin. Her monograph, *Paradise Discourse, Imperialism and Globalization: Exploiting Eden* was published with Routledge in 2010. Her research interests include world-systems approaches to world literature, postcolonial environmental criticism, and world-ecology. She is currently coediting a special issue of the *Journal of Postcolonial Writing* on world literature, and has edited an issue of Green Letters 16 on Postcolonial/Global Ecologies. She has multiple articles forthcoming on Lindsay Collen and the Indian Ocean, Roberto Bolano and peripheral realism, Rana Dasgupta and the global ecogothic, and storm ecologies in Caribbean literature.

Ferial Ghazoul is Professor of English and Comparative Literature at the American University in Cairo and Editor of *Alif: Journal of Comparative Poetics*. She has published extensively on comparative medieval literature, postcolonial criticism, and gender studies. She has written and edited books on the *Arabian Nights*, on Edward Said, on Arab writers, and on Iraqi creative women writers. She has translated Arabic novels and collections of poetry and English and French literary theory. Her essays cover European, African, Asian, and Latin American literary texts.

Walter Goebel is Professor of English and American Studies at the University of Stuttgart. His main fields of interest are postcolonial theory, African American literature, and the history of the novel. He has published books on Sherwood Anderson (1982), Edward Bulwer-Lytton (1993), and the twentieth century African American novel (2001), and has coedited *Modernization and Literature* (2000), *Renaissance Humanism– Modern Humanism(s)* (2001), *Engendering Images of Man in the Long Eighteenth Century* (2001), *Beyond the Black Atlantic: Relocating Modernization and Technology* (2006), *Postcolonial (Dis)Affections* (2007), and *Locating Transnational Ideals* (2010).

Noha Hamdy is Assistant Lecturer at the University of Alexandria, Egypt. She is currently working on her PhD at the University of Stuttgart on networking and intermedial interfacing as narrative techniques in postmodern American Fiction, with a special focus on Don DeLillo. Her areas of interest include postcolonial theory, postmodern cyberpunk, the New Media Ecology School, Media Studies, especially intermediality, and theories of remediation in general.

Nadia El Kholy is Professor and Chair of the Dept. of English Language and Literature at Cairo University. She serves as Director of the National Council for Children's Culture, and is President of the Egyptian Book Council for Young Readers. She was a member of the jury for the Hans Christian Anderson international award for Children's Literature, and is currently a member of the IBBY (International Board of Books for Young Readers) Executive Committee. Her research interests include writing and translation for children, Comparative and Postcolonial Literature, and Gender Studies. She has contributed to the *Oxford Encyclopaedia of Children's Literature*, was coeditor of the *Women Writing Africa* series published by the Feminist Press in New York, and the ASTENE publication *Egypt in the Eyes of Travellers*. She has published a number of articles on the modern Arabic and English novel and has translated *Alice in Wonderland* into Arabic.

Sue Kossew is Professor of English at Monash University. She has published widely on South African, Australian, and postcolonial literatures. Her publications include *Pen and Power: A Post-colonial Reading of J.M. Coetzee and André Brink* (1996), *Critical Essays on J.M. Coetzee* (1998), *Re-Imagining Africa: New Critical Perspectives* (ed. with Dianne Schwerdt, 2001), and *Writing Woman, Writing Place: Australian and South African Fiction* (2004). She has recently published two edited collections, *Lighting Dark Places: Essays on Kate Grenville* (2010) and *Strong Opinions: J.M. Coetzee and the Authority of Contemporary Fiction* (coedited with Chris Danta and Julian Murphet, 2011).

Mpalive-Hangson Msiska is a Reader in English and Humanities at Birkbeck College, University of London. Among others, he has published the following books: *Writing and Africa* (1997), *Soyinka* (1998), *Post-colonial Identity in Wole Soyinka* (2007), and *Chinua Achebe's Things Fall Apart* (2007).

Saskia Schabio is assistant professor at Stuttgart University. She has written a book on Mary Wroth and published on Montaigne, Shakespeare, and the eighteenth century culture of sensibility. Recent work addresses the languages of the emotions from a postcolonial perspective, and is concerned with revisionary readings of modernity and the transnational. In these areas she has coedited *Beyond the Black Atlantic* (2006), *Postcolonial (Dis)Affections* (2007), and *Locating Transnational Ideals* (2010).

Harish Trivedi is Professor of English at the University of Delhi, and has been visiting professor at the universities of Chicago and London. He is the author of *Colonial Transactions: English Literature and India* (1993; 1995), and has coedited *The Nation across the World: Postcolonial Literary Representations* (2007; 2008), *Literature and Nation: Britain and India 1800–1990* (2000), *Post-colonial Translation: Theory and Practice* (1999), and *Interrogating Post-Colonialism: Theory, Text and Context* (1996; rpt. 2000, 2006).

Dirk Wiemann is Professor of English Literature at the University of Potsdam. His research areas include Postcolonial Studies; seventeenth century English radicalism; science and Gothic in late Victorianism; and theories of modernity. His recent publications include *Genres of Modernity: Contemporary Indian Novels in English* (2008); the coedited volumes *Global Fragments: (Dis-) Orientation in the New World Order* (2007) and *Discourses* *of Violence–Violence of Discourses* (2006). He has also published numerous articles on British and Indian cinema, on John Milton and Thomas Hobbes, on republican theatre in the period of Cromwell, on the cultural afterlives of the English Civil War, on secularism and cosmopolitanism, and on Indian writing in English.

Patrick Williams is Professor of Literary and Cultural Studies at Nottingham Trent University, where he teaches courses on postcolonial theory and culture, film, diaspora, and race and nation in twentieth century Britain. His publications include *Colonial Discourse and Post-Colonial Theory* (1993), *Introduction to Post-Colonial Theory* (1996), *Ngugi wa Thiong'o* (1999), *Edward Said* (2000) and *Postcolonial African Cinema* (2007). Forthcoming books include *The Routledge Companion to Diaspora Studies*, and a collection on Orientalism in Routledge's 'Major Works' series. He is on the editorial boards of *Theory, Culture and Society*, *Journal of Postcolonial Writing*, and *Maghreb Journal of Cultural Studies and Translation*.

Index